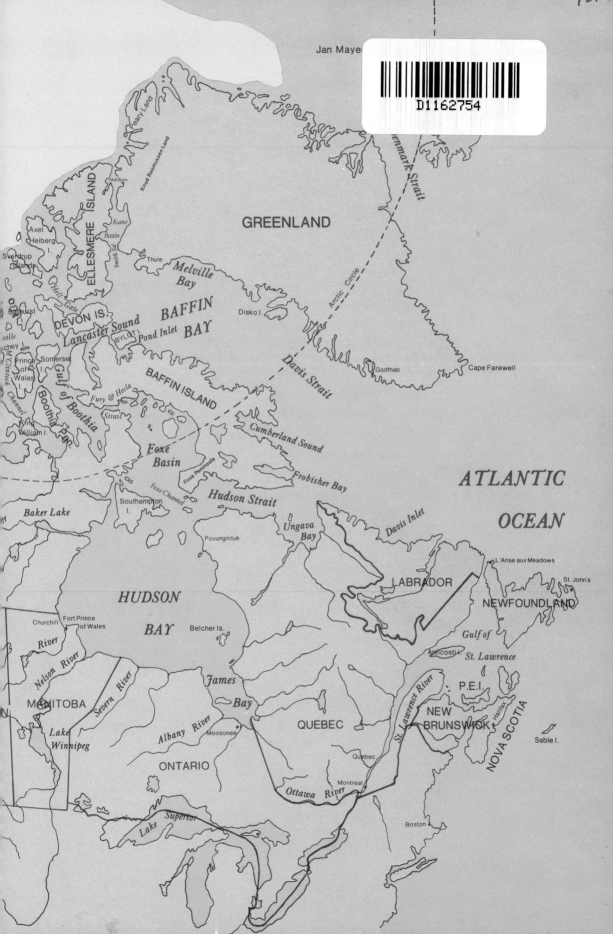

The Polar Voyagers

EXPLORERS OF THE NORTH

The Polar Voyagers

FRANK RASKY

McGraw-Hill Ryerson Limited
Toronto Montreal New York London Sydney
Auckland Johannesburg Düsseldorf Mexico Panama
São Paulo Singapore Kuala Lumpur New Delhi
St. Louis San Francisco Bogotá Madrid Tokyo

The Polar Voyagers

Copyright © Frank Rasky, 1976
All rights reserved. No part of this publication may be reproduced, stored in a retrieval system, or transmitted in any form or by any means, electronic, mechanical, photocopying, recording, or otherwise, without the prior written permission of McGraw-Hill Ryerson Limited.

ISBN 0-07-082405-3

1   2   3   4   5   6   7   8   9   0   THB   5   4   3   2   1   0   9   8   7   6

Printed and bound in Canada

Canadian Cataloguing in Publication Data

Rasky, Frank, date
   The polar voyagers

At head of title: Explorers of the north.

Bibliography: p.
Includes index.
ISBN 0-07-082405-3

1. Explorers — Arctic regions. 2. Arctic regions.
I. Title. II. Title: Explorers of the north.

G620.R38   919.8'04'0922   C76-017140-8

A Dedication

To my two *Inuit* friends — Inorak Olsen, the young radical teacher at Knud Rasmussen School in Holsteinsborg, Greenland, who helped me comprehend the tragedy of being an Eskimo anachronism trapped in the twentieth century; and Tommy Gordon, the Eskimo pilot from Inuvik, Northwest Territories, who flew me over the Beaufort Sea in a little two-engine Cessna with the marvellous skill once demonstrated by his ancestors in paddling kayaks around ice floes. In their intellect and hands lies the destiny of future Eskimo explorers.

CONTENTS

Disankering on a time from the pillars of Hercules, *the winde fitting mee well for my prupose, I thrust into the Northern Ocean: the occasion that moved mee to take such a voyage in hand, was onely a curiositie of minde, a desire of novelties, and a longing to learne out the bounds of the Ocean, and what people inhabit the farther shoare.*

Lucian of Samothrace, 125 A.D.-180 A.D.

Chapter 1

The People at the End of the Earth

I t is one of the most famous sketches in the annals of Arctic exploration. It shows a first encounter between the white man and the most northerly of Eskimos. For the whites it was the beginning of myth, and for the Eskimos it was the end of innocence. Yet for all its significance, it is a deceptively simple drawing, like a scene staged in an English pantomime.

We see in the forefront the commanding figure of Captain John Ross. The Scottish explorer is leader of the British Admiralty's expedition of 1818 to discover the elusive will-o'-the-wisp, a northwest passage to the Indies. He stands imperiously on the ice field in his grandest blue uniform. He is a-glitter with gold lace and brass buttons and wears white gloves and a Royal Navy cocked hat. As a backdrop, we see scalloped icebergs looming out of northeast Baffin Bay; also Union Jacks fluttering from the masts of His Majesty's sailing ships, *Alexander* and *Isabella*.

They are ships made of iron and wood. That is the most astounding spectacle to the Arctic Highlanders, the rather precious name given by Captain Ross to the polar Eskimos of north Greenland. He has handed them mirrors and beads, and they are seen capering and dancing, as he phrases it, "like monkeys." But it is the sight of the magical boats, fashioned out of exotic building materials, that seems most marvelous to the stone-age people.

"What great creatures are these?" they asked, pointing in terror to the ships with their strange sailing skins. "Do they come from the sun or the moon? Do they give us light by night or by day?"

"They are houses made of wood," said Sir John's interpreter, a Christianized Danish Eskimo from south Greenland named John Sacheuse.

"No. They are alive. We have seen them move their wings."

Though Ross imitated their ritual of greeting—pulling one's nose and hallooing "Heigh! Yaw!"—they still found it difficult to believe he was mortal.

It was vastly amusing, he wrote, to witness "the wild amazement, joy and fear, which successively pervaded the countenances, and governed the gestures, of these creatures." A ticking watch was held up to the ear of one native, who, supposing it was alive, wanted to swallow it. They touched the glass of the ship's skylight with awe and wondered what kind of ice it was. They shrank back in horror when shown a grunting Shetland pig on deck. And on seeing their faces in a magnifying mirror they peered behind it in hope of finding the evil spirit that had distorted their features.

Not everything impressed them. They regarded a pet terrier with contempt. It was too puny, they felt, to pull an Eskimo sleigh. They spat out the biscuits and salt port offered to them. Instead they preferred their bag of auk birds which they devoured raw. They were bored by the violin and flute that the sailors played for them. In exchange they performed a lusty native dance, which largely consisted of bending their knees, rubbing noses and, to a female chorus of *Ay yaw yaw*, miming what the puritanical Ross considered to be "indecent allusions."

Neither group was free from cupidity. Everything made of metal or timber was understandably coveted by the Eskimos; and, holding to their tradition of communal sharing, they tried to take masts, hammers, a smithy's anvil, even a ship's anchor. On his part, Captain Ross noted that the Eskimos' whale fisheries were waiting to be exploited: "The fish here are not only large and numerous, but, probably from their having never been disturbed, tame and easy to be approached." He forecast a fortune for commercial traders taking over their supply of narwhal ivory tusks: "The horn is of a finer texture, and takes a better polish, than the elephant's; and the Kings of Denmark have a throne formed of it, which is esteemed more valuable than if composed of gold." And, with uncanny accuracy, he foresaw that the aborigines could be subdued and set to trapping arctic foxes for their future European masters: "There can be no doubt that people of so harmless a disposition as the Arctic Highlanders might be easily instructed to collect these skins, which they do not seem to value."

Captain Ross palavered with the Eskimos for only six days. But his brief encounter—and the idyllic drawing which he had Sacheuse sketch of their meeting—set the pattern of mythology for an entire people. They were, in Ross's view, God's frozen children, unchristian, unwashed, and definitely inferior. "Though good humour was fully expressed in his countenance," he described one of these typical, perpetually grinning Highlanders of the north, "it also bore that indescribable mixed appearance of ignorance and wildness that characterizes all uncivilized people." And so the explorer sailed away from the people who laughed and lived like children at the end of the earth, and he concluded: "May I not say . . . that the man of these lands may be considered a 'virtuous savage'?"

It is a myth that has survived to this day, the stereotype of the primitive, though childlike, Caliban. Later explorers helped perpetuate this superficial image. Thus we have commander Robert E. Peary, the American who is credited with being the first man to set foot on the North Pole, speaking with paternal indulgence: "Plump and rounded figures, emphatically expressive countenances, bronze-skinned, keen-eyed, black-maned inhabitants of an icy desert; simple and honest, occasionally sulky; wandering, homeless people; these are my children, the Eskimos."

It was, of course, a grossly oversimplified picture that both romanticized and underrated the most ingenious and complex of cultures that had to withstand one of the cruelest environments in the world. It was a successful culture because it worked, and the white men who corrupted it had no comprehension of how perfectly adapted it was to the harsh rhythms of the north country.

The Eskimos had reason to be proud of their supremacy, for only the most intelligent and hardiest were able to survive. They called themselves simply *Inuit*, meaning they were "The People." The name Eskimo was imposed upon them. It was a rough French translation of the scornful Indian term *Eskimantsik*, which meant their northern neighbors were eaters of raw flesh. The Inuit were no less disdainful. They referred to the Indian as *Adlit* which meant "egg of the lice." And the white man, because of his excess hair which froze so easily in a blizzard, was known as *Kabloona*, "the bushy brows."

Before the Kabloona arrived there were perhaps one hundred thousand Eskimos. Thanks to the diseases introduced by the white man, their population was reduced drastically and today it is estimated to be no more than eighty thousand. Nobody really knows where their

This first meeting of Captain John Ross of the British Admiralty with the most northerly of polar Eskimos in Greenland set a pattern of mythology. The Scottish explorer nicknamed them "Arctic Highlanders"—God's frozen children who were naive "virtuous savages" to be exploited. The quaint sketch, drawn by Eskimo interpreter John Sacheuse, reflects the comedy of their

encounter in 1818. The Royal Navy officers strut in cocked hats, gold lace and white gloves. The Eskimos, more intelligently dressed for the cold climate, are awed by their images in gift mirrors, but most impressed by wood and metal in white men's ships.

ancestors came from. The nomads evidently originated in Asia. About five thousand years ago they probably stepped across a bridge of land then linking Russia and Alaska in the Bering Sea. Then they roved for six thousand miles until they were thinly spread across the roof of the world. Their Eskimo domain stretched from Siberia, Alaska and the Canadian North to the shores of Denmark's Greenland.

It was mainly a maritime domain. With some exceptions, they lived not far from the shores of the more than five million square miles we now call the Arctic Ocean. And it was mainly an arctic desert. For rainfall was meagre and nature was grudging in Eskimo country. The average yearly precipitation was less than ten inches, and perpetually frozen ground permitted a thin skin of just a few inches of top soil. So roots of the fluffy arctic cotton grass had to be tenacious to endure in this slim margin of life; yellow poppies and purple orchids were midget-sized when they blossomed in the brief, lurid summers; and the occasional patches of dwarf willow and stunted spruce were treasured as rare prizes when they were discovered hugging close to the frost-tortured earth.

To the Indians, the boundary separating their own bush country from treeless Eskimo territory was "the land of little sticks." They seldom dared venture across this border zone for they feared it was haunted by giants. To the white men, the flat tundra was "the barrens" or "the barren grounds." About a thousand years ago, the Vikings believed in their sagas that the *Skraelings* ("screamers") who howled on these bleak shores were macabre pygmies—"small, ill-favored men, with ugly hair on their heads." As late as the 1570s, the British navigator, Martin Frobisher, thought their women were witches, and when his sailors captured an aged Eskimo woman they "had her buskins pulled off, to see if she was cloven-footed."

Superstitions to the contrary, the Eskimos were not outlandish freaks. Though racially first cousins, they differed in subtle ways from the Indians. They tended to be short and compact, though some were surprisingly tall. They had straight black hair; flesh-padded, dark brown eyes; flattish broad cheekbones; and a complexion that ranged from a yellowish-brown to a pale bronze. Like most people of the Mongoloid races, they were born with a blue spot at the base of the spine.

They were a handsome, stocky people and some traits appeared uniquely suited to help them combat the polar climate. Their facial hair was relatively scanty, an advantage in preventing the accumulation of frost. Their nasal cavities were narrower than the nostrils of other races, thus protecting their lungs from freezing when they breathed. Their arms, legs and feet, though well-formed, were proportionately shorter than those of the North American Indians. "Is this because in a very cold climate it is easier for the heart to pump warm blood into short limbs than into long ones?" wondered the Canadian explorer-anthropologist Diamond Jénness. He confessed he was as perplexed as the tourist in Africa who asked his guide: "Does the giraffe strip leaves from tall trees because his neck is so long? Or has his neck become phenomenally long from the habit of stripping tall trees?"

It was not the only thing that bewildered Kabloona observers of this fascinating people. Almost every explorer who visited the Arctic tried to tabulate the vices and virtues of the natives as though they were some subhuman species, to be examined and judged according to how they conformed to the white man's imported values. But the Esquimaux, to use the old fashioned terminology employed by the early social scientists, refused to be pinpointed that neatly. The Esquimau way of thinking proved to be as elusive as the arctic butterfly—the delicate *ta-ka-lee-kee-ta*, which in their language means "spots on the wings." As for the Esquimau way of life, close students of their civilization were astonished to discover ultimately that it was as rich in contradictions as any society created by the Kabloona.

It was true that the Eskimos gave the impression of being among the world's happiest people—jovial, gregarious, funloving, more given to gaiety than Tahitians luxuriating in the tropics. But it was sometimes a defensive veneer, for beneath their smiling masks they often hid a terrible feeling of stoic helplessness. A common expression in their vocabulary was "*Ay-ung-a-mut*" or "*I-or-ana-mutt*"—"It can't be helped." It was like the Turkish kismet, a shrugging acceptance of the fates, and since one was impotent in the face of the relentless and unpredictable whims of nature, one might find release by laughing at one's own helplessness, and embrace the inevitable with serenity. It was with this sense of fatalism, "when life weighs heavier than death," that burdensome old invalids would resign themselves to suicide and hang themselves with a cheerful smile on their lips. A Greenland missionary was told this poignant story by an Eskimo woman: "Once an old woman, who was ill but could not die, offered to pay me if I would lead her to the top of the steep cliff, from which our people have always thrown themselves when they are tired of living. But I, having ever loved my neighbors, led her thither without payments, and cast her over the cliff."

Other Eskimo customs were equally paradoxical—usually rooted in brute survival and frequently a curious mixture of the tough and the tender.

It was true, for example, that the Eskimos practiced an ideal collective communism of a kind never achieved by the Marxists. Except for their prized family songs and private kit of weapons, family utensils and clothing, they owned nothing individually, but shared their wealth with the group. And, except for the exalted tribal wise man, or *angekok*, they had no class system, no capitalists or paupers. No man need be a beggar because he never had to ask for charity. "Just as by whips one makes dogs," said the Eskimos, "so by alms one makes slaves." Yet woe betided the acquisitive rich man who hoarded his food. The commune would sometimes elect an assassin. Then the selfish miser would be executed—usually stabbed in the back—and his provisions divided equally among the villagers.

The Eskimos practised a form of democracy superior to the Athenians'. They had no rulers, no government, no prisons. So strong was their belief in individual freedom that a man had the right to kill himself unimpeded, as long as his action didn't interfere with group solidarity. Yet it was not anarchy. As with the Japanese, "saving face" was a vital part of their code of honor, and often any man who tried to dominate the community was punished with the most humiliating kind of justice. The would-be tyrant had to defend himself before the assembled villagers in a *nith* song duel. His selected opponent would lampoon his behavior scathingly with derisive ballads, and if he lost this ruthless trial by public opinion, his sentence was equally merciless—ostracism from the community.

The liberality and tolerance of their social welfare system might have been envied by the Swedes. They sanctioned nudity, polygamy and bastardy. They were, by the white man's standards, shameless about swapping mates freely at midnight parties when the lights were put out. Widows were pitied and often became the second wife of the closest bigamous brother-in-law. Orphans were immediately adopted and pampered—the infant sons being regarded by their foster parents as "my walking stick," meaning social security for their old age. And yet, despite their prodigal sharing of family affection, love was sometimes sacrificed pitilessly when it conflicted with the struggle for existence. Since they were potentially unproductive in the hunt for food, female babies were often smothered in the snow at birth. In times of famine, the weakest members of the family were abandoned on the ice floes to freeze. And though they were averse to it, cannibalism sometimes became a grim necessity. It was, however, a rare practice which produced a remorseful guilt. "For having eaten human flesh," wrote the explorer, Samuel Hearne, "the pariah is shunned . . . forlorn and forsaken even by his own relations, like Cain after he killed his brother, Abel."

"Netsik," the seal, was a main staple in the Eskimos' feast-or-famine economy. Capturing one of these 800-pound submarines of blubber was a festive communal occasion.

Like the ancient Jews, the Eskimos used a language that could be either ambiguously subtle, or witty, or poetically forceful in its imagery. They had more than a hundred words to define the particular quality of a flake of snow. Superb mimics, they could parody exactly the crash of an iceberg being calved by a glacier, the chatter of the orange ground squirrel that they knew as the *siksik*, and the precise sound of the wind, whether it was whispering, or wailing, or as they phrased it, "grinding its teeth." Their vocabulary included such refinements as "he who is without shadow" for the polar bear; "the wind-loved spot" for a stormy cape; and "brain robber" for the liquor introduced to them by the white man.

They could be as clannish as the Arabian Bedouins. Their scattered encampments were linked by intermarriages, and family etiquette required that they sled for hundreds of miles to make a courtesy call on *arnaquatiga*—"my cousin." But if that relative were murdered, the etiquette of blood revenge demanded that the male next-of-kin pursue the killer remorselessly until one day he be made to "look up at the sky," stabbed to death when his nemesis was least expected. "The paradoxical position will occur," observed the Danish ethnologist, Kaj Birket-Smith, "that when a man has killed a rival in order to take his wife, he will, as a loving stepfather, bring up his victim's son who has some day to exact blood vengeance upon him!"

They could be as fanatically superstitious as the natives of Haiti. They believed that their eerie world of the northern lights was haunted by a whole host of supernatural forces, and they turned to *angekoks* ("sorcerers") to propitiate the malevolent spirits. Usually a gifted conjuror, the wizard would seemingly pierce himself with a harpoon; conduct a ghost seance by the adroit use of ventriloquism; and exercise autosuggestion to perform witchcraft. "I command you to die!" he might cry out to the sacrificial victim, and such was the power of his black magic assistant—a carved ivory image called the *tupilik*—that the doomed one would indeed languish and die. And yet they could be as orthodox in their religion as any Old Testament fundamentalist. Their taboos about not mixing the seal meat of the sea and the caribou meat of the land were more rigid than the kosher food laws of the Hebrews. And though it was a geographical reversal of our Christian Bible deities, they widely believed in Sedna, the benevolent sea goddess, who sheltered virtuous souls in a delightful heaven underground where it was always warm and the seal forever plentiful. And they believed in Sila, the satanic weather goddess, who created thunder and lightning and blizzards by rubbing caribou hides together, and kept wicked souls wandering in a wretchedly cold and gameless hell on top of the mountain glaciers.

Finally, the Eskimos could be as neurotic and tension-racked as any modern slum dweller forced to cope with a precarious hand-to-mouth existence. Their conversation was often sprinkled with the word *imaka*— "perhaps"—for such were the uncertainties of life that they never knew whether they would perish tomorrow. Their suffering was revealed by Knud Rasmussen, the Greenland-born explorer and folklorist; he was himself part Eskimo and therefore exhibited a sensitive insight in penetrating their peculiarly Asiatic politeness and getting at the roots of their feelings. Once, he was questioning an Eskimo named Aua about the mysteries of life. Aua replied by gesturing toward his neighbor's children, who were gaunt with hunger, and shivering in a corner of an unheated snowhouse.

"*Why*?" demanded Aua. "Why should all be chill and comfortless in this little home?"

Then Aua showed him his aged sister, Natseq, who obviously had not long to live and was coughing her lungs out.

"*Why? Why?*" asked Aua. "Why should we human beings suffer pain and sickness?"

When Rasmussen could not answer, Aua declared that the mystic forces of life were beyond explanation:

"We do not believe, we only fear.
"We fear the elements with which we have to fight in their fury to wrest out food from land and sea.
"We fear cold and famine in our snow huts.
"We fear the sickness that is daily to be seen among us. Not death, but the suffering.
"We fear the souls of the dead, of human and animal alike.
"We fear the spirits of earth and air.
"We *fear*!"

And yet, despite the malignant caprices of the fates, life was sweet, and they rejoiced in it and were grateful for it with a buoyancy that was a triumph of the human spirit. In springtime, when the great Dark was diminishing and the sun was awakening from its six-month slumber,

ARKTISK INSTITUT CHARLOTTENLUND, DENMARK

An early Greenland Eskimo artist drew this charming picture of a topknotted mother and child. The infant sat straddle-legged in a kind of enlarged pouch inside the mother's parka, where its moss diaper could be easily changed.

they celebrated the occasion with a jubilant salute to their own survival. At daybreak Alaskan Eskimos came out naked on the beach and stood facing the dawn.

"I am not asleep!" they exclaimed defiantly. "I am alive! I greet with you the life-giving light!"

How they kept alive was a supreme example of human adaptability. Keenly observant, inventive and resourceful, these untutored artisans, without knowing the word in their unwritten language, were peerless natural scientists. Their mechanical aptitude was particularly outstanding. Long before the Kabloona came, they were making an ivory set of false teeth from walrus tusk, an artificial leg from a narwhal tusk, an incubator for a prematurely born infant from the waterproof bladder of a seal, and setting broken limbs with driftwood splints. Later, though they could not tell you *why* it worked, they astonished the white men by their ability to take apart and put together a broken watch or a snowmobile engine, with an automatic understanding of *how* it worked.

The white men have yet to match their genius for being able to protect themselves from the cold. Their instinctive knowledge of the laws of physics was such, wrote the Canadian explorer, Vilhjalmur Stefansson, that the Eskimos hermetically sealed themselves inside a virtually tropical climate.

The early explorers, perspiring and yet shivering in their bulky coats and sweaters, mocked the Eskimos for wearing *attigi* coats that looked like light swallow-tailed evening suits. In fact, the natives had mastered the principle of air insulation; and their two sets of loose-hanging, buttonless caribou garments were practically cold- and sweat-proof. The Eskimos knew that trapped dead air, which is a poor conductor, made an ideal buffer against the arctic cold.

Each hair of the caribou itself contains a hollow pocket of air. So when you put on two pairs of caribou tunics—the fur hairs of the innercoat pointing inward, those of the outer coat pointing outward—you were well layered with warmth. At the same time, because the lightweight garments were worn loosely, the body heat was circulated sufficiently to prevent undue absorption of sweat. In addition, the Eskimos wore boots made of waterproof sealskin and hoods framed with wolverine—a fur not prone to freeze into a mask of icicles from the condensed moisture of the breath. Finally, the frock coat's hanging tail supplied a comfortable cushion for seal hunters who sat crouched on snow blocks for hours with harpoons poised over a breathing hole in the ice; and their ivory snow-goggles, with a narrow slit for each eye, were wonderfully improvised appendages for keeping out the reflected glare of the sun.

Their curved, wind-resistant winter homes were models of engineering design, perfectly in harmony with their environment. To this very day arctic architects have been unable to improve upon them. Despite popular misconception, the word *igloo* to an Eskimo simply meant "house." In summer it was a bell-shaped skin tent or *tupik*; in winter it could be made of sod, stone, driftwood, or skin-covered whale ribs. Their dome-shaped, snow-insulated igloos were remarkable for the way they kept the cold out and warmth in. Several families might live semi-nude in a single dwelling heated to sixty degrees or more by their body heat plus the warmth cast by a small oil-blubber cooking lamp. A partially fur-stuffed hole in the ceiling was supposed to act as the "nose" or ventilator of the house. But since the gregarious Eskimos loved to cram together snugly when the blizzards were raging outside at fifty below zero, the place was often as steamy as a Turkish bath. "Like bees in the centre of a hanging swarm, we almost suffocated," Diamond Jenness once complained. "But," the ethnologist added, "we were warm."

No modern stone mason was as efficient as an Eskimo in building his snowhouse. Like a snail constructing its own shell, the sculptor worked inside the site which he had carefully selected on a hard-packed snowdrift. Each rectangular block was rapidly carved out with his fifteen-inch-long snow knife—a sharply honed caribou antler known as his *pana*. As the layers spiralled upwards at an increasing inward tilt, each bricklike slab was firmly cemented into place with adhesive snow and a whack of the fist. The keystone, or topmost block, of the arch was usually juggled into position from inside. With a little extra whittling, trimming and filling in of chinks, the whole job could be accomplished within forty minutes.

Snow was also the basis for most of the furniture. A sheet of clear freshwater ice was fitted into the wall over the tunnel entrance as a window pane. Two platforms of excess snow, blanketed with caribou skins, served as tables and chairs by day and as communal beds by night. Family life centred around the seal-oil lamp. This was a shallow half-moon-shaped vessel carved out of soft soapstone, containing oil, with a constantly lit wick of white moss placed along the straight edge, dipping into it. Suspended over it was usually a pot of boiling soup, and if the stew lacked water the housewife would merely scrape snow from the igloo wall and toss it into the pot. Trimming the wick of the lamp so that it would not smoke up the dwelling was a domestic art of no mean order. And since it was cumbersome to light a fresh fire by striking two pieces of

Igloos were built of rectangular blocks of snow, the topmost bricklike slab juggled into position from inside.

In sleigh races, an Eskimo dog was a "kingmik" (not a husky), goaded on with a cry of "Huk!Huk!" (not "Mush!").

pyrite together, a housewife took pride in keeping her lamp continuously burning. Knud Rasmussen painted a delightful word-picture of one house-proud Lady of the Lamp—a widow of fifty named Iterfiluk, who welcomed fifteen overnight guests into her igloo. "While her visitors are asleep, she herself sits stark naked by her lamp," he wrote, "like one of the holy virgins guarding the lamp, so that the precious light shall not be extinguished during the night."

Male Eskimos were vainglorious about their ability in three pursuits: dogsledding, kayaking and hunting. A sledge with driftwood runners and crossbars was ranked so precious in certain regions of the Canadian Arctic that a wife might be traded for one. Marvelous at improvisation, some woodless Eskimos were known to lash together sleighs using frozen salmon or slabs of walrus meat. "The meat, as hard as a plank, is the driver's seat," wrote the American explorer of the 1850s, Dr. Elisha Kent Kane. "It is secure from the dogs; and when it is wanted for a cold cut, which is not seldom, the sledge is turned upside down, and the layers of flesh are hacked away from between the crossbars."

Often the sled was made of whalebone or walrus tusks. The cross slats were lashed to the runners with sealhide thongs, and in Greenland caribou antlers at the back served as handles for steering. The driver carefully shod the bottoms of the runners with a kind of frozen mudpack—a blend of earth and squirts of water which formed a thin coating of ice. This icy patina reduced friction and enabled the sled to glide smoothly across the snow while bearing a load of up to one thousand pounds.

Prized almost as highly as a wooden *komatik* (the Eskimo word for sled) was a well-trained *kingmik* (the Eskimo word for a husky). The word "husky" is a white man's term. Cockney English fur traders, who added an "h" when pronouncing vowel sounds, used to refer to the natives as "Heskimos." An Eskimo dog was called a "Heskimo" dog. "Heskimo" was shortened to "Hesky," and eventually corrupted to "Husky."

Whether known as a *kingmik* or a husky, the sled dogs were magnificent creatures, with pointed ears and a plumelike tail curling over a wolf-gray, black or white back. Like wolves, they never barked but only howled, and they had an undercoat of dense, oily, six-inch-long hair to protect them from the searing cold. But their masters sometimes provided them with additional sealskin shirts as well as rawhide dog shoes to prevent their pads from being cut by sharp ice.

Every Eskimo youth aspired to be an expert dog team driver. A promising litter of puppies would be given a sort of ceremonial massage. Each fuzzy ball of fur had its legs pulled, so that it might be able to run twenty to thirty miles a day; its back kneaded, so that it would be strong enough to carry a summer packsack load of up to fifty pounds. The youth would whisper into its ears to make its hearing keen enough to detect the coming of *tuktu*, the caribou; blow breath into its nostrils, that it would be able to scent out the breathing hole of *netsik*, the seal. Then he would give the puppy a name, usually that of a dead relative. Thus it was not uncommon for a dog team driver to say: "I must tie up my grandfather."

When about half-grown, a team of anywhere from three to six young dogs would be broken in to a harness made from strips of sealskin. They were not guided by reins and, despite the popular fallacy, the driver never used the word "mush" to urge them on. They obeyed the swishing flick of the driver's twenty-foot-long whip and his goading, almost whistling cry of either "Whit! Whit!" or "Huk! Huk!" Harnessed to the sled in either a fan-shaped hitch or a tandem-style long towline, the team battled ferociously for the position of leadership. The so-called boss dog, if he was a pugnacious scrapper and a speedy racer, might be given a more glamorous name, like "Split-the-wind," and to maintain his supremacy over the pack it was protocol for him to conquer the leader of every rival team he might meet.

To watch one of these bloody hairpulls in action was like having a ringside seat at a championship wrestling match fought by a "howling, snarling, biting, yelping, moving mass of fury," wrote Matthew Henson. He was the Negro servant who accompanied Peary on his trek to the North Pole (and who was given the Eskimo name, *Maktokkabloona*, meaning "black white man"). "The arrival of the first dog of the new party was the signal for the grandest dog fight I have ever witnessed," said Henson of the combat. "I feel justified in using the language of the fairy, Ariel, in Shakespeare's *Tempest:* 'Now is Hell empty, and all the devils are here.'" Then Henson added wryly, "I have often wondered what chance a cat would stand against an Eskimo dog."

Nanook, the polar bear, was the great quarry of an Eskimo dog. The very scent of this polar monarch (a male might weigh up to a thousand pounds and be eight feet tall) would throw a dog team into a frenzy of anticipation. They literally leaped at the prospect of being cut from their traces; of holding the enemy at bay by harrying its shaggy hindquarters, until their master plunged his fatal lance. When *nanook* was sighted, dog team drivers competed like Roman charioteers to be the first to reach the prize who was bounding over the ice floes ahead.

CATCHING AUKS.

THE BEAR AT BAY.

Hunters were proud of their ability to slither stealthily across ice to harpoon a seal or net auks on cliff tops, but the number one sport was spearing a 1,000-pound polar bear.

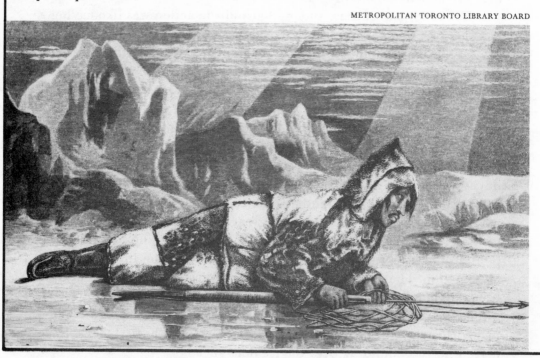

Greenlanders were master kayakers. Encased in a waterproof raincoat of seal intestine, they enjoyed somersaulting their slender, elegantly designed craft in stormy waves.

The "umiak" was a large, dorylike workhorse of a boat commonly rowed by women who sometimes hoisted a triangular sail of seal gut. It could carry a two-ton load.

"It was a beautiful sight to observe the two sledges racing at full speed to the same object, the dogs and men in full cry, and the vehicles splashing through the holes of water with the velocity and spirit of rival stage coaches," Captain George Francis Lyon, the British explorer of the 1820s, described the sport. "There is something of the spirit of the professional whip in these wild races; for young men delight in passing each other's sledge, and jockeying the hinder one by crossing the path."

Kayaking was a trickier sport, requiring as delicate a sense of balance on stormy seas as that of a first-class water skier or tightrope walker. The Greenland and Alaska Eskimos, who excelled in it, began mastering the art as boys of ten. Their equipment consisted of a long double-bladed paddle and a slender, elegantly designed craft that was perhaps the world's most seaworthy canoe. A kayak was so light, weighing as little as twenty-five pounds, that a portaging Eskimo could carry it with one hand.

In water the kayaker was absolutely watertight because both he and his craft were sheathed like footballs. The canoe's willow or driftwood frame was wrapped entirely by a taut sealskin, except for its circular cockpit. Seated snugly in this manhole, the paddler was encased in a waterproof raincoat of seal intestine, which was tightly laced around his wrists and face. When the hem of this translucent gut slicker was lashed by thongs to the rim of the porthole, paddler and canoe became one—an impregnable unity.

After years of practice, an adroit kayaker was practically unsinkable. In case his frail craft was gashed by ice, he carried a lump of blubber that was used as a temporary plug. He could improvise a raft by lashing two kayaks together. In Greenland if the rollers of a gale threatened to engulf him, the stunter could turn his canoe bottom side up, roll with the breakers, and then right himself with consummate ease.

Fridtjof Nansen, the Norwegian explorer, took lessons in kayaking, but found that balancing the cranky little vessel was as difficult as his own feat of skiing across the great Greenland Ice Cap: "One feels as if he were swinging on a knife-edge, and it is very necessary, so to speak, to keep your hair parted well in the middle. Yet when one sees the Eskimo dancing like sea birds on the crests of the waves, the whole performance seems simply child's play." An agile kayaker, after somersaulting his canoe, could right himself without his paddle, merely by using one arm. "The height of accomplishment is reached when he does not even need to use the flat of his hand, but can clench it," marvelled Nansen. "And to show that he really does so, I have seen a man take a stone in his clenched hand before capsizing, and come up with it still in his grasp."

Though not suited for such intrepid acrobatics, the larger, skin-covered *umiak* was an efficient dory. Less streamlined, with a flat bottom and an exposed top, this workhorse of a boat could transport a two-ton load. A triangular sail of seal gut was sometimes hoisted, giving it the gay appearance of an East Asiatic dhow. Since it was commonly rowed by as many as a dozen women, it was called a "women's boat." When Sir John Richardson was exploring the Canadian Arctic coast near the Mackenzie River, the Eskimos were puzzled to see his English sailors rowing a boat. Do all white females, they asked, wear beards?

In the stern of the umiak, however, there presided a male Eskimo steersman. And invariably a flotilla of men followed in their kayaks, looking, as Kaj Birket-Smith observed, "like torpedo boats escorting a dreadnought." The parallel was apt, for they usually worked as a team to attack two of the most formidable monsters of the polar seas.

The one-ton bull walrus (from the Swedish *hvalrus*, meaning "whale horse") was the more deceptive-looking of these primordial mammals. Sunbathing on an ice floe, the snoring creature resembled a caricatured member of an Englishman's club, with its wrinkled potbelly, clam-strainer moustache, buckteeth-like tusks, and the baggy eyes of a jaded *roué*. But, when embattled, the bellowing walrus was no Colonel Blimp. Its tail carried a clout, its head was a powerful claw hammer, and its ivory tusks could lacerate paddler and kayak with swift and horrifying viciousness.

Polar whales (known to the Eskimos as the *aggawek*) looked truly fearsome. Most freakish was the narwhal. The unicorn of the Arctic, it wielded like a rapier the single ivory tusk that spiraled eight feet out of its upper left jaw. The Greenland right, or bowhead, whale was the colossus of the Arctic. It was a blubbered Gargantua whose huge head accounted for a third of its total length of fifty to sixty feet. Almost as strange was the arctic white, or beluga, whale—a leaping acrobat up to fifteen feet long and, because it was endowed with an eerie musical voice, usually nicknamed by Kabloona whalers the "sea canary."

The Eskimos used an ingenious harpoon, called the *siatko*, to hunt down their aquatic prey. The weapon was a six-foot-long shaft with a detachable ivory head that was easily loosened when it hit. Attached to the head by a long rawhide line was a sealskin float, inflated like a balloon or a bladder. When the quarry was harpooned, the released shaft fell off and floated around to be picked up later. The head was barbed on one side, so that when the line was taut, the barb turned in the flesh and held firm like an anchor. No matter how often the wounded mammal dived into the water, it could not escape from the twisting barb and

A set of strong teeth were vital domestic utensils for an Eskimo woman, used to gnaw and cure hides into silky suppleness or keep her husband's wet "kamik" boots in good shape.

Children loved dancing to the tomtom beat of a hoop drum while their mothers chanted a chorus of "Ai-yai-ya-ya."

Seldom rooted in one spot, the nomadic Canadian Eskimos would travel hundreds of miles, erecting transient villages.

Primitive perhaps but ingenious was this Eskimo's mode of travel: a whalebone paddle and inflated seal bladders.

METROPOLITAN TORONTO LIBRARY BOARD

sealskin buoys. Exhausted by loss of blood and additional stabbing from the Eskimos' hurled spears, the stricken creature eventually gasped its last breath.

The hunters vied fearlessly to strike the fatal blow. "They are sometimes so daring," wrote Hans Egede, the Greenland missionary of the 1720s, "that they will get upon the Whale's Back, while there is yet Life in him, to make an End of him, and cut away his Fat."

The whale's fatty epidermis, or *muktuk*, was considered a great delicacy, and some epicure explorers claimed that a twelve-inch strip of it swallowed raw tasted as piquant as walnuts. But Dr. Elisha Kent Kane, the American explorer, maintained that it couldn't compare with a pâté of raw walrus, which was fit for the palate of Lucullus himself. In gourmet raptures, he exclaimed: "The liver of a walrus (*awuktanuk*) eaten with little slices of his delicately permeating fat—oh! call it not blubber—of a verity it is a delicious morsel. Fire would ruin the curt, pithy expression of vitality which belongs to its uncooked juices. Charles Lamb's roast pig was nothing to *awuktanuk*."

But it was *tuktu*, the caribou, and *netsik*, the seal, that formed, along with the fish of the sea, the bread-and-butter staples of the Eskimo diet. To keep their larders well cached, the breadwinners had to exercise to the utmost their power of mimicry and cunning ruse.

The bull caribou (an Indian name meaning "the shoveler," or "animal that paws through the snow for its food") had a keen scent and was not easy to stalk on the treeless tundra. Despite its five hundred pounds of brown and silvery hulk, its six-foot rack of antlers, and its broad splayed hoofs that acted as snowshoes, it was a shy creature. Caribou took refuge in numbers. Vast herds of them migrated north to the Arctic each spring; at the first blizzards of fall, massed columns of them returned south to forage in the subarctic forests. It was an awesome spectacle to see an army of thousands on the march. Their bobbing antlers suggested lanced cavalry regiments and the clinking of their ankle bones was like the clinking of armor.

But they were nearsighted and inquisitive, and the hunters took advantage of these frailties to lure them astray. Keeping to the lee side of a herd, two archers would disguise themselves in caribou skins. Sometimes they wore a caribou head and brayed like a caribou and held their bows and arrows upright to imitate the antlers of a caribou. If a curious member of the herd followed, one of the decoys would drop behind a rock while his companion would continue trotting in a caribou-like gait to entice the unsuspecting victim forward. As soon as it was at close range, about twenty paces away, the concealed hunter would kill it with an arrow through the kidney.

Another stratagem was a community sport somewhat akin to a tiger beat in India. In a valley where the migrating caribou herds customarily passed, the Eskimos erected rows of turf-capped stone cairns known as *inukshuit* ("semblances of man"). Women and children howled like wolves and flapped skins to stampede the caribou down the dummy lanes. The panicky herd surged into a cul-de-sac of pits, where they were ambushed by crouching archers; or they were driven into a lake, where they were speared in the hundreds by waiting kayakers.

To the Eskimo family, the caribou was a walking department store. It supplied, among other things, the child's doll, skipping rope and football; the mother's thread, thimble, needle case and suntan oil; the father's weapons, tools and clothes from mitts to socks. Moreover, a juicily fatted buck was a mobile snack bar: from its eyeballs (which were gulped down avidly like olives) to the half-digested mosses in its paunch (which the white men came to appreciate as "tundra salad"). The sweet jelly from its split marrowbones, oozing out like melted butter, was esteemed a special treat. "Huxley says that only savages eat marrow," sniffed Diamond Jenness; then he contradicted his fellow scientist by joyfully helping crack two dozen caribou leg bones at one sitting. "If that be true," Jenness concluded, "our epicures are neglecting one of nature's choicest viands."

Equally succulent, *netsik,* the seal, was far slipperier a prey, and required infinitely more patience and guile to catch. Like the caribou, it had a myopic eyesight. But the flippered submarine of blubber, though seemingly ponderous at up to eight hundred pounds, was swift and alert. At the slightest strange noise, it would submerge quickly into one of its *agloos*—its underwater ice caves or blow holes.

In winter time, the hunter knew that this warmblooded fish-eater must surface periodically to breathe through one of its circuit of a dozen cone-shaped air vents that it had gnawed through sheet-ice and snow. So the Eskimo took extraordinary precautions. He crept toward the breathing hole on slippers of thick polar bear fur that muffled the creaking of the snow. He silently probed through the top layer of drift snow with his knife, so that he could better aim his harpoon. He inserted into the hole his drifting indicator, a long caribou bone, slim as a knitting needle, with a colored swan feather on its forked tip, whose bobbing would signal the seal's arrival. Then the sentinel assumed his solitary vigil. Sometimes he sat on a block of ice, but usually he stood poised over the blow hole, immobile as a marble pillar, a seeming troglodyte tirelessly waiting in his classical stance, posed to strike his prey.

Time meant nothing to him. Gontran de Poncins, the French scientist, told of a fellow Kabloona who returned from a sealing expedition, empty-handed and disgusted.

"How long did you wait at the hole?" an Eskimo asked him.

"Four freezing hours!"

The Eskimo shrugged politely. "Four days are not too many."

Stalking the seals in springtime, when they lay dozing in the sun, was a sport that required accomplished acting talent. The Eskimo mimic had to talk, look and waddle like a seal. Costumed in a seal skin, the masquerader slowly wriggled toward his victim, using his elbows. His props consisted of a bearskin mat which helped him glide noiselessly, and artificial flippers that he occasionally scratched on the ice like seal's claws.

The sensitive seal, awaking from its catnap every minute or so, might bark in alarm and flip its tail nervously. The hunter would reply with a reassuring bark and toss his right leg up in a simulated tail flip. The satisfied seal would go back to sleep and the actor would propel himself forward a few more feet on his bearskin stage, until his next performance.

After perhaps fifteen minutes to two hours of this pantomime, the hunter would crawl near enough to harpoon the seal; he sometimes cracked its skull with a club or a blow of the fist if the harpooning wound was not fatal. "I knew an Eskimo who was so expert at this kind of sport," claimed James W. Tyrrell, the Canadian geologist-surveyor of the 1890s, "that he was able to catch seals with his teeth."

This was undoubtedly true. Though worn down to stumps, their edges looking as if they had been rasped off with a file, an Eskimo's incisors were powerful weapons and masticators. Frozen seal entrails, tough as cast iron, were chewed pleasurably for hours, like taffy. Seal liver and chunks of its rich white blubber were demolished, smoking hot, immediately after the kill and were deemed even by the white men to be dainties. Everyone raved about the flavor of seal-blood soup. The discriminating palate of Dr. Elisha Kent Kane considered it "not fishy, but *sealy.*" His fellow American gourmet-explorer of the 1860s, Captain Charles Francis Hall, soared into ecstasies: "I challenge any one to find more palatable food in the world. It is ambrosia and nectar! Once tasted, the cry is sure to be 'More! More!'"

To be sure, Captain Hall was a little taken aback by the table manners of his Eskimo hostess who served him boiled meat from a seal stew. "Before the igloo wife hands any one a piece of meat," he noted, "she *soups* it all over, that is, *sucks* out all the fluid from the meat that would probably otherwise drip out. Furthermore, if there be any foreign matter upon it, such as seal, dog, or caribou hairs, she *licks* them all off with her pliant tongue."

Along with her curved *ulu* kitchen knife, her teeth and her tongue were an Eskimo housewife's most versatile domestic utensils. With her arc-shaped *ulu* chopper, she was deft at butchering the seal, scraping its creamy white skin free of all fat (which was then cached in big blubber bags); tailoring clothes, which required seven prime caribou hides for a single suit; and scraping dirty snow off the floor. Her busy teeth were used to gnaw, munch and cure hides into silky suppleness; to yank off her husband's wet *kamik* boots when he returned from the hunt; and sometimes to bite off the umbilical cord of a neighbor who had just given birth to a child. As for her "inimitable pocket handkerchief, the tongue" (to borrow Captain George Francis Lyon's phrase), it was a lamp cleaner, dish washer, and, like a cat licking her kitten, the mother's chief means of bathing her baby.

A child was king of the Eskimo household. The infant was carried everywhere pick-a-back fashion, riding enthroned on the bare back of its mother. It sat straddle-legged in a kind of enlarged pouch inside the mother's parka, where its moss diaper could be easily changed. It was a lovely sight to see a mother feeding her baby. In a delicate birdlike gesture, half kiss, half mastication, she would turn her head over her shoulder to slip a morsel of meat she had tenderly chewed into the upthrust lips of the child nestling in her pouch.

The father would always take time to caress the rosy cheeks of the baby and give it plenty of loving *kooniks* — the Eskimo kissing which was done by rubbing noses. Both parents were exceedingly indulgent and permissive. No child was ever punished. The youngsters were allowed to play day and night at their cat's cradle game of weaving figures out of string or playing football with a seal bladder or spinning tops on ice. For childhood was short, and it was understood that only too soon would they have to acquire the skills so vital in the unending struggle for survival.

A boy would be taken out at an early age to spear the red arctic char salmon with a bony barbed trident, or to lasso the green-winged teal with a set of bone bola balls attached to ropes of seal sinew. A girl quickly learned to preserve the flavor of caribou tongues by boiling them with the tips upward; and to become a gifted seamstress.

As soon as a twelve-year-old girl started menstruating (which taboo decreed was an "unclean period" requiring her to live secluded in a separate igloo), she was ready to be taken in marriage. There was no ritualized wedding and little romance in the courtship. The girl's permission was never asked. Her parents usually pledged her as a bride at birth in exchange for a small dowry.

But if women were scarce and the girl was an outstanding needlewoman and an exceptionally plump, well-fed beauty, rival wife-hunters would duel for the right of possession. A wrestling match, a boxing bout or a tug of war were not uncommon. Sometimes the disputants pelted each other with dog excreta. In some regions the contestants grappled with hooked caribou horns, with which each sought to snatch the girl from his opponent.

The girl was by no means an innocent pawn in the caveman struggle. The coquette would play one suitor against the other. As David Crantz, the Greenland missionary of the 1760s, observed, "Eskimo women are as well skilled in the language of the eyes as a Turkish courtesan." She exercised the wiles of an actress. No matter if she liked the winner of the duel, modesty demanded that she pretend to put up a stiff resistance—caterwauling, and pummeling the victor who was dragging her off to his igloo.

Neither was the bride treated like a mere chattel. She was a true liberated woman. A husband could not *order* a wife to do anything; and if her mate didn't suit her fancy, she had the right to "walk away" from him in a simple divorce. Indeed, a woman might go through the purgatory of four or five trial marriages before deciding to settle down. Where females were in short supply, the polyandrous woman might rule over a household of two husbands. And even if she was one of an Eskimo sheik's harem of several wives, she was no subservient slave girl. With good reason, according to Knud Rasmussen, one female-dominated wretch with three wives bore the nickname of *Oqartaqangitseq* ("the tongueless"). "A census would certainly show a higher percentage of henpecked husbands among the Eskimos than in a civilized country," reported Kaj Birket-Smith, "except, perhaps," the ethnologist dryly added, "the United States."

The Eskimos could not understand why white people were so shocked by *kipuktu*—their practice of wife-sharing. Artificial morality had little to do with sex. A woman considered it an honor if she appeared comely to many men and could give them sexual pleasure; just as it was strange for a man to find pleasure in only one woman. It was good manners to share a wife's favors with a guest; it was likewise a practical necessity for a man going on a hunting trip to borrow a friend's wife if his own was sick or pregnant, since a female was needed to handle the scraping of hides and other domestic duties. Furthermore, a temporary exchange of mates helped relieve the tedium of the long winter nights. "There's no harm in it," an Eskimo told Gontran de Poncins. "A wife doesn't wear out. When I get mine back, she's always as good as before."

Usually the wives were consulted if two male friends sought to trade partners for the night. Sometimes the two wives themselves would hint gently to their respective spouses that a temporary switch of bed mates might be fruitful, particularly if one of the menage seemed impotent. Jealousy, of course, sometimes broke out, and a cuckolded husband might kill if he discovered his wife had been promiscuous without first consulting him. If her paramour was a stronger man, though, the cheated husband would invent a caustic nickname for her lover, which would cause him to lose face. Thus, according to the Canadian anthropologist, Asen Balikci, one notorious seducer was taunted as *Amusa* ("one who pulls"), "because of his habit of accosting absent hunters' wives and trying to copulate with them by pulling down their pants."

Nevertheless, despite the freedom of their sex mores, a deep and abiding love often developed between long-married couples. Diamond Jenness recounted how he once arranged to take an Eskimo named "The Runner" with him on an expedition to hunt those antediluvian behemoths, muskoxen (*umingmaks*, meaning "the bearded ones"). When the hunter's wife, Leaf, heard of the trip, she wasn't scared of her husband's being gored by one of the seven-hundred-pound bulls which form such a menacing ringed phalanx of horns when attacked. But she did plead with Jenness to protect "The Runner" from being enticed away by alluring women in the muskox country. "Men are so foolish with women," she said, uttering the universal sigh of wives.

An aging wife accepted with equanimity that the whips of too many winters had left their mark on her. Yet while she eked out her remaining years, though withered and semitoothless, her face now tattooed with hardship, the high-spirited crone was indomitable and invincible. Old age had earned for her the honored place in the ceremonial dance igloo. For hours on end, she dipped her knees and swayed to the tom-tom beat of the *ayayat* hoop drum and the rattle of the puffin seaparrot beaks,

To an Eskimo, "igloo" simply meant "house." It could be made of sod, stone, driftwood, even skin-covered whale ribs. Their curved, wind-resistant snowhouses were architecturally perfect for their environment. Polygamy and wife-sharing were common, but women were truly liberated and had a strong voice in the affairs of the community.

chanting her interminable chorus of *Ai-Yai-ya-ya.* Old age had won for her the title of *anaiyukok*—"the one to whom all listen." To her fell the role of sprinkling sacramental water on the slain seal or whale and crooning magical incantations to appease the wrath of the deprived "Fleshpot of the Sea."

And no matter how aged, she knew her son would always be devoted to her wishes, even if she wished for death. The Canadian missionary of the Mackenzie River district, Reverend C.E. Whittaker, told the moving story of an Eskimo traveling from Bathurst Inlet who met the elderly mother he had not seen in years. The ancient woman lifted up the front of her parka, exposing her pendulous breasts, and the son, with affection and obedience, stooped down and touched them with his lips. "However rude and uncultured the Eskimo may be," pondered the Reverend Mr. Whittaker, "the bond which binds the mother to her child is an enduring one, lasting as long as life itself."

An elderly man would be revered as *ihumatak*—"he who thinks"— and won respect as a soothsayer and story-teller. When the seal-oil lamps were darkened in the ceremonial igloo, he would hold a seance. Commanding his familiar spirits, he would take flight to the moon or to the bottom of the sea, and his audience would swear they could hear the swishing and whirring noises as of falcon's wings and feel the rush of the wind itself pass their faces.

The Eskimos, of course, were mystics, with a luxuriant sense of fantasy, and it was this that often baffled the Kabloona. Though the white men were equally superstitious, they could not understand the Eskimo need to people the faceless immensities of their land with trolls and goblins and supernatural beings. One man who did understand was the part-Eskimo explorer, Knud Rasmussen. He listened sympathetically to their folklore and he recognized in it a kind of primeval poetry. One old Eskimo minstrel named Blind Ambrosius, who referred to his songs as his "comrades in loneliness," tried to put in words to Rasmussen how he felt about his homeland:

Our country has wide borders; there is no man born has travelled round it.
And it bears secrets in its bosom of which no white man dreams.
Up here we live two different lives: in the Summer, under the torch of the
*   Warm Sun; in the Winter, under the lash of the North Wind.*
But it is the dark and cold that make us think most.
And when the long Dark spreads itself over the country, many hidden things
*   are revealed, and men's thoughts travel along mysterious paths.*

41

Rasmussen listened to this philosophy and was deeply affected. This most perceptive of explorers reflected: "These songs of theirs, their harmless fun, and a wistful sense of beauty, of loneliness, all struggling for expression, do show them rather as children in the wide, strange world; but as children like ourselves. . . . Intimately studied, the Eskimos are much more spiritual-minded, much more intelligent, much more likeable than the average man has been led to expect. They prove to be human beings just like ourselves—so like, indeed, that we cannot avoid drawing them into the fold and saying, 'These people belong to our race! We recognize them as brothers.' "

Chapter 2
The Viking Sea Darers

"Here goes Sea Darer" was the inscription emblazoned on one of the swan-necked, dragon-headed pirate ships that put terror into the hearts of men. "From the fury of the Northmen, Good Lord, deliver us" was the prayer that echoed throughout all the civilized world as the Norsemen raided and raped, plundered and pillaged.

They were called Vikings (from the Scandinavian *vik*, pronounced "veek," meaning fjord or bay) and from the eighth to the eleventh centuries A.D., these sea rovers from the northern fjords were dreaded as "the Viking scourge." Riding their high-prowed longships, a hymn to the war gods Odin and Thor on their lips, the freebooters slashed and hacked their bloodstained broadswords through the sea ports of England, Ireland, Scotland, France and Germany, and as far south as Sicily and Spain.

But it was *Vestervegen*—the westward way—that led them to glory in the annals of polar exploration. The buccaneers came westering in search of land and they became the first colonizers to leave their imprint on Iceland, Greenland and the upper reaches of North America.

The Viking colonizers were not altogether the helmeted barbarians depicted in Hollywood films. One might describe them as pagan outlaws, with a highly acquisitive streak and an unbridled passion for freedom. They were outcasts from overpopulated Norway and Sweden, where they feuded and brawled in an extremely hierarchical society:

clans of farmers banded under aristocratic chieftains, not unlike the Irish and Scots they frequently captured as slaves.

Their *hersir* (literally, "battle leaders") were arrogant, adventuresome, independent-minded war lords who gloried in such epithets as "Leif the Sword" and "Eric the Bloodaxe." In their own aggressive way they were good pioneer material. "A man who wishes to despoil others of their lives and goods must be up betimes," ran one of their maxims based on the wisdom of Odin. "A loafing wolf never gets fat, a sleeping man never wins a battle."

They were out-battled by Harald Fairhair, the would-be king of Norway, who wished to consolidate their land holdings into one realm. The archetype of the Viking, he was big, blond and burly, said to be an uprooter of oak trees, a ferocious warrior, and a great lady's man. The defeated noblemen could not bear the yoke of royal taxation and the deprivation of their liberty, so they set out across icy seas to take land.

Their "land-taking" was graphically described in their sagas, a body of folk literature that is still disputed today by scholars. For the Norse sagas were a romantically embellished form of hero worship; ancestral lore that was part *Arabian Nights*, part Homer's *Odyssey*, part authentic snippets of family history. In splitting hairs over what was fact and what was yarn-spinning embroidery, the bickering pedants have so obscured the genuine achievements of the Norse explorers that one is reminded of Mark Twain's witticism: "Researches of many commentators have already thrown much darkness on this subject, and it is probable that, if they continue, we shall soon know nothing at all about it."

From the crowded portrait gallery of the saga family genealogies, six land-takers emerge in clearest focus. They were Eric (the Red) Thorvaldsson, discoverer of Greenland; Eric's two sons who adventured to Vinland, Leif the Lucky and Thorvald the Luckless; Eric's bastard daughter, Freydis, a true Valkyrie cast in the role of villainess; and Eric's daughter-in-law, the golden-haired heroine, Gudrid, and her third husband, Thorfinn Karlsefni, who together produced little Snorri—the first white child born on the North American continent.

For three hundred years, generations of Icelanders passed on by word of mouth epic tales of Eric the Red's clan in the New World. And hair-raising tales they were: of blood feuds and homicides, of treachery and derring-do, of battles with the Eskimo-like *Skraelings*, and exploits that included an encounter with a fabulous breed of one-legged men known as the Unipeds.

The most fantastic story was left untold. That was the saga of how the seafarers cleaved their way through the impenetrable fogs, the blustering squalls and hammering ice floes in the northern seas. Archeological findings in the blue clay of Norwegian burial grounds have since revealed that the westering voyages were not negotiated in the famous dragonships. For those sleekly elegant longships were essentially men-of-war designed for speed and maneuverability.

Instead, the land-finders traveled in sturdier vessels known as *knarrs.* The sagas often referred to "knarr-beamed" women (meaning bountifully endowed), and these colonizing ships were indeed constructed along capacious lines. Some were eighty-tonners, about a hundred feet long, broad of beam and stoutly built of oak and pine, yet supple enough to take hard beatings in the pitching seas. A single square woolen sail bellying in the breeze, sixteen oars flashing from the black-and-yellow shielded portholes on each side, she was steered by a rudder board on the right side of the stern—hence the present seaman's term "starboard." But there was no compass to steer by. So the Vikings had to rely on the North Star (known to them as their Guiding Star), as well as the winds, the currents, the smells, plus an instinctive directional sense that might be called steering by guess and by God.

Some carried birds with them to locate land. In 865 A.D., this device was used by the Norseman who gave Iceland its forbidding name. He released three ravens at intervals until the third one guided his knarr to a fish-laden southern shore of the forty-thousand-square-mile island. Floki the Raven, as he was henceforth nicknamed, stood on a glacier mountain top one bitterly cold spring day, the sagas tell us, "and saw a fjord full of sea ice. Therefore he called the country Iceland." His cattle had perished that freezing winter, and the disgusted Floki "spoke very unfavorably of the country."

But on their return to Norway, it was his companion, Thorolf, who was believed. It was true that Iceland, hanging like a glaciated pendant from the Arctic Circle, was a weird land of frost and fire, full of boiling mudholes, spewing geysers, smoldering volcanoes, and moonlike deserts of petrified black lava. But Thorolf had seen lush pastures in this bleak and tormented landscape as well, and he reported ecstatically that "butter dripped from every blade of grass." The Vikings dearly loved epithets and thereafter the forty thousand Norse settlers who had flocked to Iceland by 930 A.D. to scratch out a living from the scrub birch and rocky plains had nicknamed the exaggerator—perhaps with an edge of irony—Thorolf the Butter.

*A swan-necked upthrust prow characterized the sleekly elegant Viking
longships. This ninth-century beauty, 70 feet long, was excavated from the blue
clay of a royal burial mound in Oseberg, Norway, and is now displayed at
Oslo's Viking Ship Hall. Leif the Lucky used a sturdier "knarr" vessel in 1001
A.D. to cross the 200 nautical miles of Davis Strait separating Greenland and
Canada.*

If recorded legend is to be believed, Iceland had been identified centuries before. About 330 B.C., an adventuresome astronomer named Pytheas set out from the Greek Mediterranean colony of Massilia (Marseilles), slipped past the Pillars of Hercules (at the eastern end of the Strait of Gibraltar), and sailed northward in the Seas of Darkness (the unknown Atlantic Ocean) to test his scholarly theories. Pytheas had spent long nights studying the stars. Now the geographer wanted to discover firsthand which star gave the more precise indication of the North Pole: Polaris (the North Star) or the Arctic (a Greek word meaning "bear," from the constellation of the Big Bear).

Pytheas never did reach the North Pole, but his squaresailed bireme galley ship, propelled by about ninety slave oarsmen, reputedly raised the coast of Iceland. Pytheas called it *Ultima Thule*—"the Outermost Boundary." His fellow astronomers called him a liar, because Pytheas claimed that Thule was lit by the midnight sun. Furthermore, his ship had been halted by a mysterious barricade of what seems to have been sludge ice—a "curdled" or "congealed" sea that was neither "land or sea or air, but a compound of all three elements."

A more entertaining, if less credible, account of voyaging to Iceland at the turn of the sixth century A.D. was given by the Irish sailor monk St. Brendan the Bold. The Brendan travel tales were larded with wild Irish blarney and streaked with pious Celtic fantasy, and they enjoyed a tremendous popularity in their day—a kind of priestly version of *The Adventures of Baron Munchausen.*

Apparently Brendan and his fourteen praying monks "glided into the misty darkness of the coagulated sea" aboard a square-sailed, oxhide-covered vessel known in the Middle Ages as a *curragh.* Marvelous were the miracles they witnessed: griffon birds that croaked psalms in Latin; a whale that obligingly let them cook a potful of stew on its back while their boat was accidentally anchored there; a siren of a mermaid whom they promptly baptized; horrible monsters of the deep that reverently swam away as soon as the holy brethren sang God's Mass; and the spectacle of Judas Iscariot cooling himself on an iceberg during his annual day's leave from hell.

It was preposterous stuff, of course, but there were nuggets of accurately observed geography. The Brendan chronicles, for example, gave a pretty good description of Mount Hecla erupting amid the mountains of Iceland. After rowing northward through "frozen waves" for eighty days, the monks skirted a lava-scarred island. It was "without trees or herbage," its high cliffs "black as coal and upright like a wall,"

"Here be dragons" was inscribed on early maps warning navigators who braved the unknown Seas of Darkness of the northern Atlantic. The monstrous sea serpent shown here was a figment of the imagination. But the Norse Sagas claimed that Leif's brother, Thorvald the Luckless, indubitably met his doom in Vinland pierced in the guts by a one-legged freak called a Uniped.

and a smoke-belching summit reminded them of a smith's forge with its "noise of bellows blowing like thunder and the beating of sledge hammers on anvils and iron." A favorable breeze caught the boat and drove them southward; and as they looked back, they saw the volcano peak "shooting up flames into the sky, which it drew back again to itself, so that the mountain seemed a burning pyre."

St. Brendan also preserved for posterity the first word picture of an iceberg. In a region where "the sea seemed to them transparent like glass," the monks gaped at "a great and bright jeweled crystal temple" whose summit appeared to pierce the skies. "It was covered over with a rare canopy, the material of which they knew not; but it had the color of silver, and was hard as marble, while the column itself was of the clearest crystal."

We do not know the exact location of these exotic sights. One of the many versions of the Brendan chronicles tells us that the monks penetrated "where the sea sleeps and cold runs through their veins." Yet much of Iceland has a relatively temperate climate, warmed by a branch of the Gulf Stream, and the independent republic's modern capital city of Reykjavik (pronounced Ray-kya-veek, Norse for "Bay of Smoke") boasts an average January temperature of thirty degrees Fahrenheit.

We do know, however, that Irish priests had landed in Iceland by 795 A.D., at least sixty years before the coming of the land-hungry Norse hordes. Refugees from the Viking assaults on Ireland, these were anchorites who sought sanctuary on the volcanic island. One reliable Celtic historian named Dicuil used a picturesque phrase to describe the ascetic life they led in the midnight sun. A monastic sitting in his cell on the loftiest mountain could see to *pediculos de camisia extrahere*—pick lice out of his hair shirt—at midnight as though it were high noon. In their sagas, too, the Vikings conceded that the early Norse settlers found on the east coast of Iceland "Irish books, bells and croziers" left behind by horrified priests who "went away because they did not wish to live there with heathens."

That red-bearded, red-handed pagan Eric Thorvaldsson, undoubtedly frightened off quite a few of these gentle souls when he swaggered onto the scene in the Highrocks district of Iceland. Red Eric was a violent man, ruthless, fearless, a born leader of men, and yet, amusingly enough, henpecked by his domineering wife, the daughter of the imposingly named Thorbjorg Shipbosom. Eric and his equally hot-tempered father were forced to flee from Norway, the sagas tell us euphemistically, because they were implicated in various "manslaugh-

When the Vikings colonized the New World (as shown in this imagined engraving), they wore capes and hoods; not Wagnerian war helmets as depicted in an ancient Swedish bone carving.

ters." Eric took up farming in Iceland, but rarely put down his sword and battleaxe. He quarreled, killed two neighbors named Eyjolf the Foul and Hrafn the Duellist, lay low for a while, and then slew at least two other men.

Banished for three years by the Icelandic parliament, the outlaw fitted out a knarr in 982 A.D. and told friends he would seek refuge in a land that an earlier voyager had sighted about two hundred miles farther west. That land, of course, was Greenland. At eight hundred and forty thousand square miles, it is, after the continent of Australia, the biggest island in the world—and the closest to the North Pole.

Even today it is a haunting experience to fly by helicopter over its peaks and valleys. It is an unfinished world, a ghostly relic of the Ice Age, 90 per cent of its white wastes dominated by an ice cap two miles thick at the centre. Only part of its jagged coastline is inhabitable, and here glaciers reach out into the fjords, break off with a roar like cannons and launch monstrous floating icebergs. A later explorer, John Davis, shuddered when he saw the "sugar loaf" mountains looming out of the mists off ice-rimmed Cape Discord. To him, it was "the most deformed, rocky and mountainous land that ever we saw," and the British mariner named it "The Land of Desolation." But Eric the Red, like Thorolf the Butter, had the flair of a tourist travel agent—the wily real estate promoter tagged it Greenland, because such an alluring name "would entice men to go thither."

On his return to Iceland, he enticed twenty-five boatloads of colonists to go there. But the winds blew hard that spring of 986 A.D. and only fourteen knarrs made it; the others foundered amid the ice floes or were forced back. Eric led the hardy pioneers up the most fertile fjords on the southwest coast and established two colonies—the Western Settlement being located near modern Julianehaab, the Eastern at Godthaab.

Archaeological digs conducted in the 1920s indicate there were ultimately about three hundred farms, and a population of perhaps four thousand. Houses were built of turf or stone and there were barns to protect the runty sheep, goats and cattle. The women spent their time weaving woolen hoods or making the sour milk curd delicacy called *skyr*. The men went up as far north as Disko Bay to collect precious driftwood and to hunt for the Arctic exotica that were traded with Europe. In exchange for narwhal tusks, white falcons and live polar bears, which were prized by royalty, they got in return shipments of grain, lumber and beer. Much of the beer was quaffed at the great banqueting hall in

Eric's mansion, Brattahlid (Steep Hillside). There the chieftain held court at baronial feasts and heard minstrels sing the praises of Earl Eric. "He was the man held in highest esteem," the sagas said, "and was respected by all."

His son, Leif, brought him new honor—as well as a certain amount of anguish. The sagas picture Leif as "a big, strapping fellow, handsome to look at, and in every respect a temperate, fair-dealing man." He may have been handsome, but he wasn't particularly temperate or fair-dealing in the year 999. On an expedition to Norway that summer, he was blown off his course to the Hebrides.

"There," the saga runs, "Leif fell in love with a certain woman whose name was Thorgunna. She was a woman of fine family and Leif believed she had supernatural wisdom."

Leif seduced her and dallied with her until far into the summer. Then when Leif was preparing to depart, the Scottish aristocrat begged to go with him.

Leif told her he did not consider it a wise move to abduct so high-born a woman, in a foreign country, and "we so few in numbers."

"Then," said Thorgunna, "I must tell you that I am not the only one concerned, for I am pregnant, and you are responsible."

Nevertheless, our hero jilted her. He gave her a gold finger ring, a Greenland wool cloak and a belt of walrus ivory. Then he hastily sailed away in his knarr while the going was good.

In Norway, Leif fell under the proselytizing spell of King Olaf, who baptized him and packed him off back to Greenland with a priest to preach Christianity there. On his way home, Leif rescued a shipwrecked crew, and because he was able to salvage their rich cargo of lumber, he was thereafter named Leif the Lucky.

But his heathen father, Eric, according to the sagas, swore blasphemously "that one thing cancelled out the other. For Leif had rescued a ship's company, but had also introduced a shyster (for such he styled the priest) into Greenland."

What was worse, all this holiness disrupted the old pagan's sex life. Eric's wife zealously embraced the Christian faith, and spent most of her time praying at the new church she had built. And when her husband refused to be converted from heathenism, reported the sagas, the zealot "would not have sexual intercourse with Eric, which made him extremely angry."

Leif the Christian tried to make amends by persuading his father to take charge of a bold new land-finding expedition. A merchant seaman named Bjarni, while blown off course, had caught a tantalizing glimpse of unknown land to the west. Norsemen were criticizing him because he had lacked the enterprise and curiosity to step ashore. Leif had bought Bjarni's knarr and outfitted her with a crew of thirty-five, but he thought it only fitting that the head of the clan lead the voyage of discovery.

At first Eric begged off. He reckoned he was getting on in years and didn't have the strength to endure the hardships of the sea as in days of yore. Leif argued that, of all Vikings, the original discoverer of Greenland commanded the most luck. Eric gave in. But on the day of sailing, Eric was thrown from his horse, and with a cry of "Ai! Ai!" considered the accident an omen of warning that he would bring bad luck if he accompanied the expedition. He told his son with sorrow: "It is not in my fate to discover any more lands than the one on which we now live. We shall not travel together any farther." He died within the year.

In the year 1001 A.D., Leif the Lucky became the first European to step onto North American soil. The sagas tell us that his initial landfall was a grim disappointment. He cast anchor at a shore that struck him as being "barren and useless. There was no grass to be seen, and the upperlands were covered with huge glaciers, and between glaciers and sea the shore was like one single flat slab of rock."

Leif announced philosophically: "Unlike Bjarni, we have at least set foot on this land. I shall now give the country a name, and call it *Helluland*—Flatstone Land."

Leif evidently had set foot on Baffin Island, the biggest island rampart that guards the most easterly rim of the Canadian Arctic. It is so naked and austere that early Breton fishermen called it *Terre Sterile*. Slashing like an icy scimitar down the ragged east coast of its some two hundred thousand square miles are the Iron Mountains. These are the Alps of the Arctic. They are greenstone and gneiss cliffs stabbing more than eight thousand feet high, and they spill glaciers and granite rock in plenty into the fjords of Davis Strait.

Leif is now believed to have landed at Cape Aston, a Baffin Island peninsula that juts into Davis Strait. It lies almost directly opposite Greenland's Disko Bay, and Leif would have sailed just two hundred nautical miles across Davis Strait to beach there. Most important, the beach is slabbed with rock as flat as flagstones, and Leif would have easily observed the glacier-riven mountains towering in the background before he "sailed out to sea and lighted on another land."

This second land, according to the sagas, was "flat and wooded, and wherever they went there were white sandy beaches shelving gently down to the sea." The "Marvel Strands" of beach were wonderful, but Leif was more impressed by the stands of forest. "This country," he decided, "shall be named after its natural resources, and we will call it *Markland*—Wood Land."

This is now believed to be Labrador, the subarctic region of the Canadian province of Newfoundland. After coasting past its looming black Torngat Mountains (Eskimo for "demons"), Leif would have seen patches of black spruce. As for the Marvel Strands, they have been identified as the thirty-mile-long sandy white beaches stretching uniquely on that sere and sawtoothed coast from the spruce woods down to the sea just south of Labrador's Cape Porcupine.

The third land that Leif discovered has been more difficult to trace, for it appears to have been a virtual Shangri-la. After sailing southward for two more days, the voyagers finally reached a balmy place. "They went ashore and looked about them, and the weather was fine," the sagas rhapsodized. "They saw that there was dew on the grass, and they cupped it in their hands and put it to their lips, and they thought they had never before tasted anything so sweet."

There were so many eider ducks in the region that there was hardly any place to step between the eggs. There was a river flowing nearby, and it was brimming with the biggest salmon they had ever seen. "The land was so bountiful that it seemed to them that the cattle would not need fodder during the winter. There was no frost in winter, and the grass hardly withered."

Most remarkably, one of Leif's German-speaking crew members, seems to have got drunk on fermented berries. He blurted out in thick-tongued Norse, "I can report on something new. I have found vines and grapes."

"Is that true?" asked Leif.

"Certainly," replied the addled German sailor, "for I was born where there is no lack of vines and grapes."

After wintering there in this winterless paradise, Leif had his men stock the *knarr* with a full cargo of felled timber and berries. And he sailed home after giving the land a name "in accordance with the good things they found in it, and he called it *Vinland*."

Armchair explorers have since located Wineland the Good everywhere from Nova Scotia's Cape Breton to Martha's Vineyard in Massachusetts and as far south as the Carolinas. Each theorist has his personal axe of propinquity to grind. Professor Eben S. Horsford of Harvard University, for instance, was determined to place Leif as close

Fierce figureheads, like this carving excavated from the Viking burial mound in Oseberg, Norway, were designed to ward off evil spirits and frighten enemies. The Viking settlements vanished; so did their warships bearing such poetical names as "Lion of the Waves", "Raven of the Wind" and "Sea Darer."

as possible to the Harvard Yard and argued that the Viking had landed within one mile of its principal gate.

Only one Vikingologist has taken Vinland out of the realm of speculation and anchored it with irrefutable evidence. He is the distinguished Norwegian author and Arctic explorer, Dr. Helge Ingstad. In 1960, after diligently following Leif's trail, the geographic sleuth traced the Viking colony down to a grassy estuary at L'Anse aux Meadows—French-Canadian for Bay of Meadows. It sits on the north tip of the Island of Newfoundland, overlooking the Strait of Belle Isle, the narrow body of water that separates the island from its northerly region of Labrador.

In the face of scholarly sceptics, Dr. Ingstad had translated Vinland's *vin* to read not "wine," but to adhere to its ancient Norse meaning of "grass" or "meadows." And the meadowlands of L'Anse aux Meadows were not the sole features that matched the clues he found in the sagas. Nearby flows Black Duck Brook, a river alive in summer with spawning salmon and bobbing eider ducks. There are forests of spruce trees. For good measure, amid its purple iris and violets, there are plentiful currant, cloudberry, cranberry and squashberry bushes, from which a potent beverage can be brewed.

Though L'Anse aux Meadows enjoys a relatively mild maritime climate, it is not, however, a frost-free paradise luxuriant with vines and grapes. Dr. Ingstad could argue that Leif exaggerated to entice settlers and hence put the grape in Wineland just as his father put the green in Greenland. But Dr. Ingstad, who is married to the archeologist, Anne Stine, believes in science rather than surmise. From 1961 to 1968, his wife headed teams of archeologists from five different nations who conducted excavations. Their carbon-14 datings of the ruins dug out at L'Anse aux Meadows prove indisputably that a Viking settlement was built there about the year 1000.

The eight major house sites they unearthed have yielded a treasure trove. The most spectacular of the rectangular sod buildings, seventy feet long and fifty-five feet wide, was designed strikingly like the Viking great halls in Greenland and Iceland, where the Norse pirates used to gather around the hearth to feast and sing. Another site revealed burned and fire-cracked stones, apparently the remains of a steam bath. Also exhumed were relics of four boat sheds, an Icelandic-style stone lamp, a whetstone for sharpening needles, a smithy, and hundreds of chunks of smelted bog iron (significant because neither Indians nor Eskimos knew how to smelt or hot-forge iron).

Two of the artifacts bared were especially outstanding. One was a soapstone spindle wheel, an inch and a half in diameter, part of a spinning device once used by Norsewomen to twist raw wool into yarn. The other was a bronze ring-headed pin, the kind commonly used by Vikings to fasten their cloak on the right shoulder, so that the right arm would be free for wielding a sword.

That pin might have been worn by Leif's luckless brother, Thorvald. Apparently there was sibling rivalry between the two sons. For on Leif's return from Vinland we are told that "Thorvald considered the land had been explored in too restricted a fashion." He wanted to outdo his brother.

So Thorvald borrowed Leif's knarr, enroled a crew, and in 1004 sailed for Vinland. The ship was moored beside a pleasing cape, and as he walked ashore on a gangplank, Thorvald exulted, "It is beautiful here. Here I should like to make my home."

But it was here that the Vikings had a bloody encounter with those controversial aborigines, the Skraelings. Though they may have been Newfoundland's Indians, it seems more likely that the natives were Eskimos. One of the sagas describes them as dwarfish, evil-looking men, with coarse hair, extraordinary eyes and broad cheekbones. Their "skin boats" were evidently kayaks, for we are further informed that the Skraelings paddled them with "waving sticks as if grain were beaten with flails."

Thorvald made the mistake of killing eight of these pygmylike folk who were found sleeping beneath their skin boats. One of the kayakers escaped and returned with a great swarming fleet of Skraelings brandishing bows and arrows.

"Hang the war shields over the sides of the ship," cried Thorvald, "and we shall defend ourselves as best we can."

They fought until the Skraelings fled, but Thorvald was killed by one of their arrows. The last speech of the dying Viking has a Wagnerian ring to it. As he drew out the fatal arrow, Thorvald exclaimed, according to one saga: "Though there is fat around my belly, this arrow will be the death of me. We have won a fine and fruitful country, but I will hardly be allowed to enjoy it."

Then Thorvald urged his men to carry him to the headland where he had first walked ashore and wished to make his home. "It seems," he said, "I spoke the truth when I said I should dwell there for a while. For there you shall bury me, and set crosses at my head and feet, and call it Cape of Crosses for ever more."

It was a heroic speech, but it is marred somewhat by another version of the sagas. This version had the Norse party enter fabulous Uniped Land. There Thorvald the Luckless was ignominiously struck in the guts with an arrow shot by a mere one-legged assailant. The sailors ran after the fellow, but though he had only one foot, the Uniped had no trouble hopping away in triumph. One Viking who failed to catch him later admitted defeat in a dirgelike ballad:

We men were chasing, this is true,
A One-Footer down to the beach,
But the weird creature streaked away,
Hopping speedily across the sea shore.
Hear this, Karlsefni!

The ballad was addressed to Thorfinn Karlsefni, leader of the next expedition to Vinland. Karlsefni was a wealthy merchant trader, an intrepid seaman from a noble Icelandic family. Among his ancestors were the staunchly named Thord Horsehead, Thorvald Backbone, Bjorn Ironside and Ragnar Shaggypants. With a family tree of that sort, he was able to woo and win in Greenland the hand of the fair Gudrid. She was the wise, beautiful and tactful widow of one of Leif's brothers.

In 1011, partly due to the gentle persuasion of Gudrid, Karlsefni decided to embark on the first serious attempt to colonize Vinland. Besides a good supply of livestock, his three ships carried one hundred and sixty men and women. One passenger was old Eric's bastard daughter, Freydis, a bellicose, knarr-bosomed wench. "She was very much the virago," the sagas said of her, "who had married her nobody of a husband mainly for his money." Another person aboard was one of Eric's old heathen cronies, Thorhall the Hunter, described as "giant-statured and foul-mouthed, a trouble-maker always egging people on to the worst."

When they reached the Marvel Strands of Labrador, the trouble-maker incited nine crew members into a mutiny. Thorhall was disgusted because the paradise had produced no vaunted wine, no grapes, just a stranded whale on the beach whose blubber had made everybody ill. As he helped the mutineers carry buckets of water aboard a ship before sailing off, Thorhall recited a mock ditty:

When I came, these brave men told me,
Here the best of drink I'd get.
Now with water pail behold me,
I who wore a warrior's helmet,
Wine and I are strangers yet!

And, as he hoisted sail, Thorhall bade farewell to the landlubbers and cheered on his thirsty crew with another verse:

Comrades, let us now be faring,
Homeward to our own again,
Let us try the sea steed's daring,
Give the chafing courser rein.
Those who will may bide in quiet,
Let them praise this chosen land,
Feasting on a whale steak diet,
In their home by Marvel Strand!

As far as Karlsefni was concerned, it was good riddance to bad rubbish. For he later learned that westerly gales drove the mutineers to Ireland, where Thorhall was slain and his crew cast into slavery.

The persevering Karlsefni cruised his remaining colonists southward to a land-locked bay, and there he discovered the land of promise. There were grass and wild oats flourishing everywhere, and the fields were awash with purple wine berries, and the river was teeming with fish. There his wife, Gudrid, gave birth to their son, Snorri, the first white child born in the New World. But there also the settlers ran into the Skraelings.

At first Karlsefni had his men raise their white shields of peace, and the Skraelings accepted that symbol and there was brisk trading. In exchange for red cloth and *skyr*, the natives bartered silver fox furs and grey pelts. And so it went peaceably for two winters.

But then a Skraeling who tried to steal some Viking battle axes was slain by one of Karlsefni's house servants. "We had best lay our heads together now," said Karlsefni, "for I fancy they will be paying us a hostile visit in full force." He urged the women to stay behind in the stockade, while the men met the vengeful savages in a clearing in the forest. And since the bellowing of the colony bull had frightened off the natives previously, Karlsefni said, "We must take our bull and let him march at our head."

A flotilla of kayakers swept around the headland, "so many that the bay appeared sown with coals." They clashed in battle, the Vikings raising their red shields of war, while the howling Skraelings showered them with arrows and rocks from slingshots. One missile was hurled from a slinglike pole—a blueish black, ball-shaped object, "the size of a sheep's belly," possibly a walrus hide. It so terrified the Vikings that they fled to the hills.

Freydis, the fierce Valkyrie, then stepped into the fray. Though pregnant, she ran from the stockade to rally the retreating Norsemen.

"Why do you run from such pitiful wretches, brave men like you?" she taunted. "You should be able to slaughter them like cattle. If I had a weapon, I'm sure I could fight better than any of you!"

Then she noticed a dead Viking, whose skull had been split by a flat stone. His drawn sword lay beside him. "She snatched up the sword," the sagas say, "and when the Skraelings rushed towards her, she pulled out her breasts from her bodice and slapped the naked sword on them, and this sight so frightened the Skraelings that they fled back to their boats and hastened away."

Karlsefni praised Freydis for her courage, but decided it was time to sail home to Greenland. The war-like Skraelings were too much for them. Besides, blood feuds were beginning to break out as the bachelor colonists quarreled over the sexual favors of the few wives on the expedition.

The formidable Freydis soon demonstrated that she would not be pestered or outfought by any man. For in 1014 she became the first woman leader to head the final—and goriest—expedition to Vinland.

Utterly without scruples, she struck a double-dealing bargain with two Icelandic brothers, Helgi and Finnbogi, who had arrived in Greenland on a trading vessel from Norway. She convinced them that a voyage to Vinland would yield honor and riches. So she and the brothers, each in their own ship, would carry thirty fighting men plus womenfolk to the new country, and there they would go halves with her on all profits. After shaking hands on this equal-sharing partnership, Freydis got permission from her half-brother, Leif, to borrow his old colony house in Vinland.

Freydis immediately violated the agreement by sneaking five extra warriors aboard her knarr. And when they reached Vinland, she further doublecrossed her partners. She forced them out of Leif's settlement house on the claim that it belonged to her.

The ousted brothers were reduced to building a hut nearby, and one of them swore at Freydis, "We are no match for you in evil."

Freydis was not yet through with her skulduggery. Before dawn one winter morning, we are told, she slipped out of bed and wrapped herself in the cloak of her no-account husband, Thorvard, and walked barefooted through the heavy dew for a seemingly innocent tryst with one of the brothers. At the doorway of the hut she called out to the slumbering Finnbogi, "Come outside, for I want to talk to you."

He did as she asked, and they sat down on a log that lay close to the hut. "How do you like things here?" she asked.

"I am happy with what the land produces," he replied. "But I am ill-pleased with the cold wind blowing between us, for I gave no cause for it."

"True enough," said she, "and that goes for me, too. And so I have come to propose something. I would like to trade ships with you two brothers, for yours is larger than mine, and I plan on leaving this country."

"That can be done," said he, "if it is your pleasure."

After this amiable exchange, Finnbogi went back to sleep and Freydis tiptoed home through the dew. When she climbed into bed, she awakened her husband, Thorvard, with her cold feet. He asked her why she was so chilly and wet.

She raged at him with passion: "I have been to those brothers, asking to buy their ship—I wanted to buy a bigger one. And they took my request so badly they assaulted me and roughed me up. But you! Spineless wretch that you are! You will not avenge my shame or your own! And here I am far away from home in Greenland. I swear I'll leave you unless you take revenge for this insult!"

Stung by her jibes, he marched his warriors over to the brothers' hut, seized the sleeping men and bound them, and led the captives out of the hut one at a time. And Freydis had each man killed as he came out.

With all the men of the brothers' party butchered, only their handful of women remained, but nobody would kill them.

Freydis spoke up: "Hand me an axe."

Then she slew the five women and left them there.

After this wickedness, the sagas say, the murderess loaded her ships with the richest cargo of lumber ever taken from Vinland and sailed back to Greenland. She swore she would kill any of her accomplices who denied that the partners' party had remained behind voluntarily in Vinland. But some of the crew members couldn't keep their mouths shut and Leif seized three of them and tortured them until the full story of the crime was confessed.

"I have not the heart to treat Freydis as she deserves," said Leif. "But this curse I prophesy for her and hers: no offspring of hers will ever come to any good."

And the end of the matter was, concluded the sagas, that from that time on nobody thought anything but ill of that family.

On that note of doom the Norse thrust into the New World began to fade into history's oblivion. The Vikings made no other recorded attempt to colonize Vinland. And by the fifteenth century the two settlements that Eric the Red had planted in Greenland seem to have withered completely. Nobody knows what happened to those some four or five thousand pioneers. Were they struck down by the same Black Plague that almost decimated the population of Iceland? Did they perish in a deteriorating icy climate? Were they slaughtered by Skraelings or absorbed by intermarriage with Greenland's Eskimos?

The mystery has baffled scholars for centuries. All they know is that the westering Vikings vanished, their settlements swallowed up in the Seas of Darkness, their deeds and discoveries preserved only in those northern lights of folk literature, their sagas. If for no other reason, they ought to be remembered for at least one ancient Norse chronicle, *The King's Mirror*. It was recorded by an anonymous scribe in the mid-thirteenth century. And though it was about the Vikings' sea venturing to Greenland, it described universally the motivating forces that impelled all later polar explorers to dare the ice and the cold and the mists of an unknown world:

"If you wish to know what men seek in that land, or why men journey thither in so great peril of their lives, it is the threefold nature of man that draws him thither. One part thereof is the spirit of rivalry and the desire for fame; for it is a man's nature to go where there is likelihood of great danger, and to make himself famous thereby. Another part is the desire for knowledge; for it is man's nature to wish to know and see those parts of which he has heard, and to find out whether they are as it was told him or not. The third part is the desire of gain; for men seek after riches in every place where they learn that profit is to be had, even though there is great danger in it."

Chapter 3

The Cabots in Quest of Cathay

He had a portrait of himself painted when he was an old man, and it gives us an insight into his intriguing personality. We see an imposing figure with a white forked beard and long spidery fingers, spreading a pair of dividers across the Arctic regions of a globe. His sharp brown eyes stare out at us with all the shrewdness and guile of a sixteenth century sage or wizard. He is splendidly attired in the gold chain and ermine robes of the two high offices he then held.

It is with good reason that "pilot" is derived from the Basque word for "magician." After having served for thirty years as Pilot Major of Spain, he was now Grand Pilot of England, and he gives the impression of knowing very well that he was a powerful Merlin. The second title he held when his picture was painted was equally portentous. He was "Governor of the Mysterie and Companie of the Merchants Adventurers for the Discoverie of Regions, Dominions, Islands and Places Unknowen."

To make sure that everybody would recognize his eminence, he had a Latin inscription painted on the left-hand corner of the portrait. It identifies the subject as: "Sebastian Cabot, Englishman, son of John Cabot, Venetian Golden Knight, first discoverer of the New Found Land under Henry VII, King of England."

The inscription was characteristically misleading on at least three counts. Sebastian Cabot was not an Englishman but an Italian. His father, John Cabot, was never knighted but died in obscurity in 1498. And, most significantly, the Latin is phrased with intentional ambiguity,

EFFIGIES SEBASTIANI CABOTI
ANGLI FILII IOHANIS CABOTI VEN
TI MILITIS AVRATI PRIMI INVET
ORIS TERRÆ NOVÆ SVB HERICO VII ANGI
IÆ REGE

MASSACHUSETTS HISTORICAL SOCIETY

Sebastian Cabot, the great Machiavellian confidence man of Arctic exploration, tried to steal from his father, John Cabot, the credit and glory of being the first to discover North America.

so that one couldn't tell whether Sebastian or his father was being credited with the discovery of North America.

We know now that it was John Cabot who, at five o'clock in the morning of June 24, 1497, unfurled the flag of King Henry VII and first took possession of those northerly Canadian shores on behalf of England. But our present knowledge is not due to his status-hungry son. For almost four hundred years, until near the end of the nineteenth century, Sebastian was to mislead the historians. He fooled them by having denied the achievements of his father and grabbing the glory for himself.

Sebastian was the great Machiavellian confidence man of exploration. To Henry Harrisse, the magisterial scholar and historian whose detective work finally unearthed the incriminating evidence in the late 1800s, no words were too black to paint his villainy. Besides being unfilial and an ingrate, Sebastian was a liar, an intriguer, a self-advertiser, a conniver, and even a bungler at his job of piloting an explorer's ship.

All evidently true. And yet, because rascality is more interesting than virtue, we can't help but be fascinated by the rogue's career which overshadowed his father's for so many years. This is regrettable, for John Cabot deserves more from history. He merits at least as much fame as his rival Italian explorer whose path kept crisscrossing his—Christopher Columbus.

By one of the caprices of history, Columbus is revered today for having discovered America. Yet to his dying day Columbus insisted that the New World he had reached in the Caribbean was none other than Asia. It is a further irony that Columbus never stepped on the mainland of either North America or Asia. On the celebrated landfall of October 12, 1492, when he knelt to kiss the earth and plant the banners of King Ferdinand and Queen Isabella of Spain, the "Indies" he took possession of was the coral island of San Salvador in the Bahamas. Not until his third voyage, on August 5, 1498, did he land briefly on the Venezuelan coast of South America, and that expedition was to end with the disgraced Columbus being sent back to the Spanish court in the chains of a convict.

Like Cabot, Columbus died a broken and nearly forgotten man. But unlike Cabot, it was his good luck to have a devoted son, Ferdinand, who wrote a biography to glorify his father's memory. It was John Cabot's additional bad luck that he left behind not a single scrap of paper, neither a journal, nor a letter, nor a map, describing his accomplishments. Almost all our knowledge of his momentous discovery comes from second-hand sources, and that frequently muddied up by Cabot *fils*. History, as Oscar Wilde once jested, is merely gossip recorded, and the Cabot story bears him out. Historians have been forced to piece it together from bits of hearsay and fragmentary asides in other people's letters.

From these sketchy sources, "the most honest man, John Cabot," emerges as an enterprising mapmaker, spice trader, and sea captain. "A man of the people," a contemporary describes him, ". . . of kindly wit and a most expert mariner." He was eloquent and convincing and yet without braggadocio when recounting his feats; for a rather cynical Italian diplomat writes of an interview with him, "He tells all this in such a way, and makes everything so plain, that I also feel compelled to believe him." But it was his brilliance as a self-taught geographer that most impressed people. Richard Hakluyt, the great explorers' Boswell of the period, called him a peerless cartographer, who "made himself very expert and cunning in knowledge of the circuite of the world . . . as by a chart and other demonstrations reasonable he showed."

Giovanni Caboto—to give him his proper name before it was Anglicized—acquired a love for mapmaking and sailoring in the Italian seaport of Genoa. The son of a merchant, he was born and brought up there about the same time as that moody, red-haired wool weaver's son, Cristoforo Colombo, who was born near Genoa in 1451.

As boys, the two would-be explorers were enraptured as they read of the adventures of another Italian, Marco Polo. Some two hundred years before, while jailed in Genoa, the Venetian had dictated to a fellow prisoner his *Book of the Marvels and Wonders of the Kingdoms of the East*. It told in extravagant terms how as a seventeen-year-old youth he had traveled to the kingdoms of the Mongol king of kings, Kublai Khan. And wonderful were the riches Polo had seen.

In the kingdoms of Cathay (actually *Khitai*, the Tartar name for a Chinese Manchu province), the Grand Khan had palaces "roofed with fine gold" and courtyards paved with gold "over two fingers in thickness." In *Cipango* (or Japan), the Oriental potentates were decked out with sumptuous silks and gems and rose-colored pearls, "very beautiful, and round, and large." And somewhere in the China Sea (presumably he meant the Moluccas of East Indonesia) were more than seven thousand spice islands, each perfumed with trees "more valuable than aloes wood"; and there the warm winds fanned the fragrance of "truly prodigious amounts of precious spices," such as nutmeg, cloves, cinnamon, spikenard, galangal, black pepper, as well as "a kind of pepper that is as white as snow."

Marco Polo had not been believed when he returned to Venice. The merchants at the Rialto—the trading centre of the Venetian Grand Canal—called him "Marco of the Millions," because they thought he exaggerated a million times. It was beyond imagination that one place could produce such an abundance of spices, for these were luxuries esteemed all through the Renaissance period as highly as jewels. At a time when there was no refrigeration, pepper and allspice served as vital preservatives. The gentry carried about with them a nutmeg in a little silver box fitted with a tiny grater, prepared to season otherwise unpalatable meat. And in an age when daily baths were considered ungenteel, the unwashed rich hung a spicy pomander of cloves around their throats to mask their musky aroma. The merchants of Venice made a fortune by trans-shipping to Europe the dribble of spices that came via the overland camel caravan route from the faroff "Indies," and the incurious traders scoffed at the tall tales of Messer Marco.

Indoor geographers, sticking by their hazy concepts of the unknown globe, did not believe him either. "Here be dragons," their maps warned of the Seas of Darkness—that terrible abyss that no navigator could possibly traverse. Yet Marco Polo hinted that the riches of Cathay, some twenty-five hundred nautical miles away, could be reached by ship; Cipango (Japan) was a mere twelve hundred miles from its golden shores; and, as for the spice islands in the China Sea, Polo wrote confidently, "I will add that this sea, though I have said that it is called the Sea of Chin, yet it is nothing but the Ocean Sea."

But Colombo and Caboto believed him. Each of these Genoese mariners nursed his independent dream of discovering a westerly sea route to those fabulous spiceries. Columbus felt it could be accomplished by voyaging southward; Cabot, northward.

A religious mystic who heard the voices of biblical prophets in his sleep, Columbus relied on theology rather than geography to help him find a route. "In carrying out this enterprise of the Indies," he later declared, "neither reason nor mathematics nor maps were of any use to me; fully accomplished were the words of Isaiah." His divine guidance led him to some rather curious conclusions; he was certainly the first explorer to contend that the North Pole was a forbidden Garden of Eden. "I have come to another conclusion respecting the earth, namely, that it is not round as they describe, but of the form of a pear," Columbus affirmed, "upon one part of which is a prominence like a woman's nipple, this protrusion being the highest and nearest the sky.... I believe it is impossible to ascend thither, because I am convinced that it is the spot of the terrestrial paradise, whither no one can go but by God's permission."

A more down-to-earth man, Cabot first established himself as a merchant sea trader in Venice. Then he voyaged to Mecca, the holy city of Arabia, to seek first-hand knowledge about the chain of spice caravans. When he asked the Arabian camel drivers where their spices had originated, Cabot later told a friend, "they answered that they did not know, but that other caravans came with this merchandise to their homes from distant countries, and these again said that the goods had been brought to them from other remote regions." Eastern Asia, "the place where the spices grow," was obviously very far east and probably extended very far north. So Cabot reasoned that, since the world is round and distances decrease polewards, a northwest passage would ultimately prove to be the shortest route to take traders to the spiceries of northeast Asia. It would be cheaper than paying toll to the middlemen, the customsmen, and the bandits that made the overland camel route so costly.

Each with his illusions of a shrunken globe, Columbus and Cabot both sought backing for their expeditions from the courts of Portugal, Spain and England, the three nations that were beginning to vie keenly for world trade supremacy. The Bible-quoting Columbus was rejected by Portugal (the Portuguese court considered him a "big talker") and Henry VII of England did not think much of his traveling promoter (Columbus's brother, Bartholomew, who was captured by pirates en route to London). But Cristoforo's religious fervor did win the ear of that ardent Catholic, Queen Isabella of Spain. She even offered to pawn her personal jewels to launch Columbus; for she saw in his divine mission a golden opportunity of bringing millions of new souls to Christ and at the same time diverting the treasures of the enslaved infidels to the royal coffers.

Portugal and Spain turned down the sponsorship of Cabot's more northerly expedition, for what reason we do not know. We do know, however, that Cabot was evidently in Barcelona in April, 1493, when Columbus was making his triumphal return to the Spanish court. Cabot must have felt chagrined when he saw his rival, now proclaimed the "Admiral of the Ocean Sea," parading through the streets with his six painted and bedizened Indians, his parrots and herbs and a few gold nose rings, all purported trophies of the riches of Cathay. Cabot knew from his research that Cathay had *not* been reached, and he was determined to be the first man to do it.

THE NATIONAL MARITIME MUSEUM, LONDON

King Henry VII, the tight-fisted monarch of Tudor England, signed a discoverer's licence made out to "our well-beloved John Cabot, Venetian citizen." The explorer discovered lucrative Newfoundland codfish. Frugal Henry rewarded him with ten English pounds.

So Cabot packed up his maps and his globes, his Venetian wife, Mathye, and his three sons, and sailed for England to persuade Henry VII to lend his name to a proper voyage of discovery. King Henry did not need too much persuading. He sorely regretted having turned down the Columbus brothers; their project would have brought him the glittering prizes of the West Indies. He had further lost out in the jockeying for monopoly control of the spice trade; the Spanish-born Borgia pope, Alexander VI, father of Cesare and Lucrezia Borgia, had issued a papal bull dividing all southerly new found lands in the western hemisphere between Spain and Portugal.

Furthermore, Henry, a notorious pennypincher, had nothing to lose and everything to gain from Cabot. First of the Tudor monarchs, the Welshman was still paying for the Wars of the Roses, which had ended with his costly victory of the red rose emblem over the white. Henry had coined the word "sovereign" and he carefully initialled each page of the exchequer accounts before spending a single sovereign. Yet here was Cabot proposing to find a shorter route to Cathay "on his own proper charges"—meaning it wouldn't cost Henry a ha'penny. And, to boot, he was offering to cut the royal exchequer into one fifth of the profits gained from the venture.

It is little wonder therefore that the thrifty Tudor signed with a flourish on March 5, 1496, a discoverer's licence made out to "our well-beloved John Cabot, Venetian citizen." It granted him and his three sons, Sebastian, Lewis and Sancio, the right to sail in five ships on a voyage of exploration to any heathen lands except those southward which "before this time were unknown to all Christians."

Cabot did not sail in five ships. He was a poor mapmaker in a foreign country and he had to rely on the financing of the cautious merchants in the English port of Bristol. The Bristol merchants outfitted him with a single oaken *navicula* ("little ship") of fifty tons, the size of a small yacht. It was probably a double-decked, three-masted tub, with two sails of woven flax, square-shaped, and the centre one rigged "lateen", or Latin triangular style. Cabot named her the *Mathew*. We do not know for sure, but it was probably the Anglicized version of "Mathye, my beloved wife," to whom Cabot had willed seventy-five gold ducats. It is pleasant, at any rate, to think so, for it would have been the only ship any great explorer had named after his wife.

Cabot's nautical leap into the dark was hardly attractive to most of the eighteen crew members he enlisted. Two of the exceptions were

John Cabot, about to depart from Bristol,
England, on his first voyage of discovery on
May 20, 1497, with 18 crew members
aboard the 50-ton oaken navicula, Mathew
receives the blessings of the Lord Mayor of
Bristol. This painting, entitled "The
Departure of John and Sebastian Cabot from
Bristol on Their First Voyage of Discovery,
1497," is an imagined conception by artist
Ernest Board. Cabot thus initiated the quest
for a Northwest Passage to the spice islands
of Cathay via the upper reaches of North
America. That will-o'-the-wisp was to lure
mariners for the next four centuries and led to
the mapping of the Arctic.

CITY ART GALLERY, BRISTOL

probably lured by greed—a Burgundian merchant friend of his as well as Cabot's Italian barber. Sebastian Cabot, then about fifteen, may or may not have been a crew member, though he later claimed he conducted the entire expedition out of a personal thirst for glory. "All men, with great admiration, affirmed it to be a thing more divine than human to sail by the West into the East, where spices grow, by a way never known before," declared Sebastian. "By this fame and report there increased in my heart a great flame of desire to attempt some signal deed."

No flame burned in the hearts of the other crew members. Like the sailors on the first Columbus voyage and on Cabot's second expedition, they were doubtless convicts who had been released from jails. For wages of about two pennies and two pints of beer per day, the dragooned men had to survive for weeks in between-decks quarters filthy with rats, cockroaches and bilge water. The cramped space, as one voyager put it, was "right evill and smouldring hote and stynkynge." In the Arctic exploration orders later issued by Grand Pilot Sebastian Cabot, prayers had to be said twice a day and "blasphemy of God or detestable swearing" was strictly forbidden—though heaven knows the rations of salt pork and hardtack biscuits were maggoty enough to warrant curses. The seamen then impressed into the service of the British Navy began each meal by hammering their food on the table—to shake free the swarming weevils.

If they didn't die of scurvy, seamen on voyages of exploration almost went out of their wits with fear. Those aboard the *Mathew* were just a little better equipped than the Vikings to probe the unknown. Though a primitive quadrant helped fix latitude, they had no means of determining longitude. They used a half-hour glass of trickling sand which told the time, a crude astrolabe which told the altitude of the North Star, a compass whose mariner's needle pointed to the magnetic north pole, and dreamlike maps whose blank spaces were filled in with pictures of ship-swallowing whirlpools and demigorgons. To superstitious seamen, the most horrendous bogy was the prospect of tumbling off the edge of the world. They had an adage that ran, "Beyond all things, ocean; beyond ocean, nothing."

On May 20, 1497, having "committed himself to fortune," John Cabot slipped the *Mathew* out of Bristol and sailed northwest into the oceanic nothing. The Bristol Art Gallery today exhibits a painting in which the artist, Ernest Board, imagines the pomp and pageantry when the Lord Mayor, on the cobblestoned quay, offered his blessings to the departing Cabot. One can also imagine the little navicula tiptoeing her way through the red granite gorges of the Avon River, the banks vivid with yellow primroses and bluebells which continue to bloom there in May to this day.

One can further imagine the bells of the ancient Bristol church, then known as "St. Mary's on the Red Cliffs," pealing a cheerful bon voyage. The church, built in 1140 by the local merchants who traded woven woolens for Iceland's dried codfish and the sherry from Spain and Portugal (already known as "Bristol milk"), claimed as its parishioner the John Cabot who rented a house at nearby St. Nicholas Street at two English pounds a year.

Indeed, one can still see today hanging over the church archway of St. John's Chapel what purports to be the rib of a whale or a walrus that Cabot brought back as a thanksgiving souvenir from his 1497 voyage. Records preserved by today's Redcliffe Church describe the relic as a "rib of the Dun Cow" (meaning cow-whale) and a notation in the city treasury records reads:

"1497—Item. Paid for settynge upp ye bone of ye bigge fyshe and . . . hys works brote over seas, *vid.* For two rings of iron iiijd."

Unfortunately, records spelling out the actual details of Cabot's thirty-five-day North Atlantic crossing are vexingly skimpy. The skipper, we are told, after passing the Dursey Head of Ireland, "then bore towards the north and the west," keeping the North Star on his right hand. Northeasterly winds whined through the riggings, and he "wandered about for some time"; but the sea was calm except for two or three days before his landfall. Then he ran into a gale and his compass needle jumped wildly. The black squall must have been a terrifying ordeal for the ex-convict crew members. They were playing blind man's buff with a mainland wrapped in fog, and dodging icebergs which had been torn from the polar seas and were being whisked southward in the Labrador Current.

But this is conjecture. The sad fact is that nobody knows exactly where Cabot reached what he called his prima terra vista—first land seen. Like the Vinland of the Vikings, the location of his landfall has been the subject of endless speculation. Guesswork of scholars in the past has placed it as far north as Cape Chidley on the most northerly tip of Labrador; as far west as Nova Scotia's Cape Breton off the Cabot Strait; as far east as Cape Bonavista (Italian for "Happy Sighting") which juts out from the coastline of central Newfoundland; and as far south as Cape Cod in Massachusetts.

Happily, new light has been thrown on Cabot's landfall thanks to a fairly recent and extraordinary discovery. In 1956, by sheer accident, a Cabot historian stumbled upon a historic letter that had been gathering dust for more than four centuries in the Spanish archives. It was written by a Bristol wine merchant, one John Day, reporting on Cabot's 1497 voyage to the "Lord Great Admiral" in Seville—who must have been Christopher Columbus himself.

From this and other evidence it now seems most likely that Cabot landed on a cape in the vicinity of the Strait of Belle Isle, that narrow slice of water that cuts off Newfoundland from its lobster-shaped region of Labrador. And the clews point to Cape Bauld, which is located on the northeast end of Newfoundland and, incredibly enough, just a few miles from L'Anse au Meadow—the site of what is now believed to be Vinland.

If this premise is correct, then Cabot must have been greeted with the mewing of a million gulls and guillemots, the fragrant scents of the inland spruce and balsam fir and the slapping of spuming waves against the slate beach when he stepped ashore at Cape Bauld. It was St. John the Baptist's Day, June 24, and to celebrate the occasion he named the blue island looming out of the morning mists to the northward St. John's; we know it today by its French-Canadian name of Belle Isle.

The cape on which he landed he named Discovery Cape. Carrying a crucifix, Cabot led a small landing party to take formal possession on behalf of Henry VII. He planted the cross and ceremoniously unfurled the banners of the English sovereign, the Pope and the emblematic lion of Venice. Then his men looked around.

They found the weather "excellent and temperate," so warm that they believed "Brazil wood and silk are native there." The subarctic summers of north Newfoundland can reach a temperature as high as 90 degrees; but they are certainly not hot enough for the breeding of silk worms. Here Cabot was laying it on thick, the first of many Northwest Passage explorers to do so. Like a traveling salesman in new territory, one had to justify one's expense account and prepare the head office for spending more cash on future trips.

Cabot was not exaggerating, however, when he claimed to have found signs of lurking natives: "certain snares which were spread to take game and a bone needle for making nets." They were either Beothuk Indians or, more probably, Labrador Eskimos, who at that time inhabited both the north and south coasts of the Strait of Belle Isle.

An artist's conception of Cabot approaching Labrador. It took him 35 days and 1,940 nautical miles to voyage there from Bristol.

Whatever the aborigines, Cabot's scouting party, peering into the silent underbrush on that sultry June day, were fearful of being attacked. John Day, after his interview with Cabot, thus reported to Admiral Christopher Columbus:

"In that particular spot, as I told your Lordship, they found a trail that went inland, they saw a site where a fire had been made, they saw manure of animals which they thought to be farm animals, and they saw a stick half a yard long pierced at both ends, carved and painted with dye, and by such signs they believe the land to be inhabited. Since he was with just a few people, he did not dare advance inland beyond the shooting distance of a crossbow, and after taking in fresh water he returned to his ship."

We are told that Cabot then spent "about one month discovering the coast" for about nine hundred miles. It is unlikely that he pushed westward through the ice-clogged Strait of Belle Isle or tried to grope his way up the stony northeast coast of Labrador. Clawing through the same strait thirty-seven years later, the French explorer, Jacques Cartier, cursed the "frightful rocks" of the Labrador shore and damned the whole place as "the land that God gave to Cain." And today Labradorians themselves cheerfully acknowledge that their serrated coastline is as "rough as a dogfish's back."

The evidence suggests rather that Cabot steered the *Mathew* southward and, hugging the eastern coastline of Newfoundland, made a reconnaissance investigation as far as the island's most southerly point at Cape Race. There he turned around and sailed back, as John Day informs us, to his original Discovery Cape landfall.

What did he see? Cabot must have felt dismay when his tiny bark dodged icebergs to nose into those rockrimmed, fog-sheathed mantraps of his "newe founde lande" that today bear such cruelly deceptive names: Tickle Cove, Tickle Bay, Little Heart's Ease, Heart's Delight, Heart's Desire, Heart's Content, Paradise. Cabot found no Paradise, no incense islands off Cipango, no glittering gold roofs of Cathay.

But he did find something just as precious: the fisheries off the Newfoundland Grand Banks. Newfoundlanders speak affectionately of their island as a "land of fog, bog, rock and cod." And though the smell of codfish was not as piquant as the fragrance of cinnamon, salted "stockfish" or "bacallaos," as cod were then called, smelled sweet to Englishmen who had to pay heavily to import this bread of the sea from Iceland.

Cabot hurried home to report the big news to King Henry. He believed he had reached the north end of the island of Cipango, where "all the spices of the world have their origin, as well as the jewels." As a bonus, his crew members confirmed that "the sea there is swarming with fish, which can be taken not only with the net, but in baskets let down with a stone, so that it sinks in the water.... They say they will bring thence such great quantity of fish that England will have no further need of Iceland." Adding a decorative touch, Sebastian later claimed that the shoals of "great fish like tunnies" were packed so thickly "that at times they even stayed the ship's passage."

The frugal Henry Tudor rejoiced to have this bejewelled platter of spiced codfish served up to his kingdom so cheaply. In reward he gave out money recklessly—a gift of ten pounds sterling, so that his "well-beloved John Cabot" could "have a good time." A pension of twenty pounds per annum was to follow, plus the pick of the local jails to help colonize the land of Kublai Khan.

Cabot's discovery created a sensation. He was lionized as the Grand Admiral, a title that English folk deemed loftier than that of his rival, Columbus, who was the Admiral of the Ocean Sea. "My Lord the Admiral esteems himself at least a prince," wrote one amused chronicler. As for Cabot's Burgundian passenger and his Italian barber, the Grand Admiral had given them an island apiece, "and both consider themselves counts." The Admiral, attired in silk doublet and hose, appeared to enjoy his brief celebrity. He was mobbed as he swaggered through the streets of London. "Vast honour is paid to him," observed an envoy from the Mediterranean, "and he goes about dressed in silk, and these English run after him like mad, and indeed he can enlist as many of them as he pleases, and a number of our rogues as well."

Those rogues were Italian or Portuguese adventurers who sought rich pickings in Codfish Land. Some were poor Italian friars who hoped to get bishoprics if they accompanied Cabot on his next expedition. Another who appears to have enlisted was a certain João Fernandes, a Portuguese *llabrador*, or "landowner," of the Azores. Sketchy records suggest that he tried to interest Cabot in pursuing a northwest passage via Greenland. In any event, his landowner's designation was first attached to Greenland and eventually stuck to our modern Labrador. Teen-aged Sebastian also seems to have come along as cabin boy with the unruly gang of ex-convicts.

Whatever his crew, Grand Admiral Cabot embarked on his second voyage with great fanfare. He commanded a fleet of five ships, one of them fitted out by King Henry, the others equipped by the merchants of Bristol and London. The vessels were laden with "coarse cloth, caps, laces and other trifles" thought to be proper trading trinkets for the infidels of Cathay. Cabot lifted anchor and on a sunny day in May, 1498, sailed out of Bristol—into the seas of controversy.

What happened to him? We can only conjecture. According to the contemporary reports, John Cabot and his fleet appear to have vanished mysteriously. "After that voyage he was heard of no more," a London chronicler noted cryptically, "for he found his new lands nowhere but on the bottom of the ocean."

Modern historians, however, have not been content to let him rest on the bottom of the frozen seas. For the records show that at least one of the five ships limped back to the Irish coast after a fierce storm. And if Sebastian Cabot is to be believed, he himself was aboard one of two other ships, with three hundred men who survived a voyage as far north as the polar latitudes. The scholars have wrangled over the mystery since, each one projecting theories based on the many conflicting yarns that Sebastian later spun out about the trip.

Weighing all the evidence, and keeping in mind that Sebastian was a dubious witness who arrogated to himself leadership of the expedition, we can reconstruct the 1498 voyage this way:

After the storm-tossed ship bearing the Italian friars straggled back to Ireland, the fleet evidently headed north to Greenland. They rounded Greenland's treacherous southern Cape Farewell (which they aptly named Cape Get-Sight-of-Me-and-Leave-Me) and left it to thread their way by the old Viking route across ice-infested Davis Strait toward Baffin Island.

Sebastian claimed that they penetrated past the Arctic Circle to 67½ degrees north latitude. He does give a credible description of the bobbing icebergs and the midnight sun. They found "monstrous heaps of ice swimming in the sea," which were "bigger than their ships," and "which drifted hither and thither propelled by the currents," and "the ships were in great danger of colliding with them. In that region the nights are not like ours," but rather were "in a manner continual daylight" and the sun shone "eighteen hours long and the nights are very clear and bright."

It was too risky butting against bergs, so they coasted south looking for a gulf that trended westward. The late leading Cabot scholar, Dr. James Williamson, of the British Hakluyt Society, argued that

Sebastian's ships may well have found that opening at 64 degrees north latitude. He contended they actually entered Hudson Strait and wrestled with the ice as far west as inland Hudson Bay. This surmise may possibly be accurate. For Sebastian, in one of his many enigmatic accounts, hinted it was there he had personally discovered the "hid secret of nature"—the true Northwest Passage which would allow him to "pass towards Eastern Cathay." He claimed he would have made the passage, except that "the cold killed almost the entire company" of three hundred men; and "he would have done it if the ill-will of the master and sailors, who were mutinous, had not compelled him to turn back."

Evidently the ships then headed southward, past the icy pyramids of Labrador's Torngat Mountains, and paused to refresh themselves in the swarming codfish territory that Sebastian called "Land of the Bacallaos." That name still adheres today to an island off the east coast of Newfoundland in its modified form as Baccalieu Isle."

The evidence indicates that this time the voyagers met the natives when they landed and exchanged trinkets for Eskimo furs. Portuguese explorers three years later captured seven tattooed Eskimos in the region, and one shy youth was wearing souvenirs which he had apparently obtained in barter from the Cabot party: two Venetian silver earrings and a broken piece of an Italian gilt sword. Sebastian himself described the natives as a fur-bearing people, armed with bows and slings, to kill "hawks black like crows" and "very large stags like horses" and "many white bears."

Perhaps Sebastian's most entertaining yarn was his account of how the polar bears in that "very sterile land" hunted codfish. It delighted Sebastian and his companions to watch two polar bears wade into the water and, linking their claws as though holding hands, try to ambush a shoal of the large, tunny-shaped cod. But the fish were strong and slippery, and refused to be scooped up that easily, and plunged back into the sea uncaptured.

"So it is a great sport," said Sebastian, "to see these two creatures being grappled together, now the one under the water and now the other on top, splashing the foam into the air. And in the end the bear pulls the cod ashore and eats him."

It was an age in which stay-at-home folk loved to hear travelers' tales of the fantastic, and Sebastian satisfied them with a farrago of marvels. His best seller was a 1544 map, whose accompanying legends may have been ghostwritten for him yet bear the stamp of Sebastianized hyperbole. Sebastian enchanted his readers with creepy legends of lampreys in the Arctic seas so "large and monstrous" that the serpentlike leviathans gulped down sailors. He told of dog-faced men with ostrichlike feet and pig-headed men who communicated with piglike grunts and giants with flapping ears "so large that they cover the whole body."

Sebastian's most implausible whopper, though, was his claim that he had traveled a total of some six thousand miles on his odyssey. "Despairing of finding a gulf, I turned back to examine again the coast," he later boasted, "always with the purpose of finding a passage to the Indies, and came as far as that part now called Florida. All my victuals being short, I decided to return to England."

Some historians maintain that silent John Cabot may have slunk back to Bristol, so unsuccessful in his mission that his homecoming was ignored by chroniclers. Others contend that he perished in the northern seas, his remaining ships possibly foundering on the rocks near Grates Cove north of Newfoundland's Conception Bay. However he died, John Cabot, his second voyage obliterated from recorded history, must have died a bitter man. He had failed to outreach Christopher Columbus and, like his rival, Admiral of the Ocean Sea, his quest for Cathay had been thwarted by a barrier continent undreamt of in his cosmography.

His opportunist son was troubled by no such regrets. Sebastian was a resilient survivor, wily in the art of currying favor with the right people. During his long and devious career, he won renown as a great explorer, his reputation outdazzling by far that of either his father or Columbus. "Honour of England, brave Sebastian," he was saluted in a sixteenth-century ballad. By a series of Byzantine intrigues, underhand dealings and suave court flattery, he rose to become the chief navigational expert for both Spain and England. The kings of those countries vied to pay increasingly high sums for his services. The bluffer kept them bidding by playing close to the vest his trump card. That ace, of course, was the "hid secret of nature" he claimed to have discovered — the Northwest Passage that was the open sesame to the treasures of Cathay.

One can't help but be amused by Sebastian's slippery behavior. Like a double agent in a spy thriller, he was forever betraying the kingdom that had just hired him and scheming to sell his alleged secrets to another kingdom. No sooner was he Pilot Major of Spain, for example, than he was already plotting to peddle the secret passage to the Venetian Republic.

"For I have discovered it," he whispered furtively behind locked doors in Spain to a Venetian fellow conspirator. "But I must earnestly beseech you to keep the thing secret, as it would cost me my life."

And when he had switched employers to become Grand Pilot of England, Sebastian was writing on the sly to the King of Spain, "I was almost ready to start on my journey to kiss the hand of your Majesty . . . but before I arrive at such an end I wish to declare unto your Majesty the secret which I possess."

Sebastian must have been a smooth and ingratiating talker, for royalty never doubted his word. Ordinary sea merchants, however, were more skeptical. In 1521 (though he was in the service of Spain), Sebastian persuaded King Henry VIII of England to let him lead a five-ship fleet on an expedition to his secret Northwest Passage. But the Drapers' Guild of the city of London stoutly refused to put up the money on grounds that Sebastian was an impostor.

"He was never in that land himself," objected the merchants. "He knows only what in his youth he heard his father and other men tell in times past." Sebastian was a cunning man whose seamanship they wouldn't trust with the lives and goods aboard five good English ships, and they cited the old mariners' proverb: "He sails not surely that sails by another man's compass."

Despite his many claims otherwise, we have clear proof of only one expedition that Sebastian actually commanded. In 1526, Pilot Major Sebastian set out with a fleet of four ships and two hundred and twenty men on a voyage of exploration under the colors of King Charles V of Spain. Bewilderingly enough, he had promised to find a shorter route that would lead simultaneously to the Moluccas Spice Islands, Ophir (King Solomon's African Mines) and, naturally, Oriental Cathay. Instead, he steered for the Argentine, suddenly deciding to go on an Inca treasure hunt, and spent four feckless years stumbling about the swamps and jungles of the Rio de la Plata, his Spanish name for the River of Silver.

Undaunted as ever, Sebastian promised that "His Imperial Majesty will no longer want either cinnamon or pepper, for he will have more gold and silver than he requires." But the expedition was an unmitigated disaster. As Captain General of the fleet, Sebastian lost three ships, one hundred and seventy men, and any shred of respect among the surviving crew members for his alleged piloting ability. When his flagship accidentally struck a reef, Captain General Sebastian was the first man to abandon the wrecked vessel. As a result his crews either deserted or mutinied. They scorned him for his cowardice. They mocked his leadership. "And with all his astrology," they taunted, Pilot Major Sebastian "could not handle an astrolabe or quadrant!"

Sebastian retaliated ruthlessly. He cut their ears off. He nailed their hands to a board. He sent several of them to the gallows. We are told that one poor wretch, whose head had slipped from the noose, was hanged a second time. Other crew members were eaten by Indian cannibals, not so much out of vindictiveness, it was said with a touch of gallows humor, but to "ascertain whether their flesh was as salt, and had the same unpalatable savour noticed in the other Spaniards they had previously tasted."

Sebastian struggled back to Seville with his lone ship and a handful of men ready to face the music. He returned "without profit and without glory." His promised treasures consisted of a single ounce of silver, a few earrings, and fifty Indian slaves he had bought on credit.

He was put in jail and tried by the Spanish Council of the Indies. In various lawsuits, the survivors charged him with needlessly stirring up the Indians, being reckless with the lives of his men and steering his ships ineptly. He was even accused of being an ineffectual governor of men who was led around by the nose by his bossy wife, Catalina. The Council found him guilty of many of the charges and sentenced him to four years' banishment to the African penal colony in Morocco.

Yet this astonishing confidence artist managed to talk his way out of his tight corner. Charles V was evidently mesmerized after listening to Sebastian's glowing rhetoric about the El Dorado of treasures and slaves yet awaiting in the River of Silver country: "I found it always most beautiful and inhabited by multitudes of people, who in wonderment ran to see me...." His Imperial Majesty promptly dispatched a second— and even more disastrous—expedition to the Plata swamplands. He pardoned Sebastian for all his offences, paid off his heavy fines, and as a bonus increased his Pilot Major's pension.

Never known for his gratitude or loyalty, Sebastian slipped quietly out of Spain in 1547 and for the next decade entered the services of the infant King Edward VI and Bloody Queen Mary of England. Of the Tudors he demanded an enormous fee for his secrets—a lifetime annual salary of one hundred and sixty-six pounds, thirteen shillings, fourpence. And records of the royal exchequer show that "Sebastian Caboto, the great seaman" got it, plus additional bonuses of four hundred pounds.

Not content with this, the Grand Pilot of England managed to collect as well, for a couple of years, his Pilot Major's salary of well over fifty thousand maravedis from Spain. Indeed, he was so much in demand that he was the centre of a diplomatic tug-of-war between the two nations. "I very affectionately ask of you to grant a leave to the said Caboto and allow him to come near me," pleaded Spain's Imperial Majesty. Sebastian replied from London that he would love to kiss his Imperial Majesty's hand but the arduous journey to Spain would kill him, and the British Privy Council backed him up in his refusal. For the "goode, olde, and famuse man, Master Sebastian Caboto" had become the indispensable advisor for England's newest expeditions to Arctic Cathay.

We gain a more amiable picture of Sebastian in his old age. Wealth and status appear to have mellowed the engaging humbug, especially when he was appointed "Governor of the Mysterie and Companie of the Merchants Adventurers." The Muscovy Company, as it was later renamed, was organized by London wool merchants in 1551. Its aim was to discover a northeast passage to Cathay. Sebastian, in his role as "chief setter-forth" of the undertaking, phrased it more vaguely. By sailing through "the north east frostie seas" via the "extremitie of the North Pole," the adventurers were bound to reach the "Orient or Occident Indias."

Sebastian also set forth a code of behavior for his impressed gangs of crew members, which was widely copied by later Arctic explorations. His advice reflects the foxy side of his nature as well as an unexpected facet of genial benevolence in his subtle character. The sailors were instructed to treat all natives "with gentleness and courtesy, without any disdain, laughing, or contempt." No doubt thinking back on his experiences with the River of Silver cannibals, he warned the men to beware of "persons armed with bows . . . desirous of the bodies of men which they covet for meat." Their women were not to be tampered with or "tempted to dishonesty"; their odd religious rites were to be tolerated or at least passed over in discreet silence.

Aboard ship the mariners were exhorted to be knit with "unity, love, conformity and obedience." However, they were to be punished severely if they indulged in "ribaldry, filthy tales or ungodly talk." Dicing and card playing were to be eschewed, for such devilish games resulted in brawls and oftentimes murder.

Force was to be used on the natives ashore only as a last resort. If the natives appeared to be gathering gold or other precious stones, the sailors were urged to draw nigh and mark "what things they gather, playing upon the drum or such other instruments as may allure them to harkening, to fantasy, or desire to see and hear your instruments and voices." And his wiliest piece of advice was to entertain the natives lavishly aboard ship, for "if the person taken may be made drunk with your beer or wine, you shall know the secrets of his heart."

Sebastian didn't sail on any of the company's Arctic expeditions, but the Governor did give his skippers a merry sendoff. Stephen Borrough, captain of the *Searchthrift*, paints a rather jolly picture of the "good, olde gentleman, Master Caboto," aged seventy-four, coming down to the English wharves at Gravesend to bid him Godspeed. Going aboard the ninety-ton vessel with a party of ladies and gentlemen, Master Sebastian cracked a bottle of good cheer with the skipper. He gave the mariners right liberal rewards, and going down the gangplank handed out generous alms to the poor, asking them to pray for a prosperous voyage for the ship.

"And then at the Sign of the Christopher Inn, he and his friends banqueted, and made me, and them that were in the company, great cheer," Borrough remembered. "And for very joy of our intended discovery, he entered into the dance himself, amongst the rest of the young and lusty company. Which being ended, he and his friends departed most gently, commending us to the governance of almighty God."

God was kind to Borrough. Of the three chief commanders whom Sebastian dispatched on expeditions to Cathay via a northeast route, Borrough was the only one who lived to tell the tale. The tale in each case was that they had not reached the scented spice islands of Cipango but the icy seas of Arctic Russia.

Borrough's little *Searchthrift* penetrated well past the Arctic Circle and skirted the southern tip of Novaya Zemlaya. "New Land," as it means in Russian, is that bleak island in the Kara Sea where the Russians four centuries later were to blast huge thermonuclear weapons. A modern atom bomb couldn't have startled Borrough as much as the huge spouting whale he spotted. The whale, he observed, was "monstrous, so near to our side that we might have thrust a sword in him, which we durst not do for fear he should have overthrown our ship. And then I called my company together, and all of us shouted, and with the cry that we made he departed from us. There was as much above water of his back as the breadth of our ship, and at his falling down he made such a terrible noise in the water that a man would greatly have marvelled, except he had known the cause of it. But, God be thanked, we were quietly delivered of him."

Sir Hugh Willoughby, seen in this faded print, was dispatched by England's Grand Pilot Sebastian Cabot to find Cathay via the "extremitie of the North Pole." He died icicled.

Borrough threaded through the strait at the bottom of Novaya Zemlaya and doggedly tried to push farther northeast into the unexplored Kara Sea. But he returned to England, reporting that his way was blocked by the "great and terrible abundance of ice that we saw with our eyes" and that indeed "was a fearful sight to see."

Sebastian's second commander, Sir Hugh Willoughby, a tall, handsome court favorite with little navigational experience, was to become a legendary figure in arctic folklore. So confident was he of reaching Cathay that he had the bottoms of his ships, *Bona Esperanza* and *Bona Confidentia* sheathed with lead as protection against the gnawing worms known to attack wooden hulls in the tropical waters of the Indies. Instead, he encountered the ice pack in the frigid waters of the Barents Sea.

Sir Hugh was astounded to see polar bears and "other such strange beasts which were to us unknown and also wonderful." On a blustery September day in 1553 he was likewise amazed to strike "evil weather, such as frost, snow and hail, as though it had been the deep of winter." Buffeted by storms, his crippled ships floundered about until they were blown into Russia's Kola Gulf, somewhere in the region of Murmansk. There, because they were pathetically ill-equipped to hunt for arctic foxes or seals, which abounded in the area, all sixty-three of his men slowly starved to death.

Russian seamen discovered the bodies the following summer along with Sir Hugh's unfinished journal which told of their feeble attempts to seek help on the uninhabited coast. Their ghastly death soon became wreathed in myth. A Venetian ambassador to the English court spread the rumor that the corpses had been found frozen in statuelike postures. Sir Hugh was said to have been seated at a table in his cabin, pen in hand, his fingers iced while writing in his journal. Rather like wax figures in Madame Tussaud's museum, the mariners around him were caught in lifelike poses; some with platter in hand and spoon in mouth; others opening a locker, with their faithful frozen dogs nuzzling their feet. It was a preposterous tale, but it eventually became the basis for the legend of *The Flying Dutchman*, the ship that sails forever in an arctic limbo with a phantom crew.

Just as remarkable was the fate of Sebastian's third commander, Richard Chancellor. A gallant sea captain with "many good parts of wit," Chancellor was also known as "the odde man of his time for matters touching the sea." "Odde" meant outstanding, and he was thoroughly experienced in navigating the Mediterranean. Skippering the *Edward*

Bonaventure, a fine ship of one hundred and sixty tons, the odde seafarer sailed into the unknown until he reached where there was "no night at all, but a continual light and brightness of the sun shining clearly upon the huge and mighty sea." It was 70 degrees north latitude. Despite raging winds and ice hanging like candelabra from his riggings, Chancellor was determined to "either bring that to pass which was intended or else to die the death."

At length his *Bonaventure* put into the White Sea port of Archangel. Chancellor was surprised to find himself not in the kingdom of Kublai Khan but in the land of Muscovy ruled by Czar Ivan the Terrible. The Czar's couriers graciously conducted Chancellor's party on a sledge trip of fifteen hundred miles to the Czar's grand court in Moscow. There a Russian-English trade treaty was negotiated which was to prove highly lucrative to both countries and to the merchants of the renamed Muscovy Company.

The Czar was obviously pleased at the prospect of getting warm English woolens in exchange for his realm's seal oil and fur peltries. While entertaining his guests with many a cup of vodka, Ivan made a cordial gesture as though to belie his "terrible" title. He reached over the table to stroke the whiskers of the Muscovy Company's agent, George Killingworth. Then he pleasantly delivered the end of Killingworth's beard to the Metropolitan beside him who blessed it and exclaimed, "This is God's gift!" Which indeed it was, we are told, for "it was not only thick, broad, and yellow coloured, but in length five foot and two inches of size."

After all these pleasantries were over, Chancellor was to die the heroic death he had anticipated. On his homeward-bound voyage, he carried with him the first Russian ambassador to the English court, Ossip Gregorevitch Nepeja. On November 7, 1556, after being battered by bitter squalls off Norway, the *Bonaventure* finally put into Pitsligo Bay on the coast of Scotland. "There by outragious tempests and extreme stormes, the said ship, being beaten from her ground tackles, was driven upon the rockes on shoare, where she brake and split in pieces."

Chancellor made a last-ditch effort to rescue the Czar's envoy. The explorer and the Russian took to a small boat to escape the sinking *Bonaventure*. A huge wave swamped the boat. The ambassador managed to stagger up on the beach. The odde sea captain, after braving the rigors of the Arctic, drowned ironically while within arm's reach of his home country.

Grand Pilot Sebastian Cabot died in bed a year later, still driven by the outrageous tempests of ambition. One would have thought the seventy-five-year-old pretender content. True, he had found neither a Northwest nor a Northeast Passage to Cathay. Yet he had kindled the imagination of oceanic explorers to follow, had gained a permanent foothold in North America for England (if not himself, at least in collaboration with his father), and won commercial riches for the Muscovy Company. Nevertheless, as he lay dying, the incorrigible yarn spinner could not resist whispering that he had discovered yet another hid secret that had eluded the most expert mariners of his time—the art of finding longitude at sea.

His friend, Richard Eden, a translater of books which dealt with the navigational riddle of longitude, wrote his epitaph. "On his death bed Sebastian Cabot told me that he had the knowledge thereof by Divine revelation, yet so that he might not teach any man," said Eden. "But I think the goode olde man in that extreme age somewhat doted, and had not yet, even in the article of death, utterly shaken off all worldlye vain glorie."

Chapter 4

The Arctic Gold Rush

O f all the Elizabethan explorers who went down to the sea in ships, hoping to put "a girdle round about the world" and bring back the riches of Cathay, few were as tough as Sir Martin Frobisher. He was not unlike the Frobisher Bay he discovered on the eastern rind of the Canadian Arctic: harsh and uncompromising and often given to blustering furies. It was said of Frobisher that he swore no small oaths. During his forty years at sea he swore many large ones.

Besides being a first-class seafarer, Frobisher excelled as a pirate and slave trader, and the cantankerous buccaneer ran a tight ship. In Arctic lore he is famous for having laid down the law that any mariner on his expedition who raised his sword "in quarrelling manner" would promptly have his right hand chopped off. Frobisher was that sort of strict disciplinarian.

One of Queen Elizabeth's court artists tried to prettify him in a portrait painted in 1577. It was then the height of Her Majesty's Arctic gold rush. So it was felt that the thirty-eight-year-old Yorkshireman should be depicted in a manner befitting his rank as High Admiral of the Company of Cathay in which the Virgin Queen had invested royal funds.

The artist made a noble attempt at turning Frobisher into a court fop. We see his muscular six-foot frame caparisoned from pointed shoes to pink ruff collar in elegant lace and silk, velvet doublet and pantaloons. His brown beard, so recently icicled in the Arctic, is neatly trimmed. His downswept moustache is waxed and curled. He is posed stiffly in front of a globe showing the polar Northwest Passage where he has purportedly discovered King Solomon's Mines.

But the sea dog would not let himself be glamorized that easily into a dandy. His steel blue eyes glare truculently. There is a swagger and self-assurance in his stance. His right fist is clenched around the butt of a pistol. The strong, spatulate fingers of his left hand rest on the hilt of his sword. He looks to be quick on the draw with either weapon, and indeed he was.

Yet Frobisher was no common sea gangster. If he was rough and ready for a fight, he was also exceptionally bold and resourceful; a brave leader who thought nothing of diving into iceberg-strewn waters to rescue a drowning sailor; a Christian who carried a Bible with him on his daring voyages (as well as a book of superstitions and mythical lore about the treasures of Cathay called *The Travels Of Sir John Mandeville*); and he was a navigator of the first rank in an age when English sea rovers were just gaining their global sea legs.

Geoffrey Chaucer's pen portrait of the Shipman in *The Canterbury Tales* probably characterizes Frobisher, the sea captain, more realistically than the picture painted by Queen Elizabeth's court artist. Like Chaucer's sea-hardened mariner, Frobisher undoubtedly carried a dagger on a rope around his sun-browned neck, and walked many a tossing deck with a captain's wool gown wrapped around his broad shoulders. Doubtless too he thoughtfully tugged at his gale-blown beard while trying to plot a course through unknown waters:

> *Hardey he was, and wys to undertake;*
> *With many a tempest hadde his berd been shake . . .*
> *And, certeinly, he was a good felawe.*
> *Ful many a draughte of wyn had he y-drawe . . . .*

Chaucer likewise caught the flavor of the man when he wrote:

> *Of nyce conscience took he no keep.*

Frobisher could certainly be an unscrupulous pillager and remorseless taskmaster. In his favor, though, it must be said that he was a child of his times, and the times were callous and cruel. One needed a stout body and a stout heart merely to survive. Richard Hakluyt, the great Boswell of Elizabethan voyages of discovery, rightly described the sixteenth-century seamen who served under Frobisher and the other Queen's privateers as "the most infamous for outrageous common and daily piracies."

Sir Martin Frobisher, with his broken nose and muscular frame, seen here clutching a pistol with one hand and ready to grasp his sword with the other, was a tough customer to meet in a battle. Yet the Yorkshire sea dog, after whom Frobisher Bay is named, was a first-class explorer. The three expeditions he spearheaded during the course of the Arctic gold rush were blunted against Baffin Island ice mountains and were financially valueless. They cost roughly 20,000 pounds and produced "fool's gold" which were glinting flecks of biotite mica. But he bequeathed a virtual manual of Arctic seamanship that was priceless.

BODLEIAN LIBRARY, OXFORD

Frobisher and his men were indeed pirates. But they were far from being the rollicking buccaneers pictured so romantically in the Hollywood movies of Errol Flynn. The life of an Elizabethan privateer— the equivalent of a mariner serving in the Queen's merchant marine— was unmitigated hell.

Most crew members were desperate men, dragooned into service by the press gangs. Few of the early explorers' voyages were devoid of incipient mutiny, bloody arguments over the spoils, or the threat of desertion. There was reason enough, for the surly, protesting crews wished for nothing better than to escape from the torture of their shipboard purgatory. Unwilling tailors, butchers, students, farm boys, paupers handed over by local authorities—all found themselves forcibly recruited for two- or three-year voyages that frequently meant certain death. In the words of John Donne, the poet laureate of Elizabethan expeditions:

Long voyages are longe consumptions
And ships are carts for executions.

The discovery ships were dank, squalid and over-crowded floating coffins. Their rotting oaken timbers were riddled by the teredo worm. Despite the efforts of the ship's cat, swarms of rats transmitted the plague and typhus fever. Crews, trying to sleep on the bare decks, using their coarse wool sea gowns and cotton hose as pillows, were almost devoured by cockroaches. "They eat the labels off the slop chests," wrote one impressed sailor. "They will gnaw your toenails and eat your boots and will fly in your face; on one occasion they drove all the watch below on deck."

The stale water, covered with a slimy green scum in rain barrels, was so foul that it caused dysentery. Any man who drank it must have been dying of thirst. It was one reason why the men on Frobisher's Arctic voyages were issued so much beer—seven gallons per man each week. The remaining weekly food rations were vile: four pounds of maggoty brined beef or pork (called "salt horse"); seven pounds of verminous hardtack biscuit (known as "scouse" when mixed in a stew with the salt horse); four and three-eighths sun-cured codfish ("stock fish"); and a Sunday "plum duff" or "dandy funk" (an evil mixture of boiled powdered hardtack, drippings and raisins, often consumed with one's weekly rations of fourteen ounces of olive oil and two-and-a-half pounds of cheese).

Invariably this vegetable-and-fruit-free diet, deficient in vitamins, gave rise to deaths from scurvy. The men's weakened bodies festered with blisters. When they chewed weevily hardtack, teeth fell from swollen gums; black blood gushed from sores. To move aching joints brought a shriek of pain.

But that torment was trifling compared to the cruel punishment inflicted by sadistic sea captains exerting the power of life or death over their crews. A marline-spike might be thrust into a seaman's gagged mouth if he was heard uttering profane language. A laggard reluctant to attend Sunday Communion or daily prayer services was severely penalized. He could be ducked from the yardarm; or be tied to the mizzen shrouds with weights hung from his neck and nettles stuck in his hands; or be put in the bilboes, meaning he was lashed to a capstan bar and forced to wear a kind of wood-and-iron collar for the duration of a four-hour watch.

A seaman plotting mutiny would "get a red checked shirt at the gangway"—meaning he was flogged with the cat-o'-nine-tails until his flesh was raw and bloody. The cat was a short, wooden stick covered with red baize; the tails were of tough knotted cord about two feet long. Three dozen lashes on a bare back were usually sufficient to bring a would-be mutineer whimpering to his knees. A relatively tender-hearted captain would limit punishment to a dozen lashes. A particularly sturdy seaman reportedly shrugged this off as "nothing but an 'O' and a few 'O my Gods'". But a more rebellious, vengeful victim, cut with fifty blows, wrote: "Believe me, the shirt on my back was like a butcher's apron and so stiff that every time I had to stoop down, it would tear off the bladders of blood and water that were rose on my poor mangled body. Well may tortures like these cause the unfortunate sufferers to cry out for revenge and have it at the risk of their lives."

We have no reason to believe that Frobisher was any better or worse than the other rapacious freebooters who skippered the "hell hounds of the sea" in the name of the Queen. If he was a hardboiled Christian, it must be remembered that navigators then needed iron nerves and great faith in the mercy of God to endure. If he was a ruthless disciplinarian who chopped off the right hands of quarrelsome crew members, it must be recalled that life ashore in sixteenth-century England required men to wear a calloused hide. They had to become inured to the cruelty they met on all sides: the terrible poverty, the filth, the plague; the rackings, the gibbets, the decapitated heads of alleged traitors; the witches burned at the stake and the convicts strung up on the gallows and then, still alive, cut down, castrated, and disembowelled. Life was cheap.

It was Frobisher's intrepidity as a navigator that distinguishes him.

He was compelled to suffer the hardships and the terrors of an ice-studded sea under living conditions little better than his crew's. (His chronicler's journal makes mention of the homely detail that the sole luxuries in "the captaine's cabbine" consisted of "a bed sted and a table ... the table broken.") Yet as their commander he had to inspire in his subordinates that extra ounce of nerve, that wild belligerence which in the end wins battles against oceanic punches and vicious ice mountains and performs miracles of endurance.

As a pilot Frobisher had to rely on pathetically inept navigation devices. He had no wheel to steer with; for ship's wheels did not appear until the beginning of the eighteenth century. His steering apparatus consisted of a crude rudder and an attached bar known as a whipstaffe. He had no accurate clock or chronometer; for it was not until 1765 that a Lincolnshire clockmaker, John Harrison, won a prize of twenty thousand pounds offered by Parliament for the invention of a sea watch. Frobisher therefore had to depend on a half-hour sandglass, hung in the binnacle under the eye of the helmsman, who turned the glass each time the sand ran out and marked the passage of time by ringing the "watche belle" every half hour.

He had no way of determining longitude, and for a latitude reading he had recourse to shooting the midday sun or the Pole Star at night with two elementary instruments known as the astrolabe and cross-staff. His compass, little more than a magnetized needle stuck into a cork that floated in a bowl of water, was described by a contemporary as "so bungerly and absurdly contrived, as nothing more." His maps were a pastiche of old wives' tales, cluttered with imaginary islands, aquatic unicorns and geyser-headed hippomonstrosities.

Frobisher pretty well steered by "dead reckoning." This meant he used a kind of intuitive guesswork, keeping track of the wind and the tide and his speed as he spumed through the trackless sea, and like most of his fellow Elizabethan adventurers, "doeth but grope as a blinde man doth." Like them, he was driven by the lust for plunder and glory, praying that beyond the next glimmering iceberg fabled Cathay would be revealed to him with its gold-glittering palaces, its silks and spices and immortality. All alike were inspired by the same spirit of credulous hope in the possibilities of a world of wonders, with the imagined Northwest Passage to lure them ever onwards to "the discovery of things which were hidden from other men."

But you had to be a rough-and-tumble fighter, and no sissy, if you hoped to attain your goal. Martin Frobisher, whose Yorkshire name may have been derived from the French word for "sword cutler," learned how to handle a buccaneer's sword at the age of fourteen. But the origin of his name is a matter of conjecture; an abominable speller, Frobisher spelled his name roughly fifty different ways. But we do know he was born in 1539, one of three children in a family of country gentry in Pontrefract, Yorkshire. We are certain that he spoke in a heavy Yorkshire accent, for his misspellings disclose that he wrote phonetically to recapture the sounds of the North Country dialect that he spoke.

His father died when Martin was quite young and the widowed mother sent the child to London. He was raised there by his uncle, Sir John York, a merchant whose investments in the African slave trade were so profitable that Sir John was appointed Master of the Mint.

Young Martin was a poor scholar and a worse speller. Nevertheless his uncle recognized the boy's "great spirit, courage, and hardness of body." So Sir John apprenticed the fourteen-year-old lad into the lucrative but often deadly trade of privateering.

On his first voyage to Guinea in West Africa, variously known as the Slave Coast or the Gold Coast, the teen-ager was quickly initiated into the perils of the profession. The skipper of the ship *Lion* was a Portuguese brigand reputed to be "the terror of the seas"; the skipper of the expedition's second ship *Primrose* was an English freebooter nicknamed "the terrible Hydra." Though they shared a mutual "thirst for ye fine gold," the two roughneck captains got into a terrible fight over command, in which they threatened to slice off each other's ears and nail them to the mast. In the end the ships brought back to Plymouth a rich haul of pepper, gold and ivory. But the stark records tell us that both skippers died en route; and of the total crew of one hundred and forty sailors there were only forty fever-stricken survivors.

Young Martin was likewise lucky to survive his second voyage to the Slave Coast under Captain John Lok. The boy was held captive for almost a year, first by the chief of an African tribe, then by a gang of Portuguese slave traders; yet he managed to escape with booty of four hundred pounds of pure gold. It was a cut-throat trade, but Martin soon mastered it. By the age of twenty, he was a freelance pirate commanding a ship. And by the age of thirty, he was one of the trio of English corsairs most widely dreaded along the North African Barbary Coast. His two colleagues in privateering escapades were John Hawkins, the infamous slave trader, and Francis Drake, whose looting of Spanish galleons was so notorious that he won the sobriquet of *El Draco*, "the Dragon."

The records show that Frobisher was arrested on charges of high-sea piracy at least four times, but the Queen's Privy Council invariably released him after a mild scolding. This was to be expected, because privateering in those days was part of the game of cold-war politics and illicit profiteering that Queen Elizabeth then played. "Gloriana, North Star and Queen of the Seas" dearly loved her gallant sea dogs, secretly invested in their ventures, and took her royal share of the booty that they plundered from her Roman Catholic enemies.

The immorality of dealing in the Negro slave traffic didn't bother her conscience one whit. John Hawkins once returned from an expedition, muttering apologies as pious as his two piously named slave-hunters, the *Jesus* (a galleon loaned to him by the Queen) and the *Grace of God.* He had brought back a mere 50 per cent profit, knowing the Queen had expected double that amount, and he tried to excuse himself by saying, "Only God can give the increase." Gloriana was not impressed. "God's wounds!" she stormed. "This fellow went away a sailor and hath come home a prating divine."

Neither was her conscience pricked by the duplicity she practised against her alleged allies. Francis Drake returned from his voyage around the world, his *Golden Hind* laden with Spanish plunder worth six hundred thousand pounds. Court shareholders, who had invested some five thousand pounds capital, got a regal return of 4,700 per cent profit from the spoils. When the Spaniards protested that El Draco had violated their territorial rights, Elizabeth promised publicly to punish the culprit. Privately, though, she confided to her court, "The gentleman careth not if I disavow him." She secretly climbed aboard the *Golden Hind* and told Drake to kneel on the deck while she placed the sword of state on his shoulder. "The King of Spain has asked me to strike off your head," said Elizabeth. Then she dubbed him with a smile, "I have here a gilded sword with which to do it — *Sir* Francis Drake."

Frobisher ultimately won the same royal treatment. Elizabeth was particularly grateful after he scuppered the sixteen-hundred-ton carrack, *Madre de Dios*, and seized her prize of 537 tons of spices and jewels, silks, drugs, carpets, ivory, Chinese porcelain, ebony and "elephants' teeth." Even after his crew of rowdy pirates had pilfered some hundred thousand pounds' worth of pearls, diamonds and gold plate, Frobisher was able to present the royal treasury with a cargo estimated at the impressive sum of 141,200 pounds. He was glad to be Her Majesty's "most humbly bound servant" and "while God giveth me lyfe youe shall finde me dewttefull and fathefull to youe and youres." In return, Her Majesty blessed him in a handwritten letter for "your love of

"I have the body of a weak and feeble woman, but I have the heart and stomach of a king." Thus spoke Elizabeth I, also known as "Gloriana, North Star and Queen of the Seas." Martin Frobisher, the piratical sea dog who launched the Arctic gold rush on her behalf, was knighted by her and brought her back a narwhal horn; all else was fool's gold.

our service" and saluted "Our trusty and well-beloved Sir Martin Frobisher, Knight."

But this reward was to come much later in his career. Meanwhile, as a freelance freebooter, Frobisher made the mistake of not realizing that piracy was patriotic only as long as the loot was alien. But if the cargo was owned by an Englishman, then it was considered plain burglary. After being accused of thieving the hogsheads of wine belonging to a London merchant aboard the French ship *Marie*, Frobisher was fined nine hundred pounds, and had to serve a stretch in jail like a common criminal. He emerged from prison not particularly reformed but determined to refurbish his reputation and his purse. And so the sea rover turned his hand to the business of exploring.

The Elizabethan period was a ripe period for explorers. It was a robust, greedy and expansive age just bursting with opportunities for a thrustful man who lusted "for gold, for praise, for glory." Christopher Marlowe, the poet, set the tone for acquisitive adventurers of the era when he exclaimed: "I'll have them fly to India for gold—Ransack the Ocean for orient pearl—And search all corners of the new-found world." And another of Frobisher's contemporaries declaimed with nationalistic optimism that, for an exploring Englishman, "there is no land unhabitable nor sea innavigable."

The discoverer's fever was in the air and contagious, and Frobisher caught it. He had once heard from a Portuguese captain in prison that a northwest passage to Cathay was truly possible, and for fifteen years, we are told, it became an obsession with Frobisher to discover this "one thing in the world that was left undone whereby a notable mind might be made famous and fortunate." But Frobisher was a semiliterate seaman, and he needed court favorites with the influence and financing to sponsor his expedition.

He found his principal backer in Michael Lok, brother of the John Lok who had skippered the ship on Frobisher's second voyage to the Slave Coast. Michael was a flamboyant character: a promoter, wire-puller, and merchant entrepreneur who induced court investors to take a fling in joint-stock gambling syndicates. Today we would call him a high-class bucket-shop operator. In those days, since he was the well-educated, well-traveled son of Sir William Lok, former alderman of London, he was highly regarded in court society as a speculating merchant-adventurer.

He was the sort of promoter whose cupidity and gullibility were satirized in Ben Jonson's play, *The Alchemist*. Indeed he may well have been the prototype of that comedy's Sir Epicure Mammon, who makes his stage entrance with the florid speech: "Here's the rich Peru, and there within, sir, are the golden mines, Great Solomon's Ophir! This is the day wherein, to all my friends, I will pronounce the happy word, Be Rich!" In his real-life scheme to find King Solomon's Ophir Mines via Cathay, Lok claimed purer motives than Mammon. It was all done out of patriotism: "to the intent that the whole world might be opened unto England ... to yield to the Queen's Majesty great honor, and to the whole realm infinite treasure."

It is somehow fitting that Lok had won the post of Director of the Muscovy Company; for he was a grandiloquent romancer in the tradition of its late Governor, Sebastian Cabot. You could never tell— despite his assertions that "I will now speak precisely and say the truth, the very truth"—whether he was speaking fact or fiction. Later, when accused of being a swindler who had perpetrated the Arctic gold rush hoax, Lok testified, "Words are but wind." He made many windy claims. The egotist claimed that the entire plan to discover the Northwest Passage was his own; and he drew a map assigning North America to "R. Elizabeth" and retitling the supposed Asia north of it simply LOK, capitalized. He claimed to be an expert in the art of cosmography who had spent fifteen years traveling everywhere from Spain to Greece and had captained a one-thousand-ton ship to the Levant Seas; and he had. reams of notes to prove his expertise in global geography.

According to one of the many contradictory stories he told, Lok appears to have taken over management of the expedition to the Indies after Frobisher first proposed it to the Muscovy Company in 1574. His associates, who had exclusive rights to exploiting a northwest route, rejected the idea, but Lok could see its money-making potentialities. So the promoter pulled strings at court until the Queen's Privy Council granted a licence to his separate joint stock venture. He eventually gave it the beguiling name of the Company of Cathay.

Like any modern stock promoter, Lok worked vigorously to convert Frobisher's public image from that of an uncouth pirate with a rather shady past into the "rare and valiant" Captain General embarking on a heroic mission "the like of which is not to be read in any history." The publicist had ballads written extolling Frobisher as a second Jason seeking the Golden Fleece. A particularly atrocious verse, composed by the court rhymester, trumpeted his fame this way:

O Frobusher! Thy bruit and name shall be enroled in bookes,
That whosoever after comes and on thy labour lookes,

Shall muse and marvell at thyne actes, and greatnesse of thy minde.
I say no more, lest some affirme, I fanne thy face with winde.

Despite the advance publicity, Lok seems to have had a hard time persuading subscribers to invest hard cash in the initial voyage. It took him two years, Lok later maintained, because Frobisher was a poor diamond in the rough who needed his polishing. If Lok is to be believed, the explorer was "utterly destitute of money and credit and friends." But the promoter took him in "and opened unto him all mine own private studies and labors, and showed him all my books, charts, maps, instruments. And daily instructed him therein to my skill for his better defence in talk thereof with other men. And, to be short, I daily increased my good will toward him, making my house his house, and my purse his purse, and my credit his credit."

Eventually Lok got several cautious plungers—including Baron Burghley, the Queen's Lord High Treasurer, and Sir Thomas Gresham, founder of the Royal Exchange—to buy shares worth a total of 875 pounds. It wasn't enough. Lok later claimed that he himself had to put up almost an equal amount of his own money, a sum of almost 740 pounds.

Captain General Frobisher must have sworn a large oath when he saw the three cockleshells that were to carry his crew of thirty-eight men. He was supplied with two three-masted barks—the *Michael,* named after Lok, and the *Gabriel,* apparently named after the trumpeting angel. They were each about twenty-five tons, as tiny as a modern ship's lifeboat. In addition there was a seven-ton pinnace, a mere dinghy barely large enough to hold four sailors, and so insignificant that she wasn't even given a name.

The prospect of braving the Seas of Darkness in this eggshell fleet was enough to drive a Captain General to drink. This Frobisher did, ordering for the launching on June 7, 1576, a good ten-shilling bottle of aqua vitae brandy for himself. To provide internal fuel for the expected cold weather ahead, the skipper laid in stock an additional three hogsheads of aqua vitae. His crew would have to make do with five tons of beer, which meant each seaman would be fortified on the voyage with a gallon of beer per day.

The Captain General was especially fortunate in having George Best as his pilot lieutenant. For Best was a seasoned navigator who had sailed to Muscovy; he was a daring battler, after Frobisher's own heart, who ultimately died fighting a duel with a nobleman; and he was an articulate Boswell, who recorded a vividly written log of Frobisher's three voyages to the land of "darke fogge, icie Alps, and icie seas."

Sailing down the river Thames on his first voyage, Frobisher got a royal sendoff. In answer to a cannon salute from his small fleet, Queen Elizabeth waved a jeweled hand from the window of her palace at Greenwich. She also sent a gentleman aboard to wish them God-speed and to request the Captain General to visit her at court for a personal farewell.

Frobisher was later to compose a ballad in which he wistfully dreamed of:

A pleasant ayre, a sweete and firtell soil,
A certaine gaine, a never dying praise:
An easie passage, voide of loathsome toil,
Found out by some, and knowen to me the waies.

He found little of that idyllic passage on this trip. Gales had struck one hammerblow after another by the time he reached the ice pack off the southern tip of Greenland—a "high and ragged land" where the crags rose up in the sky "like pinnacles of steeples, and all covered with snow." Never had he been pulverized by such storms. The pinnace cracked in the onslaught like a veritable eggshell; all four sailors aboard were sucked to the bottom of the green North Atlantic. The master of the floundering *Michael* was appalled by the writhing mists and the swirling icebergs; the coward turned tail and scurried home, where he gave out the cock-and-bull story that Frobisher and his eighteen hands aboard the *Gabriel* had perished.

It wasn't true, of course. Frobisher had vowed "to make a sacrifice unto God of his life rather than return home without the discovery of Cathay." Nevertheless, he almost did make the sacrifice. Wallowing in the troughs of tempestuous waves off Greenland's Cape Farewell, the *Gabriel* heeled over flat on her side. As the icy waters poured in the sailors were seized with despair. Not so Frobisher. "Like himself with valiant courage," he grabbed an axe and ran along the tilted side of the ship. Hacking savagely, he cut the foresail free. The pressure was thus relieved and the vessel gradually righted herself.

Frobisher returned to his tiller, and while his crew tried to pump out the water, he steered westward across iceberg-studded Davis Strait. When his drenched men lost heart, Frobisher remained resolute. "The sea," he cheered them on, "at length must have an ending."

And so it did. On July 21, 1576, dodging the "monstrous high islands of floating ice," the little bark nosed into "a great gut, bay, or passage, dividing as it were two mainlands or continents asunder." Frobisher thus triumphantly entered the great bight of a bay that today bears his name on the southeast coast of Baffin Island. The explorer was certain he had discovered the Northwest Passage. And as he sailed one hundred and fifty miles westward into the gut of that ice lane, he was convinced that the north-shore mountains on his righthand side formed the continent of Asia and that the south-shore mountains on his lefthand side were the back-end of North America.

It was a heady moment. Frobisher climbed to the top of a high snow-capped mountain to survey his discovery. He felt as exalted as another historic explorer. Ferdinand Magellan had discovered in 1520 the Magellan Strait on the bottom of South America that was the southwest passage to the Pacific Ocean. "So this place he named Frobisher's Straits," pilot George Best proudly tells us, "like as Magellan at the southwest end of the world, having discovered the passage to the South Sea."

Yet it was a strange Asiatic Cathay that Frobisher gazed at through his spy glass. Though glacial rivers of ice and snow snaked down the mountains, "mighty deer," huge hares and silver foxes also scampered through gravel grasslands that were blazed purplish with violets, lupins and fireweed. Like many an Arctic explorer to follow in his footsteps, he swore full-mouthed oaths at the mosquito. It was "a kind of small fly or gnat that stingeth and offendeth so fiercely that the place where they bite shortly after swelleth and itcheth very sore."

That meticulous observer, George Best, remarked on the abundance of ravens, snowy owls and ptarmigans: "All these fowls are far thicker clothed with down and feathers than any in England; for as the country is colder, so nature hath provided a remedy thereto." He rejoiced at the midnight sun which, even though it did set at 10:15 P.M. and riseth again at 1:45 A.M., "is never above three or four degrees under the edge of the horizon; so that in July all the night long, we might perfectly and easily write and read whatsoever pleased us."

But it was the variability of the climate that proved most astounding. The temperamental summer winds blew hot and cold. "On the 26th of July," it was noted with amazement, "there fell so much snow, with such bitter cold air, that we could not scarce see one another for the same, nor open our eyes to handle our ropes and sails, the snow being about half a foot deep upon the hatches of our ship." And yet, the next minute, a cat's paw of wind suddenly "cometh down from the hollows of the hills, and we shall have such a breath of heat brought upon our face, as though we were entered within some bathtub or hothouse, and we shall be weary of the blooming heat."

Like the winds, Frobisher and his party had a blow-hot and blow-cold relationship with the natives of this contradictory Cathay. As he peered through his glass on the high hilltop, Frobisher saw a number of small dots swarming among the ice hummocks in the sea. He supposed they were a school of "porpoises, or seals, or some kind of strange fish; but coming nearer, he discovered them to be men, in small boats made of leather."

They were Eskimos, of course, paddling their seal-skin kayaks. Frobisher, who thought he had reached the foreland of Asia, naturally assumed they were Asiatic. They had long black hair, flat noses, blue tattoo marks etched under their slanted eyes, and they had a tawny complexion "the colour of a ripe olive."

Both sides were wary at first. But after an exchange of hostages, nineteen of the Eskimos clambered aboard the *Gabriel* and exchanged "great courtesy." The crew bartered mirrors and needles for their bearskins and sealskins. The exchange of cultures was perhaps more interesting. The Eskimos were repelled by the ship's pork and by the taste of Frobisher's aqua vitae brandy offered to them. On their part, the mariners were horrified to see the natives devour raw salmon and seal meat. It was fun, though, when the guests climbed up the ship's rigging and nimbly competed with the English sailors at performing acrobatics.

Pilot Best, presumably reflecting the prejudices of Frobisher, summarized their good qualities thus:

"These people are in nature very subtle and sharp-witted. They are ready to conceive our meaning by signs, and to make answer, well to be understood again. If they have not seen the thing whereof you ask them, they will cover their eyes with their hands, as if to say, it hath been hid from their sight. If they understand you not whereof you ask them, they will stop their ears.

"They will teach us the names of each thing in their language which we desire to learn, and are apt to learn any thing of us. They delight in music above measure, and will keep time and stroke to any tune which you shall sing, both with their voice, head, hand and feet, and will sing the same tune aptly after you. They will row with our oars in our boats, and keep a true stroke with our mariners, and seem to take great delight therein.

An Eskimo man, woman and child were brought back from Frobisher Bay to England and John White's sketches of the so-called "Asiatic" captives are now exhibited at the British Museum. Queen Elizabeth enjoyed watching the kayaker shoot royal geese and swans on the Avon River. Unfortunately, all three natives soon died of pneumonia and English cooking.

The first European painting of Eskimos shows them, alas, involved in a battle with invading white men. Artist John White, who accompanied Frobisher on his second voyage of 1577, has preserved for posterity this rendition of the encounter at "Bloody Point" in Frobisher Bay. The upshot of the fray: one Englishman pierced in the belly and the slaughter of half a dozen Eskimos.

"They are exceedingly friendly and kind-hearted, one to the other, and mourn greatly at the loss or harm of their fellows, and express their grief of mind, when they part one from another, with a mournful song and dirges."

Alas, these friendly people were soon to be regarded as a "brutish and uncivil people." In all fairness, though, it must be said that Frobisher showed himself the brutal one. He visited a small village of Eskimos living in sealskin tents with the intention of hiring a local pilot. We are told that the natives "made signs of friendship (by laying their head on their hands) and led him by the hand into their houses." But apparently the Eskimo being held hostage in the English rowboat used that opportunity to attempt an escape. Frobisher immediately lunged forward with his long gilt-handled halberd. "He held the point thereof to the strange man's breast, threatening by signs to kill him if he did once stir."

Another frightened Eskimo was rowed back to the ship. And after being paid with bits of haberdashery, the cowed native agreed in sign language to guide the *Gabriel* farther down the channel in his kayak and apparently indicated that in two days they would reach the end of the so-called strait. The Eskimo obviously meant it would take that long to reach the end of Frobisher Bay, which is, of course, a cul-de-sac.

In any event, Frobisher was cautious. He suspected "these strange people are not to be trusted" despite any "show of friendship they might make." So the skipper ordered five crew members to row the kayaker pilot ashore to the village, but to return to the ship immediately. The oarsmen, who had secretly stuffed their pockets with trading trinkets, rounded a point and vanished from his sight forever.

Frobisher was furious. Either they had mutinied or been taken captive. And he had been hoodwinked by the Eskimo pilot, who had taken the haberdashery and not kept his bargain. After impatiently waiting two days for their return, Frobisher ordered the *Gabriel* to sail back and forth firing gun shots while he blew blasts on his trumpet. He was rewarded by silence ashore, or, what was more galling, what sounded like contemptuous laughter.

His rage turned to worry. He had no rowboat with which to land and with just thirteen sailors left, he was clearly outnumbered by these "ravenous, bloody, and man-eating people." And when he saw a flotilla of thirty-four Eskimos approach in their kayaks and umiaks, he hastily prepared for action. All openings where the acrobats might climb up on ropes were covered with canvas, and every firearm was loaded. There was no attack, and so Frobisher decided, as Pilot Best phrased it, "to deceive the deceivers" and catch one of them with a "pretty policy" of pretty toys.

Frobisher's seducing stratagem had a certain charm about it. He stood alone on deck (though with weapons cagily hidden at his feet) and began tinkling a brass bell. The sound appealed to one of the kayakers. As the music-lover gingerly approached, Frobisher flung the bell into the sea, making sure it fell short of the paddler. The Eskimo was disappointed. Then Frobisher rang a second bell and held it out as though offering the pretty gift. Tempted beyond caution, the kayaker paddled right up beside the waist of the ship. What happened next tells us how remarkably small the *Gabriel* was and how muscular Frobisher must have been. For he reached over from the deck to clutch the Eskimo by the wrists; and "suddenly, by main force of strength, plucked both the man and his light boat out of the sea and into the ship in a trice."

The Eskimo was so vexed at being tricked that he bit off his own tongue, and thus couldn't or wouldn't reveal the whereabouts of the five missing sailors. His crew members were "tired and sick with hard labour of their voyage," and so Frobisher weighed anchor on August 25 and sailed home.

When he reached London six stormy weeks later, a man returned from the dead, Frobisher received a delirious welcome. But it was his captive Eskimo with his kayak that created a sensation. Promoter Michael Lok, sounding rather like a circus barker fronting a freak show, declared that the tongue-tied infidel produced "such a wonder unto the whole city and to the rest of the realm that heard of it as seemed never to have happened the like great matter to any man's knowledge ... And because I have heard reports of many strange tales and feigned fables touching the personage and manners of this strange man, I have thought good therefore to declare the very truth thereof to satisfy the world." Lok announced that the strange man—with his Moorish complexion and "his countenance sullen or churlish and sharp withall"—was indubitably a Tartar from Cathay.

Unfortunately the Eskimo caught cold in the London damp and shortly died of a chill.

Lok was left with a large unpaid investment in the expedition and nothing to show for it. But he was a resourceful promoter. The tale soon spread that he had asked Frobisher's crew to return with souvenirs of the first things they spied in the new world. The men had brought back a clump of green grass, a bunch of flowers—and a chunk of rock black as sea coal. Lok's wife was said to have accidentally tossed the metallic lump into the fire, and then quenched it with a little vinegar, and, lo, it "glistened like a bright marquisette of gold." And when the London assayers tested it, the nugget was indeed found to hold gold, "and that very richly for the quantity."

So ran the tale. The real story, as Lok later confessed, was more complicated than that. Frobisher had handed him the black pebble, considering it nothing but a novelty. But Lok had convinced himself that it must be a precious mineral. He had it evaluated, first by the royal mint assay master, and then by two of the top professional assayers in the City. All three metallurgists dismissed it as iron pyrite—mere fool's gold.

Lok, an obdurate wishful thinker, refused to take no for an answer. Incredible as it may seem, he had consulted an alchemist, a Venetian practitioner of the black arts named Giovanni Baptista Agnello. Signore Agnello appears to have been as shady a charlatan as Subtle, the leading character in Ben Jonson's *The Alchemist* who believed that "Alchemy is a pretty kind of game, somewhat like tricks o' the cards, to cheat a man with charming." For Agnello had no trouble at all charming both "powder of gold" and "a grain of gold" from the iron lump.

Gulled by greed and his own credulity, Lok was completely taken in by the mountebank. He asked Agnello: How did the alchemist happen to find gold when the three eminent scientists had found nothing? In melodious Italian, we are told, Signore Agnello had replied to the *Molto Magnifico* and *Honorando* Lok: "*Bisogna sapere adulare la natura* —Nature sometimes needs a little coaxing."

Additional negative tests were made by the Queen's Secretary of State, the skeptical Sir Francis Walsingham. But Lok persuasively insisted that the pebble was a bonafide gold nugget. Agnello could not possibly be a bamboozler. "I must credit his honesty," Lok swore in all earnestness; for the alchemist had whispered to him the magical words: "The ore is of sufficient value to make you rich."

Those words set London agog. Salted or not, King Solomon's gold mine had been discovered in Cathay.

This time Lok had no difficulty attracting speculators. The cream of court society (even the doubting Secretary of State Walsingham) came rushing to take a flutter in the stock. Queen Elizabeth herself headed the list with a subscription of one thousand pounds. She granted a royal charter to the Company of Cathay. Lok, appointed Governor for life, shrewdly charged new investors a levy on admission of thirty pounds each to liquidate the deficit on the first voyage. It was a canny piece of financial manipulation, making new shareholders pay interest on old investments, but it worked. A total of 4,275 pounds flowed in.

Captain General Frobisher now rejoiced in the title of "High Admiral of Cathay." Besides the *Gabriel* and the *Michael*, he commanded a handsome tall ship, the two-hundred-ton *Aid*, loaned to him by the Queen. And besides brandy and beer, he was able to afford five tons of the best malmsey and sack wine, plus barrels of honey, cheese, butter, salad oil, oatmeal, almonds, raisins, licorice.

He was to head an expedition of one hundred and twenty men. Among those scheduled to sail were: thirty miners (supervised by a so-called German "goldfinder," Jonas Schultz, who was an assistant of alchemist Agnello); six convicts (deported by the Crown with the high-minded hope that the criminals might civilize the Eskimos); and, most important historically, an artist named John White from the London Painter-Stainers' Company (who left to posterity the first European painting of Eskimos—involved in a battle with the invading white men).

Before that battle occurred, the three ships left England in May of 1577 with a "merry wind" as well as a "Godspeed" from Queen Elizabeth, who allowed "our loving friend, Martin Frobisher" to kiss her majestic hand. Gloriana named their destination *Meta Incognita*—Goal Unknown —and after eight weeks of merry winds they reached their goal.

On the little island now known as Loks Land, near the cape called Queen Elizabeth Foreland, High Admiral Frobisher ascended the highest snow-mantled mountain to take possession. His party erected a cross of stones and planted the Queen's ensign. Then, with a blast of trumpets, they solemnly knelt to pray that "by our Christian study and endeavour, those barbarous people trained up in paganry and infidelity, might be reduced to the knowledge of true religion."

Apparently the unconverted pagans, like the gold, needed a little physical coaxing. Several Eskimos appeared on the mountainside, making friendly noises "like the mooing of bulls." Frobisher mooed right back, held up two fingers as a peace sign, and blew his trumpet. The natives responded by skipping, laughing, and dancing with joy. Two unarmed men from each camp went to neutral ground, and there was an amicable exchange of pins and needles for Eskimo bow cases. As a "token of affection," one Eskimo cut off the tail of his coat and presented it to Frobisher as a gift.

But Frobisher wanted more than a coattail. He signalled to his partner. Then both muscular Christians suddenly lunged forward with

EQUES auratus

MARTINUS

FORBISHERUS

FORBISHERVS ouans NEPTVNIA regna Frequentat
Pre Fatria at tandem glande Feremptus obit

Frobisher died fighting, on November 7, 1594, with his cutlass and pistol in hand, a national hero. The Latin inscription reads: "Joyfully Frobisher travelled Neptune's kingdoms for his country but finally met his death when struck by a missile."

the intent of capturing the "two salvagies" by force. The savages ran off free because Frobisher and his mate slipped on the ice. Then in a slapstick turnabout the two Eskimos grabbed their bows and arrows from behind a rock and followed hot on the heels of the escaping evangelists. The embarrassing upshot was that High Admiral Frobisher was struck in the buttocks by an aboriginal arrow. Christianity was somewhat redeemed by a Cornishman, one Nicholas Conger, "a good man on his feet and a good rassler," who pursued one of the Eskimos and "showed him such a Corniss trick that he made his sides ache against the ground for a month after."

The next Eskimo captive was taken prisoner in a skirmish that wasn't quite so comic. The pitched battle took place in a cliff-rimmed inlet farther down Frobisher Bay which was given the name of Bloody Point. Firing guns and shooting their own arrows, Frobisher's marauders in rowboats trapped a group of Eskimo kayakers in the inlet. The natives scrambled up the cliffs and replied with a fierce barrage of darts and arrows.

They may have been "crafty villains" of a "ravenous and bloody disposition," but Pilot Best was surprised at how manfully the Eskimos fought. "For after gathering up those arrows which our men shot at them, yea, and plucking our arrows out of their bodies, they encountered afresh again." In the end one Englishman was pierced in the belly and a half dozen Eskimos were slaughtered. "And when they found they were mortally wounded," Best wrote, the Eskimo victims desperately "cast themselves from off the rocks into the sea, lest perhaps their enemies should receive glory or prey on their dead carcasses, for *they* supposed *us* to be cannibals."

The cultural misunderstandings continued. The white victors captured two Eskimo women cowering behind rocks. One was so old, deformed and ugly that the superstitious sailors removed her boots to see if she was cloven-hoofed. She proved not to be a witch, but rather than take any chances, the fearful mariners let her go. The other woman was a young mother, sobbing and terrified because the white men had shot through her hair topknot and pierced the arm of her suckling child. Frobisher took her hostage and had the ship's doctor apply salves to the baby's wounds. "But she, not acquainted with such kind of surgery, plucked those salves away," noted Best, "and by continual licking with her own tongue, not much unlike our dogs, healed up the child's arm."

Best paints a sympathetic picture of how the Eskimo hostages behaved under stress. Frobisher used them in a parley with a band of their countrymen who came waving a flag of seal bladders and pleading for the release of the prisoners. While the mother and child were held in sight on top of a high hill, Frobisher took the captive caught by the Cornish wrestler with him to the bargaining negotiations.

"This captive, at the first encounter with his friends, fell so into tears that he could not speak a word," observed Best. "But after a while, overcoming his emotions, he talked at full with his companions. He bestowed upon them such toys and trifles as we had given him. Whereby we noted that they are very kind one to the other, and greatly sorrowful for the loss of their friends."

Frobisher handed the Eskimo delegation a letter to deliver to his five shipmates who had deserted and apparently been captured on his first voyage. He signed it, "Yours to the uttermost of my power," and its phrases ring powerfully with his curious mixture of Christian sincerity and pugnacity.

"In the name of God in whom we all believe," he began, "and who, I trust, hath preserved your bodyes and souls amongst these Infidels, I commend me unto you. I will be glad to seeke by all meanes you can devise for your deliverance, either with force or with any commodities within my Shippes, which I will not spare for your sakes, or anything else I can do for you. I have aboard of theirs a Man, a Woman and a Childe, which I am contented to deliver for you. . . ." Then Frobisher couldn't resist adding a note of defiance. "You may declare unto them," he wrote, "that if they deliver you not, I wyll not leave a man alive in their Country." He trusted they were serving God, and he would pray for them daily, and meanwhile he was sending them pen, ink and paper for a return message.

Frobisher waited three days for a reply, and when it did not come he vented his indignation. When he noticed a party of twenty Eskimos singing and dancing on the brow of a hill, he ordered the mightiest cannon to be fired over their heads. "It thundered in the hollows of the high hills, and made unto them so fearful a noise, that they had no great will to tarry long after." The cannonade, it was noted with Christian piety, was designed to give the heathen cannibals a taste of English strength rather than "our flesh which is so sweet meat for them."

Frobisher had better luck recovering traces of his supposed precious ore. At first his goldfinder couldn't find a piece the size of a walnut. They were fooled by the glint of mountain peaks that sparkled in the midnight sun like dazzling metal. But the stuff proved to be black iron, thus verifying the old proverb, as Best predicted with ironic accuracy: "All is not gold that shineth."

However, "God being our best steersman," He steered them to an island where goldfinder Jonas Schultz detected the genuine article. (Geologists today think it may have been mica formation.) In an act unprecedented for a High Admiral, Frobisher set an example for his English officers by democratically swinging a pick with the miners. They loaded their ships with two hundred tons of ore, and on August 23, with icicles lacing their riggings, they sailed for home.

Frobisher received a gala court welcome when he returned with his trophies. At Windsor Castle he presented the Queen with a two-yard-long narwhal horn. Elizabeth was so delighted with this jewel of the unicorn that she rewarded him with one hundred pounds. The Eskimo man, woman and child enchanted her. For entertainment, she watched the kayaker spear the royal geese and swans on the Avon River—though, unfortunately, all three natives soon died of pneumonia and English cooking.

Naturally the Queen was most pleased with the supposed treasure trove of gold. The rocks were securely guarded behind quadruple locks in the Tower of London and Bristol Castle. On the strength of Signore Agnello's preliminary tests, Michael Lok assured her that a profit of five English pounds per ton of rock could be realized. So Gloriana sponsored an even more ambitious expedition to bring back two thousand tons of the ore.

This time an armada of fifteen ships was assembled—the largest single fleet until World War II — to brave the Canadian Arctic. It established three other records. Aboard were: more than one hundred colonists who proposed to plant the first English settlement in the New World; carpenters to erect what was probably the world's first prefabricated house; and an Anglican divine, the Reverend Mr. Wolfall, the first missionary who hoped to bring the gospel to the pagan Eskimos.

After an interlude at Greenwich Palace, where the Queen slipped a gold chain around Admiral Frobisher's neck, the fleet set out on May 31, 1578 for Meta Incognita. Unknown Goal it proved to be, for in a historic accident, the ships blundered about one hundred and eighty miles down modern Hudson Strait. Frobisher named it his Mistaken Strait; yet there was no mistaking the unerring seamanship and cool bravery he displayed under the most dire conditions. Pilot Best, skippering the *Anne Frances* on this voyage, was hard put to describe the "incredible pain and peril" that the ship masters faced.

They were separated by grey walls of "hideous fogge." They were lacerated by summer's "cruel nipping storms of raging winter." They were spun around by the furious riptide at the entrance of Hudson

Strait, whirlpools that roared like "the waterfall of London Bridge." And worst of all, they ran the risk of ramming into the grinding, groaning, gyrating ice mountains, "whose hugeness and monstrous greatness was such that no man would credit it, but such as to their pains saw and felt it."

Thus compassed on all sides by mists and sleet, falling snow and floating Alps, some mariners knelt in prayer on the iced decks. "Lord, now help us or never!" they cried out. "Now, Lord, look down from heaven and save us sinners, or else our safety cometh too late!" And some, with fear or terror in their hearts, began to murmur secretly against their admiral. They would as lief be hanged when they came home, they muttered, rather than stay and submit themselves and their ships to the mercy of the unmerciful ice.

But thanks to the leadership of the steadfast Frobisher, only one ship, the *Thomas of Ipswich,* abandoned the scattered fleet and fled home like a "milksoppe." Another bark, the *Dennis,* carrying the prefabricated house, was smashed by a tossing ice pan and sank, "which so abashed the whole fleet that we thought verily we should have a taste of the same sauce." Fortunately Frobisher had ordered that any ships lost in the dense fog would sound trumpets, drum and cannon and shout the password, "Before the world was God," which would be answered by, "After God came Christ, His son." The warning signals were recognized and the foundering sailors were rescued in time.

Not Christ, but magnificent ingenuity, saved the other ships from being crushed by the menacing ice floes and bergs. Some protected the sides of their vessels with bedding, masts and junk rope against "the outrageous sway and strokes of the said ice." Some fended it off with pikes, two-inch-thick planks, and even their shoulders. Some anchored their ship to a bulwark of ice and in full sail used it as a battering ram to clear a lane free of other ice hummocks. Yet the biggest of ships were so squeezed by the ice pack that they were "heaved up between islands of ice a foot out of the sea, having their knees and timbers both bowed and broken therewith."

Frobisher finally rallied his fleet at Resolution Island, midpoint between the gateways of both Hudson Strait and Frobisher Bay. At their meeting the torn ships "hailed the Admiral after the manner of the sea, and with great joy welcomed one another with a thundering volley of shot." There was a cheerful flinging up of sailors' caps. And truly, said Best, it was wonderful "how joyful and glad every party was to see themselves meet in safety again after such strange and incredible dangers."

Officers and men pitched in heartily farther down the bay to dig for black ore. By now the Eskimos were wary of meeting Christian kidnappers, so the Reverend Mr. Wolfall had no heathens to convert. In order to "allure those brutish and uncivil people" to the ways of civilization, a limestone building was constructed. Left inside were baked bread that the natives might taste as well as toys to play with — such as whistles, pipes, Elizabethan dolls, and lead soldiers on horseback. By the end of August, icicles were making the ropes painful to handle. And so, with a farewell cannon volley, the invaders departed from what the Eskimos forever after called Kodlunarn Island (Isle of the White Men). And the ships set out for England with a cargo that Best called enough to "reasonably suffice all the gold gluttons of the world."

Back in England it turned out that the gold gluttons extracted everything out of the lumpish black rocks except gold. After so much bravery was spent in the Arctic — including the loss of forty sailors who either drowned or died of scurvy — the entire enterprise became a kind of black comedy. Signore Agnello and Jonas Schultz attempted their dubious science on the ore in the basement furnace of one of Michael Lok's knighted speculators, but the furnace blew up and the pair of alchemists were smoked out. A third alchemist was called in to try his hand at refining the ore at a giant smelter at Dartford on the Thames, but had no better luck. All three prima donnas got into a ruckus of rivalry and quarreled over whose sorcery was superior. Just before Christmas (when, he said, his unpaid mariners "cryeth out for money"), Frobisher was so furious at the delay that he allegedly drew his dagger on one of the double-talking goldfinders, and, according to Michael Lok, "he entered into great storms and rages with me like a mad beast."

Poor Lok was beset by financial storms. His reputation and his gold bubble had burst. His Cathay Company went broke. His fool's gold was transmuted into mere paving stones "cast forth to mend the highways." His courtier friends on the Queen's Privy Council, besides not paying for their own subscriptions to the company, insisted that the promoter make good for the some three thousand pounds worth of debts incurred in the name of the Queen. Lok lashed back at the hypocrites: "You have a thorn in your own foot which doth somewhat prick you, which you would pull out and put into mine, who am not able to cure it as well as yourselves."

When this didn't work, the hamstrung promoter turned on Frobisher, the one person involved with the Ship of Fools who had performed his job ably. Lok drew up a list of sins entitled "The Abuses of Captain Frobisher Against the Company." His once valiant Jason seeking the Golden Fleece was now denigrated as an arrogant, imperious ignoramus, a pirate after all, "so full of lying talk and so impudent of tongue that his best friends are most slandered by him when he cannot have his will." Frobisher retaliated by calling his backer a "bankrupt knave," a "false accountant," an embezzler who had cozened the Cathay Company out of three thousand pounds without investing a groat of his own cash.

Despite these churlish recriminations, one can't help but feel sorry for Lok, done in by the folly of his own greed. We last hear of him thrown into Fleet Debtors' Prison, where he is petitioning the Queen's Privy Council to pity himself, his wife and fifteen children who are left to "beg their bread henceforth except God turn the stones at Dartford into his bread again, and that your Honors be good unto him in this his humble suit. I must say that you have dealt very hardly with me."

Equally pathetic was the petition for relief submitted to Privy Councillor Walsingham by Frobisher's wife, Isabel. The elderly widow of a wealthy Yorkshireman, she had married Frobisher before he set off on his third voyage, only to find that the vagabond had invested her fortune in the Cathay Company. Now Isabel was "the most miserable poor woman in the world," and her destitute children and grandchildren were famishing "for want of food, ready to starve, to your poor oratrix's intolerable grief and sorrow."

Down and out he might be, but Frobisher still had his swashbuckling courage to offer. He replenished his purse by joining his fellow pirate, Sir Francis Drake, in a series of looting raids in the Spanish West Indies. His combustible temper flared in a notable dispute with his partner. Drake apparently tried to cheat him out of his share of the gold booty after they had jointly plundered the Spanish galleon *San Luis*. "We *will* have our shares," Frobisher warned, "or I will make him spend the best blood in his belly!" The Queen's Privy Council stepped in to award Frobisher five thousand pounds of the prize money.

They evidently patched up their differences. For Frobisher joined Drake and another buccaneering comrade, Sir John Hawkins, to command the English naval forces that repulsed the invading Spanish Armada. He became a national hero and was knighted.

Sir Martin Frobisher died fighting with his cutlass and pistol in hand. On November 7, 1594, he personally led the attack on Spanish Fort Crozon at the seaport of Brest in France. He climbed up the fortress ramparts on a scaling ladder and, at the head of his men, slashed away at the besieged Spaniards. An enemy soldier a few yards away fired a gun pointblank which mortally wounded him, but the fifty-five-year-old warrior kept fighting. After the fortress was captured, Frobisher was carried aboard his flagship, *Vanguard*. Before his death he managed to scribble a letter to the Queen's Lord High Admiral. Its roughhewn phrases bespeak the character of the invincible sea dog:

"We have taken this fort. They defended it verie resolutelie. And never asked for mercie. So they were put all to the sword, saving five or six, that hid themselves in the rockes.

"It was tyme for us to go through with it.

"I was shot in with a bullet at the battery alongst the huckle bone. So as I was driven to have an incision made to take out the bullet. So as I am neither able to walk nor ride. And the mariners are verie unwilling to go except I go with them myselfe. Yet if I find it to come to an extremitie, we will try what we are able."

We will try what we are able. Perhaps that ought to be his epitaph. One of his biographers, the English sailor named William McFee, expressed it in another way: "He was impatient. He was irascible. He was incapable of dissembling his emotions when roused. But Frobisher seems to have had in him not only greatness, but a human quality which made men curse him and love him, grumble at him and toil for him."

In the matter of Arctic discovery, geographers deprived him of greatness for several centuries. For some inexplicable reason, possibly because the gold rush fiasco had yielded such paltry dividends, mapmakers in his time erroneously relegated Frobisher's Strait to the southeast coast of Greenland.

Not until 1861 did Frobisher emerge in true perspective in history. It was then that an American explorer, Charles Francis Hall, wintered with the Eskimos in the landlocked bay and discovered remains of Frobisher's limestone hut still standing on Kodlunarn Island. Even more extraordinary, Hall heard from the Eskimos the detailed story of how their ancestors had taken compassion on Frobisher's five missing sailors, and had sheltered them for two years, until the five homesick deserters had sailed from the "Isle of the White Men" in a homemade boat to their doom in the Arctic. This folk memory, handed down from one generation to the next for almost three hundred years, thus showed that the Arctic is a remarkable preserver of more than limestone.

Another hundred years later, in the reign of Queen Elizabeth II, an ironic footnote was added to Frobisher's Arctic gold rush. A Canadian mining explorer named Murray Watts, taking his cue from Frobisher, followed the trail of the blue-black mountain ranges up the northeast coast of Baffin Island and discovered what is now believed to be the world's richest mountain of highgrade iron ore. And so Frobisher's lumps of iron, "black as sea coal," proved not to be fool's gold after all.

Perhaps Frobisher's greatest, most immediate contribution to Arctic exploration was the record of his voyages bequeathed to his successors. His pilot-lieutenant, George Best, wrote a stirring introduction in his published account, *A True Discourse of the late Voyages of Discovery for the Finding of a Passage to Cathay under the Conduct of Martin Frobisher, General.* It was a bugle call to all Northwest Passage adventurers:

"How dangerous it is to attempt new discoveries; either for the length of the voyage, or the ignorance of the language, the want of interpreters, new and unaccustomed elements and airs, strange and unsavoury meats, danger of thieves and robbers, fierceness of wild beasts and fishes, hugeness of woods, dangerousness of seas, dread of tempests, fear of hidden rocks, steepness of mountains, darkness of sudden falling fogs, continual painstaking without any rest, and infinite others.

"How pleasant and profitable it is to attempt new discoveries; either for the sundry sights and shapes of strange beasts and fishes, the wonderful works of nature, the different manners and fashions of diverse nations, the sundry sorts of government, the sight of strange trees, fruit, fowls, and beasts, the infinite treasure of pearl, gold, and silver, the sundry positions of the sphere, the news of new found lands, and many others."

Chapter 5

The Wizard, The Knight, and The Pilot

In the spring of 1583 Dr. John Dee, a fortuneteller with a milky white beard and a black skull cap, sat in front of a crystal ball and held a series of seances in which he tried to elicit from the spirits predictions about certain expected journeys across the ocean. Dr. Dee was no ordinary crystal gazer and his clients were making no ordinary trips.

Astrologer to Queen Elizabeth and her royal court, he was reputed to be the "arch-conjuror of the whole kingdom." Everybody who was anybody came to consult the Welsh wizard in his book-tiered study at Mortlake on the Thames. For he was the high priest of mysteries that few people understood, a seer who combined the intellect and the ignorance of the Elizabethan age.

The Cambridge University scholar was a brilliant Euclidean mathematician. He was a scientist who invented a so-called Paradoxical Compass for navigating Arctic waters. He was an influential empire propagandist who coined the term "British Empire." He was a roving James Bond spy for Secretary of State Sir Francis Walsingham (predating Bond some four hundred years by using the secret agent code signature "007"). And he was a Muscovy Company mapmaker who was the advisor to every leading explorer of his day.

Yet for all his academic wisdom, Dr. Dee was self-deluded by superstition. He was a dabbler in black magic and cabalistic numerology who barely escaped conviction on charges of witchcraft before the Star Chamber. He was an alchemist who dreamily sought the philosopher's stone that could transmute base metals into gold. He was a caster of horoscopes, so versed in the abracadabra of the stars that Queen Elizabeth had asked the prophet to fix the date for her coronation. And he was an occultist, so naively steeped in spiritualism that he paid an annual salary of fifty pounds to his private medium—a zombielike charlatan named Edward Kelly, who had had his ears shorn off in the public stocks for having committed forgery and for communicating with graveyard ghosts.

During his clairvoyance sessions of 1583, Kelly was being paid to commune with the spirits about forthcoming Northwest Passage expeditions. Dr. Dee was understandably curious because he had a financial stake in two of them. That June, Sir Humphrey Gilbert was scheduled to establish the first colony in the New World's Codfish Land, and the knight had grandly awarded to Dr. Dee title to all land north of 50 degrees latitude—virtually the whole of modern Canada. In addition, Dr. Dee had just set up a company of discovery in partnership with the knight's brother, Adrian Gilbert, and a pilot explorer named John Davis—and the enterprise was to attempt the newest polar voyage in search of Cathay.

In all the history of Arctic exploration planning there was no setting so fantastic. The seances were conducted in Dr. Dee's library, where he often amused himself with a trick carnival mirror which distorted people's images into fat or thin shapes. While the bearded sage sat in a green chair, the medium, Kelly, knelt in front of a polished "shew stone." This crystal globe of mystic properties was set in the centre of a tasselled square of red silk on a three-foot-high gazing or "scrying" table, whose four legs stood on wax seals each inscribed in Hebrew.

After a certain amount of mumbojumbo, Kelly's supernatural angel spirit allegedly emerged from the crystal ball. Her name was Madimi and she was said to be a pretty little wench dressed in white. Only the crop-eared Kelly could hear her forecasts spoken in Greek, Arabic or Syrian, which had to be deciphered by the scholarly Dee.

According to Dr. Dee's diary, the dialogue that ensued was not particularly revealing, for Madimi's prognostications were as murky as any gypsy teacup reader's.

What did the future hold in store for the expeditions?

"Behold, these things shall God bring to pass," Madimi generalized. "The corners and straits of the earth shall be measured to the depth. And strange shall be the wonders that are creeping into new worlds. Time shall be altered, with the difference of day and night."

Explorers seeking the Northwest Passage in the Elizabethan era had to rely on the crystal ball-gazing horoscopes cast by the Queen's astrologer, Dr. John Dee. In return for his occult geographical guidance to Sir Humphrey Gilbert and pilot John Davis, the wizard was granted land title to the whole of Canada north of 50 degrees latitude.

Could Madimi be more specific in her geographic description of the straits to be explored?

"Let darkness go behind thee," she warned, in an apparent reference to the midnight sun.

Well, then, what were the chances of converting the infidels from the mouth of hell to the great glory of Christianity?

"Who made thy mouth to prophesy?" she replied. "Who opened the eyes of thy understanding?" Gilbert, she added cryptically, was "not of the true faith."

How then, Dee inquired through Kelly, could God's faith be brought to the pagans?

"That," said Madimi, before she vanished wraithlike back into the globe, "is a mystery."

If this scene sounds bizarre and theatrical, so was Dr. Dee's disciple, Sir Humphrey Gilbert, the leader of the first projected expedition. Indeed both Dee and Gilbert might have been cast in the play, *King Henry IV*, written by their Elizabethan contemporary, William Shakespeare. Dee might well have been the counterpart of the Welsh oracle, Owen Glendower, who proclaimed sonorously, "I can call spirits from the vasty deep." Gilbert would have been perfect for the role of Hotspur, that impetuous, "wasp -stung" warrior who was restlessly afire "to pluck bright honour from the pale-faced moon."

Headstrong was probably the word that best defined Sir Humphrey Gilbert. His contemporaries employed many other adjectives, not all flattering. They described him as "brimful of fickleness and bragging and overflowing with vanity"; a "naughty man" given to choleric rages and tantrums and bloody sadism; a "chameleon" who oscillated between chivalric posing and reckless bravery; a highflown courtier with "an excellent and ready wit and therewith a tongue at liberty to utter what he thought"; a "learned knight with a projecting head"—meaning his brain was teeming with ambitious projects.

In a sense, he embodied the spirit of the Elizabethan age: the explorer who voyaged with the mind as well as the body. But in uniting the man of action with the man of ideas, the trouble was that the overreacher often let his ideas run to his head. *Quid Non*—Why Not? — was his family motto, and he was forever ready to embark on extravagant ventures that he himself termed rash and quixotic. Yet why not? For was he not knight errant and gallant conquistador seeking glory and gold for himself and the Queen? It was the gesture that counted, no matter how foolhardy. He truly believed in the imperishable

HVMERIDVS GILBERTVS MILES AVRATVS E@

Quid Non

THE NATIONAL PORTRAIT GALLERY, LONDON

Sir Humphrey Gilbert, the grandiose, ruthless and chivalric knight to Queen Elizabeth I, was the Hotspur among Arctic explorers. After crushing the Munster rebels in Ireland with severe cruelty, he became the first colonizer and Governor of Newfoundland. His swashbuckling credo: "The wings of man's life are plumed with the feathers of death."

phrase he coined to end his *Discourse of a Discovery for a New Passage to Cathay*: "He is not worthy to live at all that, for fear or danger of death, shunneth his country service and his own honour, seeing death is inevitable and the fame of virtue immortal."

Gilbert was imbued with fantasies of gaining chivalric renown at an early age. A son of the landed gentry, he was born in West Country Devonshire in the Valley of the Dart River. A famous painting purports to show Gilbert and his half-brother, Sir Walter Raleigh, as boys lying on the riverbank and listening entranced to deeds of derring-do told them by a mariner from nearby Dartmouth. Raleigh, who was also to become a romantic courtier-cum-seafarer, shared with Gilbert the notion that "style is the man" and that the adventure of life was a "troublesome bark." It was up to each bravo to swashbuckle his way up to "the upper deck; those that live under hatches are ordained to be drudges and slaves."

As a youth Gilbert studied at Eton and Oxford and then rapidly became a pageboy favorite in the court entourage of Queen Elizabeth. Gloriana was charmed by his "pregnant wit" and his handsome physique. He cut a dashing figure. He had haughty blue eyes and wavy red hair and moustache, an esthetic and aristocratic face set on a soldier's muscular and unusually tall body. We are told that it pleased Her Majesty to engage her court mannikin in intellectual discussions, and the flatterer enjoyed playing Harlequin to her aging Columbine. On his last journey she was to bid Sir Humphrey farewell as "a person whom she tendereth," and he was to boast that her knight had served his beloved Queen manfully through war and peace "from a boy to the age of white hairs."

His war service was violent enough to whiten any man's hair. There was a ruthless streak in him, common to many explorers, and he exhibited it most savagely during the campaigns he led to crush the rebels of Ireland. In the melancholy history of that country there was no oppressor more brutal. The Irish of Munster composed ballads about him and his atrocities. He was the legendary colonel, riding aback a black horse, killing and pillaging the helpless with such cruelty that he was accounted "more like a devil than a man." He was without pity in putting to the sword every peasant, man, woman and child, his band of horsemen encountered. Irish lords, who came to surrender, were forced to walk to his tent between two lines of butchered heads and then had to crawl on their knees to beg for the Queen's mercy.

"Neither did I spare any malefactor unexecuted that came to my hands," Gilbert reported to the Queen of his "pacification" of the wild Irish whom he hoped one day to colonize. "No conquered nation will ever yield willingly their obedience for love but rather for fear."

Between "broils and bloody wars" in France and the Netherlands, Gilbert displayed his literary bent by writing petitions to the Queen for half a dozen projects which he hoped she would sponsor. Some of his schemes were hairbrained; he squandered his wife's fortune in a get-rich-quick alchemist's plan to transmute lead into silver. Other proposals were imaginative in their scope; and they were at least enriched by his fine flair for grandiose rhetoric.

There was wisdom in his treatise which advocated a London Academy to educate the children of the gentry. It would train them in the arts of music, dancing, poetry, navigation and science as well as in the arts of war. As it was, most young gentlemen were ignorant popinjays, who knew only how to follow a hound or lure the hawk. "Better is it to have renown among the good sort," he concluded in his usual lofty style, "than to lord over the whole world."

His *Discourse How Her Majesty May Annoy the King of Spain* was more annoyingly naive than cunning. Under the guise of colonizing Newfoundland, his plan was to seize the Spanish, Portuguese and Catholic French fishing vessels off the Labrador Grand Banks, and with the profits from this codfish piracy, to raid Spanish convoys. The stratagem would "pare their nails to the stumps those that are most ready pressed to pluck the crown from Your Highness's head," he declared. "By which means also Your Majesty shall engraft and glue to your crown, in effect, all the northern and southern voyages of the world, so that none shall then be able to cross the seas, but subject to Your Highness's devotion." He urged her not to delay in thus outwitting the Spanish colossus; "for the wings of man's life are plumed with the feathers of death."

The Queen ignored these proposals, but she did pay attention to his *Discourse of a Discovery for a New Passage to Cathay.* When it was published in 1576, it had a great immediate impact, and the beguilingly ingenuous pamphlet was to mislead other Arctic explorers. A mishmash of wishful - thinking geography, it presented the Northwest Passage as an ice-free, easily navigable sea land between the island of North America and Greenland. Along the alleyway, the Queen's knight was certain he would discover marvelous rich lands abounding in "gold, silver, precious stones, cloth of gold, silks, all manner of spices, grocery wares. ..." The beauty of it all was that ownership of the strait would give the Queen monopoly control of the whole traffic. Thus Spanish traders would be left to "beat the bushes while other men catch the birds."

As if this were not incentive enough, Gilbert proposed to occupy the New World and plant a utopian colony there. Sir Thomas More's *Utopia*—his imaginary Nowhere— would become a Somewhere for deported beggars and thieves. "We might settle there such needy people of our country," suggests Gilbert, "which now trouble the commonwealth, and through want here at home are enforced to commit outrageous offences, whereby they are daily consumed with the gallows." He further envisions a lucrative trade with the Indians in handicrafted trinkets made by poor men's children; and so "there should be none occasion to have our country encumbred with loiterers, vagabonds, and such like idle persons." In short, if Her Majesty listened to her knight, he would make her rich and happy and "spin a thread proper for our English looms."

Elizabeth, whose regal nose was keen to scent profits, could hardly resist such tempting bait. On June 11, 1578, she signed letters patent which amounted to the English charter of colonial America. For the first time two words were clearly spelled out: "to inhabit." Her trusty and well-beloved knight had royal permission to discover, occupy, build on and fortify any heathen lands not already claimed by a Christian prince. She gave her empire-builder sweeping viceregal powers—to govern, punish and pardon both colonists and aborigines. He was granted as well the right to serve as supreme landlord.

Gloriana's generosity, however, did not extend to financing the utopian scheme. She was too prudent for that. On the contrary, she balked at paying the two thousand pounds she had long owed Gilbert for his services in Ireland. "A miserable thing it is that I, poor man," Gilbert wrote in a piteous dunning letter, "should be now subject to daily arrests, executions, and outlawries; yea, and forced to mortgage and sell my wife's clothes from her back, she who brought me so good a living." He had dissipated the fortune of his heiress wife, Dame Anne, his seven children were utterly undone, and "I not able to show my head for debts."

Elizabeth finally paid the money she owed him in 1582. Still strapped for cash, the landlord of North America and Cathay hatched the ingenious scheme of selling land grants in what he now took to calling the "Commonwealth of Sir Humphrey." It was equivalent to a real estate agent selling acreage in Florida, without either the agent or his customers knowing the precise location of the fabled land.

One of Gilbert's principal customers was Sir George Peckham, a Roman Catholic, high in court standing. Peckham wanted a colony for his fellow Catholics who were being persecuted for not adhering to Church of England ritual. Once they got to America, he expected the colonists to do a little persecuting of their own. But he didn't call it that. The Christians would exploit and convert the heathen idolaters for their mutual benefit. One doesn't know whether to laugh or cry over his glib rationalization. In a few sentences, Gilbert's tenant foreshadowed the fate that Eskimos and Indians of the north could expect:

In the name of Christ, said Peckham, "I say to plant, possess, and subdue. ... Christians will always be ready with force of arms to defend savages in their just quarrels from all invasions of their next borderers. ... So we shall not only mightily stir and inflame their rude minds gladly to embrace the loving company of the Christians, but also by their frank consents shall easily enjoy such competent quantity of land as every way shall be correspondent to the Christian expectation."

Peckham's Christian expectation was one and a half million acres of land, which he in turn sold in sublots to other Catholics. His property— covering about one half of modern Connecticut and Rhode Island—was to extend from what we now know as Narragansett Bay, but which was described on Gilbert's deed as Dee River.

The phantom river was named, of course, after Gilbert's geography tutor, Dr. John Dee. It was no more make-believe than the fairy-tale map which Dr. Dee had prepared for the "courageous captain" of the expedition. The spirit world had informed the clairvoyant that a far southerly St. Lawrence River cut right across the New World to the Pacific Ocean. All one had to do was cross over to the speck island of Newfoundland, adjacent to the mouth of the river, and then sail right through to Cathay. In reward for the occult information, Dr. Dee's diary tells us that Gilbert granted him rights to most of present Canada, and they shook hands on the deal over a good Saturday night dinner held at appropriately named Witchcross Street.

More backers were needed and, since apparitions and wraiths were not substantial enough, Dr. Dee summoned to his study a certain David Ingram to furnish living evidence of the treasures that could be harvested overseas. Ingram was a castaway English mariner who claimed he had walked three thousand miles in one year from Mexico up to the cod fisheries near the mouth of the St. Lawrence, where he had been rescued by a French fishing vessel in 1569. The perambulating Sindbad the Sailor was eager to testify before all potential speculators about the riches he had seen on his hike.

THE NATIONAL PORTRAIT GALLERY, LONDON

*William Cecil, Baron Burghley, Lord High Treasurer to the Queen, was not as
canny as he appeared. He invested his own money as well as Elizabeth's royal
funds in two dubious stock companies: Sir Martin Frobisher's Arctic gold rush
and Sir Humphrey Gilbert's Cathay land boom. He also hoped Dr. Dee's sorcery
would combat "my old enemy, the gout."*

THE NATIONAL PORTRAIT GALLERY, LONDON

Secretary of State Sir Francis Walsingham had such faith in Dr. Dee's occult powers that he hired the wizard as a roving spy and also believed that the alchemist could transform Queen Elizabeth's bed warming pan into gold "as fast as a hen will crack nuts." Little wonder that Walsingham was ready to put stock in Dee's clairvoyant maps.

Yes, swore Ingram, utopia was fertile beyond belief. He had seen elephants and silkworms and deer with skins of damask, almond trees and pepper trees and trees that poured forth whey-colored wine, and the earth smelled as sweet as any pomander. Yes, along the riverbank, there were towns with streets broader than any avenue in London, and in massy silver mansions, round like dovehouses; the kings of the savages were decked with four-inch-long rubies and turquoises, and their hundreds of wives, when not naked, were hooped with pearls and armored with solid gold breast plates. He himself had picked up from the streams pecks and pottles of gold nuggets, some as big as his thumb, some as big as his fist, and some as big as an egg. . . .

After listening to this delirium of myths, the Queen's courtiers scrambled to invest in the utopian land boom. Although they had already had their fingers burned in Martin Frobisher's Cathay gold rush, even such dignitaries as Secretary of State Sir Francis Walsingham and Queen's Treasurer Lord Burghley succumbed to the excitement: they, too, subscribed to the joint stock company, the Merchant Adventurers, with Sir Humphrey Gilbert. Dr. Dee was so overcome by his own propaganda that he acquired an extra five thousand acres of land from Sir George Peckham's sublease and bought shares in Gilbert's stock company as well. Sir Walter Raleigh gambled two thousand pounds in his half-brother's venture and threw in his two-hundred-ton bark, the *Raleigh.* It was the biggest ship in the fleet of five that Commander General Gilbert mustered, which included the one-hundred-and-twenty-ton *Delight,* two forty-tonners called the *Golden Hind* and the *Swallow,* and Gilbert's own ten-ton pinnace, the *Squirrel.*

At almost the last minute, the Queen had second thoughts about Gilbert's imperial visions. One doesn't know whether she had intuitive forebodings or was genuinely concerned about the seamanship of her errant knight who, at forty-six, was essentially a land sailor. In any event, she begged him through Sir Walter Raleigh to stay home from the voyage, "as a man noted for no good hap at sea."

Sir Humphrey's vanity was stung. He replied hotly that he had already withstood the "scorn of the world" from cynics who had previously held his utopian venture to be ridiculous. He would not now be denied the glory of northwest discovery.

"If the doubt be my want of skill to execute the same, I will offer myself to be opposed by all the best navigators within this realm. If it be cowardliness, I seek no other purgation thereof than my former service done for Her Majesty. If it be suspicion of daintiness of diet or seasickness, in both those I will yield myself second to no man living."

He shrewdly reminded the Queen that she was to get one-fifth of all the gold, silver and gems he obtained without cost to herself. And he added the touching plea: "I trust Her Majesty, with her favour for my twenty-eight years' service, will allow me to get my living as well as I may honestly (which is every subject's right), and not to constrain me by my idle abode at home to beg my bread with my wife and children."

Elizabeth relented. As a good luck charm she sent her knight a piece of jewelry shaped like an anchor guided by a lady. She asked him to let her have his portrait. And through Sir Walter Raleigh she wished him "as great good hap and safety to your ship as if she herself were there in person, desiring you to have care of yourself as that which she tendereth."

Raleigh appended the postscript, "So I commit you to the will and protection of God who sends us such life or death as He hath appointed," and he signed himself, "Your true Brother."

In a gale of wind the five ships set sail from Cawsand Bay off Plymouth on Tuesday, June 11, in 1583, and that same night a slashing storm of thunder and wind struck. "Our voyage undertaken with Sir Humphrey Gilbert began, continued, and ended adversely." So wrote Master Edward Hayes of Liverpool, captain of the *Golden Hind*, in his deeply moving account of the ill-starred expedition to utopia. Hayes had qualms from the outset. His Admiral, though an idealist, seemed an erratic, thin-skinned exhibitionist, who quarreled with his officers, and in one peevish burst of rage, beat up his cabin boy. Among the two hundred and sixty men recruited, there were carpenters, miners and other settlers, fainthearted and fearfully inexperienced at sea. There were landlubberly musicians, such as oboe and flute players, as well as "Morris dancers, hobby horses, and many like conceits to delight the savage people." Most mischievous were the riffraff sailors: impressed jailbirds and pirates.

Two days after they left Plymouth, pleading "contagious sickness," the *Raleigh* abandoned the fleet and sailed home, where the piratical deserters promptly pounced upon two French barks laden with salt and wine. (Gilbert dispatched an angry letter to Sir Walter praying him to make an example of the knaves.) The crew members of the *Swallow* were not much better. The former convicts slipped away in the mists to plunder an English fishing smack, and they tortured their countrymen for valuables by winding cords around their necks until the blood gushed.

The remaining ships in the fleet separated in the mists, too. After seven weeks of fog and rain and contrary winds, dodging drifting mountains of ice, Master Hayes tells us he reached his farthest north at about 51 degrees latitude. He was evidently in the Strait of Belle Isle. But he quickly steered the *Golden Hind* southward from the scoured crags of Labrador, "nothing appearing unto us but hideous rocks and mountains, bare of trees and void of any green herb."

Several days later, with much flinging up of sailors' caps, the scattered fleet joyfully united in the harbor of St. John's, and here Sir Humphrey Gilbert, the founding father of Newfoundland, finally found his utopia. Awaiting him there was a polyglot community of codfishermen. Thirty-six ships—twenty of them Spanish and Portuguese and sixteen French and English—filled the harbor. Though obviously outnumbered and an intruder in their harmonious maritime colony, Gilbert put up a good bluff. By the sheer showmanship of waving the Queen's instructions under their noses, the Commander General assumed immediate overlordship and had the various nationalities submitting to his "taxation" orders. The Portuguese and Spanish, whom he had originally planned to plunder, couldn't have been more hospitable. They feasted him with the finest wines, marmalade, sweet oils and choice rusks of biscuits. They plied him with lobsters, fresh salmon and trout. "To grow short, in our abundance at home," wrote Master Hayes, "the entertainment has been delightful."

Ashore, where Gilbert had his tent set up, he and his officers were taken for a stroll through the fishermen's garden. Everything he saw refuted notions of the desolate north: red roses as sweet-smelling as any English flowers, wild peas, fat raspberries, lush grass, thick stands of pine, spruce and witch hazel; and of course, the schools of cod, herring and whales were astounding. And far from being intolerably cold, the summer climate was hotter than any August in England.

On August 5, 1583—a day which Newfoundlanders regard as the founding of the British Commonwealth—an elated Gilbert summoned foreigners and Englishmen alike to a ceremony in front of his tent. He planted a wooden pillar bearing a lead engraving of Her Majesty's coat of arms; and then, in the name of the Queen, took formal possession of the land. The ritual was further solemnized when Sir Humphrey, as new Governor, was presented with a sod of turf and a hazel twig dug up from the soil.

Governor Gilbert then laid down a code of laws for the colony that seemed harshly un-utopian. English Catholic settlers seeking religious freedom were undoubtedly dismayed by the decree that all public worship must be according to the Church of England. Foreign cod-

"We are as near to heaven by sea as by land!" cried out Sir Humphrey Gilbert. That was the lofty death speech declaimed by the headstrong knight after he rashly took over command of the little frigate, Squirrel, to prove his seamanship. He foundered off shoal-girt Sable Island east of Nova Scotia on September 9, 1583.

fishermen were told in no uncertain terms that, if they uttered words dishonoring Her Majesty, their ships and goods would be confiscated, and they would have their ears chopped off.

Nobody complained, for we are told that the crowd voiced unanimous assent to the high-handed orders. Yet discord was stirring in utopia. Some of the convict sailors stole into the woods and plotted a mutiny against Gilbert. Some of the pirates deserted to seize a French fishing vessel, and sailed off. "Some were sick of fluxes, and many dead," reported Master Hayes. "And, in brief, by one means or another, our company was diminished."

After seventeen days in St. John's, Gilbert packed the malcontents and the invalids into the *Swallow* and sent them home. As for himself, rapturous over his rich cargoes of codfish, and with specimens of supposed silver in his hold, the enthusiast headed his three remaining ships southwestward in high hope of reaching Cathay along the St. Lawrence.

His chivalric pride and his headstrong obstinacy shattered those hopes most cruelly. The first of two tragedies struck because the knight tried to play admiral. It happened off Sable Island, that shoal-girt graveyard of more than two hundred shipwrecked vessels, just east of Nova Scotia. In arrogant dispute there, Gilbert insisted on giving steering orders to the veteran skipper of the *Delight*.

Master Hayes set the scene in Shakespearean fashion. Aboard the *Golden Hind* and the *Squirrel* that Wednesday, he quieted the fears of the helmsmen who thought they heard strange sounds in the night. Aboard the *Delight,* "like the swan that singeth before her death, they continued in sounding of trumpets with drums and fifes; also winding the cornets and hautboys; and in the end of their jollity, left with the ringing of doleful knells."

A violent storm blew up, bringing with it rain and a curtain of mist, and the *Delight* belied her name by ramming into the rocks. Almost one hundred colonists were sucked down to their doom, and the fleet's precious provisions and supposed silver ore went down with her. All that was left was her lifeboat, the size of a River Thames barge, and sixteen overcrowded mariners equipped with a single oar and not a drop of water.

One of the survivors suggested they lighten the boat by drawing lots and throwing four losers overboard. But the skipper, Master Richard Clarke, said, "No. We will live and die together." And if they did not reach land by the seventh day, he would volunteer to cast himself overboard.

Two of the poor wretches died, but the rest, by eating seaweed and drinking their own urine, did indeed survive for seven days. And when they crawled ashore in Newfoundland, Master Clarke later testified, "We kneeled down upon our knees and gave God praise that He had dealt so mercifully with us."

Master Hayes, aboard the *Golden Hind*, was meanwhile praying to God to avert a second tragedy. Sir Humphrey Gilbert, having compassion on his dispirited and decimated crew, decided to return to England. But despite the entreaties of Master Hayes, the Admiral General was stubbornly determined to take command of the overburdened little frigate, the *Squirrel*. Gilbert declaimed: "I will not forsake my little company going homeward, with whom I have passed so many storms and perils."

Master Hayes understood why his Admiral would not bend to reason, but privately considered it vainglorious posturing. This gallant man *had* to make the heroic gesture to disprove the reports that he was afraid of the sea. "Albeit this was rashness rather than advised resolution," Master Hayes thought, "to prefer the wind of a vain report to the weight of his own life."

His misgivings were borne out on September 9, 1583. A raging storm boiled up, with turbulent waves tossing high like foaming pyramids, yet Gilbert seemed strangely exhilarated by the danger. Master Hayes last caught sight of him seated in the tempest-tossed *Squirrel* reading a book, which may well have been Sir Thomas More's *Utopia*. Gilbert waved to him and joyfully cried out, with sublime nonchalance, "We are as near to heaven by sea as by land!"

His General repeated the lofty speech, wrote Master Hayes, "well beseeming a soldier, resolute in Jesus Christ, as I can testify he was."

At midnight the lights suddenly winked out on the *Squirrel* and Master Hayes lost sight of her. "And withall our watch cried, 'The General is cast away!' Which was too true. For in that moment the frigate was devoured and swallowed up by the sea."

And so Master Hayes sorrowfully steered homeward the solitary craft left from the utopian expedition, mourning the loss of the intemperate, impetuous knight who was "too prodigal of his own patrimony and too careless of other men's expenses on a ground *imagined* good."

Back in England, despite the failure of the mission, Gilbert was hailed as a hero. Though Newfoundland was not to be colonized for nearly a generation, he had delineated more clearly the nature of the subarctic region of the Canadian coastline.

Pilot John Davis is shown standing on the right, pointing out his proposed Northwest Passage route on a map to Secretary of State Walsingham, seated centre, as Gilbert and Dr. Dee look on, in this imagined 19th-century etching.

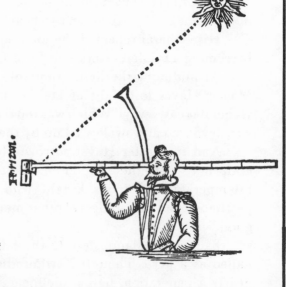

Pilot John Davis, who pushed back the geographical mists shrouding Davis Strait, was the consummate scientific navigator of his day. This illustration of the Davis backstaff quadrant he invented is contained in his book The Seaman's Secrets, *in which he expressed lyrically a love for "that sweet skill of sailing."*

Far from being deterred, advocates of further northern exploration merely regretted that "So forward a mind should have so backward a success." And Elizabethan rhymesters encouraged other voyagers with the rousing ballad:

> *You gallants all o' the British blood,*
> *Why don't you sail o' the Ocean's flood,*
> *I protest you're not all worth a filbert*
> *If once compared to Sir Humphrey Gilbert.*

Pilot John Davis, who took up the challenge, might well be compared with Gilbert. Though they were boyhood friends in the West Country Valley of the Dart River, the two north voyagers had few things in common except their consuming desire to discover the Northwest Passage. Unlike Gilbert, Davis was no court peacock, no bombastic braggart, no bullying colonizer. Above all, he was no dilettante sailor "ill hap" at sea.

Davis was the consummate scientific navigator of his time, the inventor of such nautical instruments as the Davis backstaff quadrant. In the knowledgeable book he wrote, *The Seaman's Secrets*, he expressed an almost lyrical feeling for his calling. To him it was "that sweet skill of sailing." He had little use for the stay-at-home cartographers, "epicures who sit and carp at other men's hazards, not daring to give any attempt." Rather, the true geographer should be an active pilot, able to plot his course through every creek "in the hell-dark nights"; and it was "in those Northwest voyages where navigation must be executed in most exquisite sort."

One regrets that no contemporary painting exists of Davis, for he seems to have had an attractive, sunny personality. Unlike the swaggerers of his era, he was modest and humane, a commander who inspired love and loyalty. True, he regarded himself as a "shining messenger of the Lord," bringing God's light to pagans who sit in darkness. But he believed in treating the Eskimos with kindness, and he had a whimsical humor and the tolerance of a humanitarian, which prevented him from becoming a holier-than-thou Christian.

Indeed what distinguished him most from Gilbert, the posturing soldier of Christ, was his gentle, turn-the-other-cheek Christianity. Not that Davis lacked bravery. On one of his later voyages to the Far East, he had no compunctions about stabbing a piratical Turk with his rapier; and when his mariners fled like cowards from a rabble of cannibals, he joked ruefully, "We were in muster giants with great armed bodies, but in action babes with wrens' hearts."

He had his frailties, of course. The Christian was too trusting. Typically, his trusted wife, Faith, who bore him five children, proved to be faithless. While Davis was away on a voyage, she took a lover, a scoundrelly forger named Milburne. When Davis returned from his expedition, Faith allowed her paramour to have her husband jailed on a trumped-up charge. It was only thanks to the court influence of his friends, Sir Walter Raleigh and Adrian Gilbert, that Davis managed to get released. Another weakness was his gullibility, which induced him to fall under the spell of the legerdemain and pseudo-science of his Arctic advisor, Dr. John Dee.

Davis met the Welsh wizard through the Gilberts and the Raleighs, who were the pilot's Devonshire neighbors on the banks of the Dart River. Young John Davis lacked their social status, for he was the son of a yeoman farmer; but he did share their love for voyaging into the unknown by sea and by mind. John's closest friend was Adrian Gilbert, Sir Humphrey's younger brother. They had an intimacy of shared interests. John's wife, the faithless Faith, was related to Adrian Gilbert's wife. Furthermore, John was intrigued by Adrian's interest in alchemy, geography, and astrology.

We first hear of the pair visiting Dr. Dee's house of spiritualism at Mortlake in 1579, by which time Davis was a seasoned thirty-six-year-old navigator bent on exploration. Dr. Dee's diary speaks of Davis and Adrian being reconciled to his occult wisdom after they had spurned a rival astronomer and cartographer named Emery Molyneux. Dee, a jealous visionary, claims they revealed his rival's "most unhonest, hypocritical, and devilish dealings and devices against me ... and likewise of that errant strumpet, her abominable words and deeds; and John Davis said that he might curse the time that ever he knew Emery, and so much followed his wicked counsel and advice."

Whether the mysterious strumpet was also a rival of Dee's supernatural spirit, Madimi, we do not know. But in any event, Davis and Adrian returned for several additional consultations with the seer of Mortlake. Davis seems to have been drawn by Dr. Dee's mathematical erudition, for the pilot praised highly his matchless "theoretical speculations and most cunning calculations." On his part, Dee saw in Davis a matchless navigator who could exploit the rights of discovery for all lands north of the fiftieth parallel, which he had acquired from Sir Humphrey Gilbert.

Dr. Dee didn't do much with his land deed for half a continent until January 23, 1583. Secretary of State Sir Francis Walsingham chanced to drop in at Mortlake that evening while Dr. Dee was conducting a seance with Adrian Gilbert and John Davis. "And so," reads his diary, "talk was begun of Northwest strait's discovery." The next night all three held a secret session at the home of the Queen's Privy Council clerk, and with the charts spread out on the table, they agreed upon a fresh assault on the Northwest Passage.

Dr. Dee proceeded to draft an application for rights patent for his company, which bore the odd title of the "Colleagues or Fellowship of New Navigations Atlantical and Septentrional." He and his colleagues, Davis and Adrian Gilbert, were prepared to open a "profitable traffic" in the northerly regions extending as far as the North Pole. How pilot John Davis was to pursue this course seems baffling, for according to Dee's spiritualistic map, the explorer would have to surmount an Arctic blocked by "infinite ice."

But then, of course, Madimi as a geographer seemed as absurd as Dr. Dee's compass. In his communications with her during the spring and summer of 1583, the angel spirit's bulletins from the other world were more mystifying than edifying: "What do ye seek after? Do ye hunt after the swiftness of the winds? Or go ye forth to hear the braying of an ass, which passeth away with the swiftness of the air?"

By the end of September, Dee gave up seeking arctic guidance from her. He was discouraged by news of Sir Humphrey Gilbert's calamitous utopian venture. And raising spirits seemed more profitable than raising money for another futile expedition to Cathay. So Dee and his medium, Edward Kelly, accepted an invitation from Albertus Laski, a Polish nobleman, to go on a tour staging their crystal-gazing and table-rapping seances before the crowned heads of Europe.

The fate of the two wandering clairvoyants presents a serio-comic sidelight to the history of exploration. Their partnership ultimately dissolved in shocking circumstances. Madimi appeared in a vision, not as an angelic spirit in white, but as a naked temptress, and the brazen hussy commanded Dee and Kelly to begin "cross matching"—meaning to sleep with each other's wives. Dee returned to England, further disillusioned to find that a superstitious mob had broken into his library at Mortlake and ruined his navigational instruments and his alchemy retorts. Dee died at eighty-one, an impoverished warden of Christ's College, Manchester, his name commemorated—though not permanently—in a few crags in Greenland called Dee's Pinnacles. He eked out a threadbare living in his old age serving as an expert witness in witchcraft cases and doing a little horoscope-casting on the side to maintain his brood of eight children.

The rascal, Kelly, made the necromantic arts pay off more lucratively. King Rudolph II, Emperor of Bohemia, knighted him in Prague because the forger claimed to have found through black magic the means to "maketh gold as fast as a hen will crack nuts." He apparently dispatched to Queen Elizabeth, via Secretary of State Sir Francis Walsingham, a bed-warming pan whose lid had been transformed into precious metal. We last hear of him being beseeched by Queen's Treasurer Lord Burghley to please forward quickly the secret elixir. For the sake of British patriotism, the least that Sir Edward Kelly could do was to "send Her Majesty, as a token, a good round sum of money, say enough to defray the charges of the navy for this summer," and failing that, "something of your operation to strengthen me afore next winter against my old enemy, the gout."

Gout and bogus gold bedpans notwithstanding, Treasurer Burghley and Secretary Walsingham exerted their considerable influence on the Queen in 1585 to grant a charter to Adrian Gilbert's renamed "Colleagues of the Discovery of the Northwest Passage." Fortunately his colleagues (meaning John Davis and Adrian's half-brother, Sir Walter Raleigh, whose name replaced Dr. Dee's) did not have to rely on the spirit world for fund-raising. Most of the financing for Davis's three arctic voyages came from a wealthy merchant fishmonger named William Sanderson; he had married a niece of the Raleigh and Gilbert brothers, and, more important, had a sound business interest in finding a fresh supply of fish.

On June 7, 1585, two brightly named barks, the fifty-ton *Sunshine* and the thirty-five-ton *Moonshine*, sailed from Dartmouth on a fishing-cum-Cathay-discovery expedition headed in the general direction of the North Pole. Sanderson had outfitted the vessels with a handpicked crew of forty-two men. The personnel included a by now obligatory four-piece orchestra of oboe and flute players, who were to share a fortifying breakfast in the cold climate of a pint-sized can of beer, almost half a pound of hardtack, and at least one codfish each.

Sanderson's nephew, John Janes, came along as Captain Davis's admiring recording clerk ("I conclude the world hath not any so skilfull pilots"), and they both had much to record six weeks later when they first viewed the sentinel crags guarding the east coast of Greenland. "It was the most deformed, rocky and mountainous land that ever we saw. The first sight whereof did show us as if it had been in the form of a sugar loaf, standing to our sight above the clouds, for that it did show over the fog like a white liste in the sky, the tops altogether covered with snow."

Davis tried to row ashore, but he was pestered by three miles of grinding ice floes. It was as if a chef had flipped thousands of bluish white pancakes into the sea, and they were constantly colliding with a great "whirling and brustling and rolling" racket. Icebergs being calved from the glaciers contributed to the tumult. "Incredible to report," Davis reported, "I have seen ice and snow of one hundred tons' weight, which when torn from the cliffs and falling, maketh such an horrible noise as if there were one hundred cannons shot off."

The place gave him the shudders. "The loathesome view of the shore, and the irksome noise of the ice, was such that it bred strange conceits among us," Davis added. "So we supposed the place to be waste and void of any sensible or vegetable creatures. Whereupon I called the same 'Land of Desolation'."

Davis hastily departed from these weird and desolate shores. He rounded Cape Farewell on the southern tip of Greenland and sailed up its west coast until he spotted "many green and pleasant isles." He had reached Greenland's most hospitable region where the Vikings had once settled. The inlet which he named Gilbert Sound (actually the site of the modern Danish capital of Godthaab, where more than eight thousand Greenlanders now live) turned out to be green and pleasant indeed. Though the mountains along the fjord were capped with ice, the July weather was as warm as April in England. The heather was in bloom, dwarf willows were showing off their yellow catkins, and the bog whortleberries were as sweet and full of red juice as any currants they had tasted back home.

Davis's first meeting with the Greenland Eskimos proved to be equally delightful. He stood on top of a high hill and heard them screeching and howling a welcome across the fjord. "Using the people with kindness" was Davis's custom, so he screeched a friendly halloo of what sounded like *Yliaoute* back at them. They re-echoed the greeting, and soon ten kayakers timorously paddled close to the shore.

"With courtesy to allure the people," the four-piece orchestra was immediately summoned from the *Moonshine* and ordered to strike up a gay tune. Then while the band played on their oboes and flutes, the sailors contributed to the musical allurement by dancing the hornpipe. The performance was immensely successful. At length thirty-seven kayakers arrived. Then the Eskimos entertained their English guests by staging a drumming and dancing show of their own.

"By friendly embracings and signs of courtesy," wrote John Janes, "they did trust us. So I shook hands with one of them, and he kissed my hand, and we were very familiar with them."

Trade between the two parties was brisk. In barter for English nails and knives, the Eskimos stripped the seal and birdskin clothes off their backs, and handed over five of their kayaks.

"They would by no means displease us, but would give us whatsoever we asked of them, and would be satisfied with whatsoever we gave them," Janes observed. "They are a very tractable people, void of craft or double-dealing, and easy to be brought to any civility or good order."

Davis agreed they were "a people of tractable conversation," and their conversation by sign language indicated there was a great sea towards the northwest. So on August 1, his two barks hoisted anchor and in six days crossed the two hundred and ten miles of channel that now bears the name of Davis Strait. Close to the Arctic Circle, Davis was happy to find the east coast of Baffin Island altogether void of "ye pester of ice." The air was very moderate, yellow flowers with the fragrance of primroses were blooming, and though the Iron Mountain Range seemed to offer nothing but one huge bastion of stone, it was "the bravest stone that ever we saw." They anchored under a cliff, "as orient as gold," whose glitter was not unlike the ore Martin Frobisher had brought from Meta Incognita, and while a black raven hovered proudly over its peak, they named it "Mount Raleigh."

Davis probed down the Baffin coastline, naming capes and bays as he went, not the first explorer to thus repay with immortality, if not cash, his court and merchant patrons back home. His most momentous find was Cumberland Sound, a big bay northward of and parallel to Frobisher Bay. Davis sailed some one hundred and eighty miles into the blue, oceanlike waterway and was so assured that he had discovered the passage to Cathay that he gratefully named the cape at its entrance "Cape of God's Mercy."

Davis hurried the *Sunshine* and *Moonshine* back to England with reports as glowing as the lovely names of his two barks. Secretary of State Walsingham, pleased to have a cape named after him on Baffin Island, was further informed jubilantly: "The Northwest Passage is a matter nothing doubtful, but at any time almost to be passed." The merchant prince, William Sanderson, rejoiced in the news that Davis had found porpoises that "did eat as sweet as any mutton" and "white bears of a monstrous bigness," and that the seals and whales were marvelously abundant.

His sponsors supplied Davis with two extra ships, a pinnace of ten tons named *North Star* and the one-hundred-and-twenty-ton *Mermaid*. The fleet left Dartmouth on May 7, 1586, and a month later near the outflung ice pack off Cape Farewell their paths separated. Davis dispatched the *Sunshine* and *North Star* to explore the east coast of Greenland while he tried his luck with the *Moonshine* and *Mermaid* on the west coast.

Davis didn't get much farther north than his old stamping grounds at Godthaab. He was overwhelmed by the hospitality of his Eskimo friends. It began with eighteen kayakers darting up the fjord to greet their musical entertainers of the previous year with joyful cries of recognition.

"I had no sooner landed, but they leaped out of their canoes, and came running to me and the rest, and embraced us with many signs of hearty welcome," Davis was glad to observe. "To each of them I gave a knife. They offered skins to me for reward. But I made signs that it was not sold, but given them of courtesy."

The next day as many as one hundred kayakers arrived, bearing gifts of white arctic hare, salmon, sealskins and caribou pelts. "I used them with much courtesy," became Davis's byword, but he couldn't possibly equal their grinning cordiality. When he made an exploratory boat trip up the fjord, fifty kayakers followed him, pointing out the camping spot where his party would find the warmest place to sleep. When he investigated a high hill, the Eskimos, with gentlemanly politeness, were "very diligent to attend us, and to help us up the rocks, and likewise down."

They proved to be good sportsmen, too: for Davis thought it might be amusing to stage an interracial athletic competition. In long jumping the English beat the Eskimos, but in wrestling the aborigines were stronger and nimbler. We can't tell which team won the soccer match, because the mariner who refereed admitted English foul play in the regulations of the game: "Our men did cast them down as soon as they did come to strike the ball."

Davis was fascinated by the Eskimo culture and compiled the first anthropological notes of any value about their customs. They taught him a vocabulary of forty Eskimo words (including such terms as *kuninga* for "kiss me") and he observed acutely that their pronunciation was "very hollow and deep in the throat." Some of his ethnological notes reflected his own superstition. Because they carved bone figurines as toys for their children, he supposed they were idolaters; and, amusingly for a devotee of Dr. Dee's black magic, he condemned their sorcery. "They are witches," he remarked disapprovingly, "and have many kinds of enchantments, which they often used, but to small purpose, thanks be to God."

On the whole, though, he was captivated by "these simple people" and was amused by their magpie propensity for pilfering any brightly shining metal. When they stole a sword and knife from the deck, the shipmaster pleaded with Davis, "Dissolve this new friendship and leave the company of these thievish miscreants." And the shipmaster had the sailors fire a cannon over their heads, which sent the startled natives scurrying. Ten hours later, the miscreants were back grinning and bearing propitiary presents of salmon and sealskins. But as soon as they saw iron nails lying about they were tempted to be as light-fingered as ever.

"Which when I perceived it did but minister unto me an occasion of laughter to see their simplicity," said the good-natured Davis. "And I willed that in no case they should be any more hardly used."

His tolerance was sorely tested. The mariners complained that the Eskimos had stolen their anchor, and it was the captain's "lenity and friendly using of them gave them stomach to mischief."

Davis pacified his crew. "I desired them to be content, and said I doubted not but all should be well." Determined to dispense Christian charity to the natives, Davis handed out bracelets to them. He invited a group to come aboard and try acrobatics at the top of the *Moonshine*. "Which they did willingly," he noted, "and thus courteously using them, I let them depart."

But no sooner had the sun gone down than the pranksters used their slingshots to pelt stones at the *Moonshine*, one of which struck down the boatswain.

"Whereat being moved," wrote Davis with an understandable loss of patience, "I changed my courtesy, and grew to hatred."

He pursued the culprits in an armed rowboat, but the swift kayakers easily eluded him. The next day a party of five peacemakers came aboard to make a new truce. In a vengeful pique the shipmaster seized the ringleader as hostage for the return of the stolen anchor. But a fair wind came up, and the *Moonshine* sailed off with the poor fellow aboard.

Davis, not one to lose his temper for long, took a benevolent interest in the captive. "At length he became a pleasant companion among us. I gave him a new suit of frieze after the English fashion, because I saw he could not endure the cold, of which he was very joyful. He trimmed up his darts, and all his fishing tools, and set his hand to a rope's end upon occasion."

Regrettably, the Eskimo later died on the voyage, though certainly not of the cold. It was Davis's own men who soon grew sick and feeble in freezing blasts near the Arctic Circle. They were pestered mightily with massive bergs, and the *Mermaid's* sails were shrouded with ice, and his trembling mariners begged their Captain to sail home rather than "leave their widows and fatherless children to give me bitter curses."

"This matter, in conscience, did greatly move me to regard their estates," Davis felt. And exhibiting the compassion and courage so characteristic of him, he sent the ailing crew back to England in the big *Mermaid*, while he pursued his explorations unescorted across Davis Strait and down the Baffin coastline in the little *Moonshine*. Off the coast of Labrador, using nothing but spikes as hooks, he hauled up forty fat cod in a matter of minutes. Tragically, when five of his youngest sailors rowed ashore to dry the fish near Cut Throat Tickle, a band of warlike Indians "executed their cursed fury" in a surprise attack, and with bows and arrows slew two of the crew and severely wounded the three others.

"It pleased God further to increase our sorrows," for after weathering a sharp fret of keening winds, Davis returned to England to learn that the pinnace *North Star* had been swamped in gales with all hands lost on her polar cruise to east Greenland. However, the irrepressible optimist was able to offer his mercantile sponsor, Sanderson, more than five hundred sealskins brought back by the *Sunshine*. To Queen's Treasurer Burghley, he presented the most succulent codfish caught by the *Moonshine*, which no doubt soothed that worthy's gout. And he wagered them all, "upon the peril of my life," that the Northwest Passage could be performed with assured profit for the investors; even if it cost him his home at Sandridge, "I will, by God's mercy, see an end of these businesses."

The end of the business was that on his third expedition of 1587 he sailed closer to the Pole than any European explorer of record had ever ventured. He accomplished the feat in a lone, leaky pinnace, the *Ellen*, a twenty-tonner as unwieldy as an oxcart. To hedge their bets, his backers had also ill-provided him with two other barks, the worn-out *Sunshine* and the *Elizabeth*; those two excess baggages were to restrict themselves to commercial codfishing off the Labrador Banks, and they were manned by a frightened, near-mutinous crew who would accompany the *Ellen* as far as Godthaab only "after much talk and many threatenings."

Happily, his mariners aboard the *Ellen*, including faithful recorder John Janes, were more stout-hearted men. When the tiny pinnace began leaking at the rate of three hundred pump strokes per hour, the shipmaster feared they would be hazarding their lives by continuing farther north. But John Janes tells us that Davis was "determined to end his life with credit rather than return with infamy and disgrace"; and the Captain so inspired his shipmates that they loyally dared "to live and die together, and committed ourselves to the ship."

Davis reached his farthest north at close to 73 degrees latitude. It was the site of modern Upernavik on the upper west coast of Greenland. There a gleaming granite cliff stabs up into the sky like a dagger eight hundred and fifty feet high plunging at snowy white kittiwakes fluttering in the milky arctic light. On June 30 Davis named the famous beacon "Sanderson's Hope," and a shining hope it proved to be. For it marks the point where Davis Strait broadens out into Baffin Bay; and, gazing northward, Davis marveled at the sight of "a great sea, free, large, very salt and blue, and of an unsearchable depth."

He couldn't search the seeming passage further because of frisking head winds. So he zigzagged the cranky little *Ellen* westward until he was forced south by the awesome middle ice pack of Baffin Bay. This glacial jumble was "a mighty bank of ice," eight feet thick and almost two hundred miles long, whose translucent diamond greens and blues were dazzling and shimmering in a "sun which beat with extreme force of heat."

When he finally reached Baffin Island, he was welcomed by Eskimo kayakers, who bartered a pile of sealskins for a few beads and nails; and after giving them "the gentle farewell" for their courtesy, he tried once again to poke his way down Cumberland Sound. He cruised at least as far as the present village of Pangnirtung. Here, amid blowing whales, the July air was so "marvellous extreme hot" that Davis's officers took their panting hounds ashore for a little exercise and a fox hunt. And the outlandish spectacle must have caused many a grin from any Eskimos lucky enough to have gaped at it. One imagines musicians in red coats sounding their horns, sailors sweating as they dutifully yelled "Tally-ho!", and the arctic foxes easily scampering away from the pursuers, because we are told of the "dogs being so fat that they were scant able to run."

Davis's run farther south down the coast was more perilous. His *Ellen* got caught in a "whirling and roaring" riptide at the entrance to a vast gulf. To Davis the whirlpools seemed to be "loathesomely crying like the rage of the waters under London Bridge," and the titanic, berg-bearing currents were surging out of the gateway like "forcible streams that pass through the arches of the bridge." With full sails spread, the *Ellen* endured the extraordinary experience of racing an iceberg trapped in the same current, and the pilot won by the skin of his teeth. Davis named it the Furious Overfall, like Frobisher before him making the mistake of not penetrating sufficiently into the inland waterway that we know today as Hudson Strait.

The master pilot returned to England, and on September 16, 1587, wrote exuberantly to good Master Sanderson: "I have been in 73 degrees, finding the Sea all open . . . . The passage is most probable, the execution easy . . . ."

Davis never came back to explore that open polar sea. A fervent nationalist, he instantly enlisted with his fellow captains of discovery to fight off the invading Spanish Armada. But for the rest of his life the Northwest Passage became his curse and his passion. He piloted three expeditions to the East Indies, intrepidly negotiating through the Magellan Strait at the bottom of South America, and forever obsessed with the idea of locating the other end of the Northwest Passage "upon the back parts of America."

His fixation led him through trials that tested his perseverance to the uttermost. On his first Far East voyage, he and his cabin boy were the only two of the sixteen surviving crew members able to stand on their feet. His other sixty mariners died amidst harrowing agonies: blinding hailstorms, a rotting ship, slaughter by cannibals, famine that left them eating seaweed, and scurvy-ridden flesh gnawed by lice as large as lima beans. To add to the miseries, two mutineers tried to murder Davis. Yet recorder John Janes wrote of Davis—"with whom, and for whose sake, I went on this voyage"—that his beloved Captain offered them nothing but "kind conversation" in the very pinch of death:

"I do in Christian charity entreat you all, first, to forgive me in whatsoever I have been grievous unto you. Secondly, that you will rather pray for our General than use hard speeches of him. Lastly, let us forgive one another and be reconciled as children in love and charity, and not think upon the vanities of this life."

And so, "as lost wanderers upon the sea," he pacified the mutineers and persuaded the dying men "to give God thanks, and, like dutiful children, to accept of His chastisement."

On his next voyage, suffering the attacks of Turkish pirates, poisoning at the hands of a sultan of Sumatra, and raids by dart-throwing Mozambique cannibals, Davis lost seventy men and his cargoes of black pepper. Yet he was able to view his misfortunes with self-deprecating humor. "I do most grieve over the losses of poor John Davis," he joked, "for I may conclude that, although India did not receive me very rich, yet she hath sent me away reasonable poor."

On his last voyage, his Christian forbearance proved fatal. While he was piloting the spice-laden *Tiger* and *Tiger's Whelp* past an island east of the Strait of Malacca, he took pity on ninety Japanese pirates stranded in a leaky junk which they had seized on the coast of China. He invited the desperadoes aboard for food, and deceived by their pretended humility, he paid no attention to the pleadings of his own officers to disarm his guests. In gratitude the treacherous pirates drew their swords, stabbed Davis seven times, and cast their mortally wounded benefactor into the sea. And so on December 27, 1605, at the age of fifty-five, the master pilot found his watery grave, murdered by the people of Cipango off the Cathay spice islands which he had vainly tried to reach through the Northwest Passage.

He died secure in the knowledge that his Arctic thrust had at least pushed back the geographical mists shrouding the coastlines of Greenland and Baffin Island. "He lighted Hudson into his strait," wrote Sir Clements Markham, his British Admiralty biographer. "He lighted Baffin into his bay." Davis achieved more than that. In the books he wrote before his death, *The Seaman's Secrets* and *The World's Hydrographical Description*, the pilot refuted some of the dread legends which the superstitious had spun around the polar regions. His experience had taught him that it was not all a Land of Desolation, malignant with unbearable cold.

"I found the air very temperate, yea, and many times in calm weather marvellous hot," declared Davis. "In summer, by my own experience, I know that upon the shore it is as hot there as it is at the Isles of Cape Verde. There is such abundance of mosquitoes that we were stung like lepers .... And therefore it is an idle dream that the air should there be insufferable."

To disprove the fiction of dreamers like Dr. Dee that it was a place of infinite ice, Davis helped Emery Molyneux—the rival cartographer whom Dee had once denounced—to produce the celebrated Molyneux *Mappemonde*, which traced fresh landmarks in the hitherto blank spaces on the face of the globe. Shakespeare, who kept a keen eye on contemporary discoveries, charmingly commemorated the wrinkles in that map. "He does smile his face into more lines," Maria jested in

Twelfth Night, "than are in the new map with the augmentation of the Indies."

The other myth that Davis dispelled was the notion that the high Arctic was not fit for civilized man or beast, except wretched, pigmylike, man-eating savages. On the contrary, Davis asserted, the so-called frozen zones are "inhabited with people of good stature, shape, and tractable conditions. I have conversed with them and not found them rudely barbarous, as I have found the cannibals which are in the Straits of Magellan and the Southern parts of America."

Indeed, because of the summer's midnight sun, "under the Pole is the place of greatest dignity" and "those people have a wonderful excellency and exceeding prerogative above all nations of the earth ... How blessed then may we think this nation to be; for they are in perpetual light. Which people," concluded the evangelist, "if they had the notice of their eternity by the comfortable light of the Gospel, then are they blessed and of all nations most blessed."

Shakespeare, the most inspired of Elizabethan explorers of the mind, comprehended intuitively what would happen once the explorers of the seas brought those blessings of civilization to the New World. In *The Tempest*, the dramatist foretells with the insight of a genius the tragic fate awaiting Caliban, his poetic symbol of the dispossessed and displaced Cannibal.

At first the primitive welcomes the white invader with courtesy:

I'll show thee the best springs; I'll pluck thee berries;
I'll fish for thee, and get thee wood enough.

But in the end remorse sets in, and there is a pathos in Caliban's plight that the wizard, the knight, and the pilot never did foresee in the angel spirit's crystal ball:

This island's mine, by Sycorax my mother,
Which thou takest from me. When thou camest first,
Thou strokedst me, and madest much of me; wouldst give me
Water with berries in't; and teach me how
To name the bigger light, and how the less,
That burn by day and night: and then I loved thee,
And show'd thee all the qualities o' th' isle,
The fresh springs, brine-pits, barren place and fertile:
Cursed be I that did so!

Chapter 6

Icicles on Dutch Beards

In Shakespeare's comedy, *Twelfth Night*, Sir Toby Belch is told by a servant of Olivia: "You are now sailed into the north of my lady's opinion; where you will hang like an icicle on a Dutchman's beard."

Shakespeare, who cracked many a quip at the expense of Elizabethan-era explorers, was here making a topical allusion to the icicled whiskers of an extraordinary Dutchman named Willem Barents. Though he was blessed with the kind of Dutch good humor portrayed in the Frans Hals painting "Laughing Cavalier," Barents warrants more from English history than a passing jest in a comedy.

The Dutchman was the first European to winter in the far north— his exploits, equally funny and harrowing, perpetuated in one of the most engaging of polar diaries. He ventured farther north than any of his predecessors—close to 80 degrees latitude, which is six hundred miles from the Pole. He was the first to delineate those two unknown clusters of islands—Russia's Novaya Zemlya (meaning new land) and Norway's Spitsbergen (pointed mountains). Both are located north of Russia and the Scandinavian countries in the arm of the Arctic Ocean which is today known on our maps as the Barents Sea. As if all this were not enough, he outmatched John Davis's football players in the introduction of polar sports—for Barents brought the game of golf to the Arctic.

His monument was the posthumously published book, bearing a three-paragraph title that sounds as lurid as a Phineas T. Barnum circus poster. It reads, in part: *The True and Perfect Description of Three Voyages,*

so Strange and Wonderful, that the like hath never been heard of before. . . .
Performed three years, one after the other, by the Ships of Holland and Zeeland,
on the North of Norway, Muscovia and Tartaria, towards the Kingdoms of
Cathay and China. . . . Where never any man had been before: with the Cruel
Bears and other Monsters of the Sea. . . . And how, in the last Voyage, the Ship
was so enclosed by the Ice that it was left there. . . . Whereby the men were forced
to build a house in the cold and desert Country of Novaya Zemlaya. Wherein
they continued 10 months together, and never saw nor heard of any man, in most
great cold and extreme misery. . . .

Little wonder that the thriller was the best-selling book of its time.
It had all the ingredients of Daniel Defoe's *Robinson Crusoe*, except that
the castaways were stranded on an island in the icy void of the Tartary
Sea. There were quaintly drawn illustrations of the marooned
Dutchmen, soaping themselves in their homemade steam bath or
washing their clothes around the hearth-side of their arctic hut. They
appear as snug as any Netherlands housewife tidying up her scrubbed
clean Vermeer kitchen. And the narrative was chronicled with droll
humor and immense gusto by Willem Barents's first mate, Gerrit De
Veer. He never fails to make an encounter with a polar bear or an
iceberg literally a hair-raising experience. Invariably the adventure
"made all the hairs of our heads to rise upright with fear."

Despite his purple passages, De Veer gives us a clear picture of why
the Dutch pilot was regarded as a national hero. Barents was Dutch
stubbornness personified. He was like the rebellious Netherlanders
themselves, who had recently, in 1581, declared their little republic's
independence from the tyranny of mighty Spain; he stood fast with
sublime obstinacy once he had made up his mind to go it alone. He had
an overmastering passion to find the Northeast Passage to Cathay; and
he would let nobody — neither queasy superior officers nor hesitant
merchant backers—deter him from the course of his *idée fixe*. A
sometimes prickly fanatic he may have been, but he was a likeable one.
His crew members, though cooped up with him for months in an icebox
of a shack, never questioned the authority of their "notable skilfull and
wise" leader; and De Veer obviously loved and admired him for his
camaraderie.

We get a hint of his character from a portrait of him affixed to a
chart. It was sketched when he was, roughly, in his forties. He was the
former cabin boy from Dutch Terschelling Island in the North Sea, now
risen to become an Amsterdam burgher in command of merchant ships.
We see a debonair but authoritative figure. A graying spade beard juts

Dutch explorer Willem Barents, after whom the Barents Sea is named, scored many firsts: the first European to winter in the far north; first to delineate Spitsbergen and Novaya Zemlya; first to penetrate 600 miles from the Pole; and first to introduce golf to the Arctic.

like a ship's prow over a fancy white ruffled collar. He has a barrel chest encased in velvet, short-cropped hair and fiercely pointed moustachios. It is in some ways the face of a *bon vivant*: a God-fearing Calvinist who nevertheless enjoys his schnapps; a sporting man who can appreciate the fun of his men sliding down snow hills on their backsides; a musical man who takes along a beachwood flute on his expeditions; a gambling man, even when dying, ready "to lay wagers with us that he would bring that intended voyage to an end." His set lips wear a trace of a smile. Yet one looks into his piercing, glacier blue eyes, and one detects behind that amiable façade a man of bull-headed pertinacity.

His resolve to find the chimerical Passage to Cathay was based on the usual commercial interests and geographical myths. Netherlanders had long cast covetous eyes on the flow of trade between Russia and the Muscovy Company of England. All three nations had made abortive attempts to butt through the ice barrier of the Siberian Kara Sea (then known as the Tartary Sea); and they were dimly aware of the caterpillar-shaped island of Novaya Zemlya that separates it from the Barents Sea (called the Frozen Ocean). The legend persisted that somewhere beyond the Ob River, the Mississippi of western Siberia, there was a warm, open, liquid avenue that would lead merchants northeastward to the spiceries of Cipango.

The leading Dutch astronomer, Reverend Peter Plancius, a Calvinist visionary not unlike Dr. John Dee of England, was convinced that this golden pathway could be found once one hurdled the first Kara Sea dike of arctic cold and ice. As explorers neared the Pole, the reverend divine further argued, they would discover a balmy tropical climate; for was it not true that the sun at the far north "was rather a manufacturer of salt than of ice"? The merchants of Holland believed in the learned cosmographer (as did Henry Hudson later on) and so did Hudson's precursor, pilot Willem Barents.

And so on Whit Sunday, May 29, 1594, Barents sailed out from Amsterdam in command of the hundred-ton *Messenger* to bring back news of the salty seaway to Cathay. He was accompanied as far as Siberia by two other Dutch merchant ships, the *Mercury* and the *Swan*. But differing about the best course to pursue, they parted company near a point to which they gave the wonderfully rancorous name of Cape Dispute. Barents was determined to probe easterly around the north coast of Novaya Zemlya; the disputing skippers of the other two vessels were just as adamantly bent on penetrating the Kara Sea via the narrow strait at the bottom of Novaya Zemlya.

Barents first sighted Novaya Zemlya on July 4, its rock crystal mountains seeming to glitter in the sun like diamonds. They reckoned it must be Goose Land because, though treeless, its shiny basalt cliffs were populated by millions of strutting burgomaster gulls and white-bellied Brent geese. With his marvelous freshness of observation, Barents's chronicler, Gerrit De Veer, was to record that the barnacle geese uttered a guttural Low Dutch croak that sounded like, "Rot, Rot, Rot."

It was not the only homely comparison he made. It was comforting to find five hillocks at Cape of Comfort, dappled with yellow poppies and blue palemones, and sticking up raggedly into the empty sky like the thatch-roofed huts of peasants back home. And at the marshlands off Cape Negro, the black ooze was as slimy as the diked mud bars of the Zuider Zee.

The arctic exotica, of course, won a more exotic description. Off the islands that Barents named Orange, his men bagged one of a herd of two hundred walruses basking in the sun. They brought its carcass back to Amsterdam as a souvenir, but not before the bellowing creature almost tipped over the rowboat with her ivory tusk prongs. "This sea horse is a wonderful strong monster of the sea, much bigger than an ox," wrote De Veer, "with very short hair, mouthed like a lion."

The polar bear they lassoed and shot at Willem's Island "showed a most wonderful strength" even greater than a lion's. When Barents gave the wounded bear a friendly poke with a boat hook, assuring his men, "She will there rest herself," the pet bruin took umbrage and scrambled menacingly over the side of the rowboat. Fortunately the loop around her neck got caught in the rudder, and the behemoth was strangled there until thoroughly killed with a blow of a pikestaff. Though the men had hoped to bring the curio back alive, they had to content themselves with a pretty bear skin.

But it was the ice that proved most astonishing. At first sight, the men cried out that the flotillas of drifting ice floes looked like white swans floating gracefully over grass-green and azure-blue waters. But by the time the *Messenger* reached about 77 degrees latitude, it was a pitching, angry, growling tumble of white which, when viewed from the crow's nest, stretched out endlessly "as if it had been a plain field of ice."

Barents rolled with the punches and feinted and tacked about no less than eighty-one times, seeking openings in the ice lanes. But after twenty-five days and more than one thousand five hundred miles of zigzagging along the western coast of Novaya Zemlya, the pilot had to admit defeat. The ice pack was as strangling as the rope around the throat of his choked polar bear.

It was all the more humiliating when he met the *Mercury* and the *Swan* at the pre-arranged rendezvous on the Siberian coast. The skippers gloated (incorrectly as it turned out) that they had sailed with ease into the Kara Sea as far as the mouth of the Ob River. And there beckoning before them, deep blue and ice-free, was the southeasterly alleyway that surely led to Cathay.

It was, in fact, Kara Bay. But the mercantile burghers back home were entranced by the illusory news. Prince Maurice of Orange and the Dutch States General issued a Cathay discoverers' charter as grand as any scroll put out by the English.

On July 2, 1595, a fleet of seven ships set out, laden with trading trinkets for the infidels, and there was a Rotterdam yacht supposed to hurry home with the news as soon as they spotted the tropical salty seaway. Barents sailed aboard the two-hundred-ton *Greyhound,* officially designated Pilot Major of the fleet. But he was outranked by an Admiral and Vice Admiral of the fleet, and it soon rankled in him that he had to take orders from such timorous officers.

In fairness, though, it must be said that a shuddering spectacle greeted them on August 19 when the fleet arrived at the narrow strait between Novaya Zemlya and Siberia that was the gateway to the Kara Sea. "The entire channel was closed up as far as the eye could see, so that it had the appearance of a continent, which was most frightful to behold."

The snarling ice floes made the men murmur with alarm. More terrifying was a subsequent episode. Barents's crew went ashore at Staten Island to hunt for arctic hare and the stones which they thought were diamonds. While two sailors were resting on their stomachs, one felt a cold clutch around his throat.

"Who is it that pulls me so by the neck?" he asked.

His companion glanced up and blinked. "Oh, mate, it is a bear!" he cried out, and dashed off for help.

When a party of twenty armed men arrived, according to De Veer's colorful description, the "cruel, fierce and ravenous beast had fallen upon the man, bit his head in sunder, and sucked out his blood."

The men charged with muskets and pikes. The lean female fury retaliated by seizing another sailor and proceeded to devour him alive. They fired a shot at her clean between the eyes and slashed at her until their cutlasses shivered into pieces. "Yet she held the man still fast by the neck, and lifted up her head, with the man in her mouth." Their brave pilot stepped forward and struck a mighty blow with his musket on her snout and she finally staggered to the ground with an agonized roar. As a *coup de grace*, the pilot slit her throat with his knife, and they buried their two dead comrades amid the ersatz diamonds, and returned to the *Greyhound* with a hard-won bearskin trophy.

In De Veer's memoirs, the illustrated scene bears the grisly caption: "How a frightful, cruel, big bear tare to pieces two of our companions."

It is a pity there is no illustration of the somewhat more engaging scene that occurred. It might have carried a caption on the order of Barents, the Gulliver, meeting the Samoyed Lilliputians. With eight oarsmen, Barents rowed around the ice floes to the Siberian mainland at a point across from Vaygach Island, which means "Island of the Idols." It was so called because it was inhabited by idol-worshippers known as Samoyeds. These are short, squat aborigines who are Siberian tribesmen. At that time their colony in the region of the Kara Strait was studded with hundreds of grotesque totems carved out of driftwood.

Out of the mists ashore loomed the small, shaggy, satyrlike figures of twenty fur-clad Samoyeds. They were divided into two armed infantry sections, bristling with bows and arrows, and they had cavalry units of reindeers harnessed to sledges. With a menacing air, their leader took an arrow out of his quiver and was about to shoot.

Barents's interpreter, who spoke a little Russian, cried out, "Shoot not! We are friends."

The chieftain cast his bow and arrows to the ground. "Then you are welcome," he said.

"Saluting one another," De Veer wrote of the strange encounter, "they bended both their heads down towards the ground, after the Russian manner."

De Veer described them as being low of stature, with broad flat faces, small darting eyes, long plaited hair, short legs, knees bent outward, but quick to leap. They were dressed in deerskin from head to toe. "The manner of their apparel is like as we use to paint wild men," observed De Veer. "But they are not wild, for they are of reasonable judgment."

They were reasonably suspicious of the Dutchmen. Offered a biscuit, one of the sentinels guarding their chieftain accepted it with thanks. "But while he ate it, he still looked diligently about him on all sides about what was done."

What was done was the accidental shooting off of a Dutch musket. "Wherewith they were in so great fear that they ran and leaped like mad men. Yet at last they satisfied themselves when they perceived that it was not maliciously done to hurt them. And we told them, by our interpreter, that we used our muskets instead of bows. Whereat they wondered, because of the great blow and noise that it made."

One of Barents's sharpshooters set a flat stone, the size of his palm, on a snow hill a good distance away. The marksman aimed and fired. "And when the bullet smote the stone in sunder, whereat they wondered much more than before."

In return for this demonstration of their thundersticks, Barents heard good news. The chieftain said that five days' sailing from there to the northeast would bring his ships to a point of land, beyond which there was a great sea stretching to the southeast.

"After that we took our leave with great friendship on both sides," wrote De Veer. He added a delicious comic touch: "And when we were in our pinnace, we all took off our hats and bowed our heads unto them, sounding our trumpet. They in their manner saluting us also, then went to their sleds again."

There followed, however, an embarrassing situation. The chieftain came riding to the shore, brandishing his fist and demanding the return of the Samoyed idol that one of Barents's sailors had filched. Barents shamefacedly made the guilty mariner deliver up the graven image. By the time they rowed back to where the stalled fleet was stationed he had little good humor left.

In no uncertain terms he told the Admiral and Vice Admiral that they were shilly-shallying. It was irresolute to let a pack of ice block Dutchmen from the open sea five days hence which the Samoyeds had spoken of. The Admiral heard him out and then said, "Willem Barents, what think you were best for us to do?"

"I think we should do well to set sail," said Barents bluntly, "and go forward on our voyage, that we may accomplish it."

Whereupon, according to De Veer, the Admiral replied in a huff, "Willem Barents, mind what you *say*."

Willem Barents said nothing but stalked angrily across the ice field back to the *Greyhound*. Before sunrise he had warped and twisted his vessel free from the floes. On seeing their pilot do so, wrote De Veer, the abashed Admiral and Vice Admiral "began also to hoist their anchors and to set sail."

But after a month of plugging away, they still could not breach the unyielding ice barrier. By mid-September the men were murmuring more loudly. The officers were fearful because it was growing increasingly "misty, melancholy and snowy." And yet the obdurate

Barents wanted to give it one more try. But the Admiral would not let him. Swallowing his pride, the Pilot Major grudgingly agreed to sail home, bowing to superior orders that it would be sheer Amsterdam obstinacy to continue to "run with our heads against the wall."

And yet Barents was a born head-rammer. The obstacles he had to overcome to lead a third expedition were almost as tough as the ice. The Dutch States General, disappointed in past failures, would not back a new venture, though a government reward was offered to private entrepreneurs willing to gamble on their own. Under the prodding of Barents's tutor, Peter Plancius, the merchants of Amsterdam finally agreed to make a fresh attempt closer to the North Pole. But it was to be financed on a shoestring, for they would risk the outfitting of just two tubby, nameless, oaken barks.

To Barents's chagrin, he was not asked to lead the company or even to skipper one of the two vessels. The merchants evidently thought he would be too truculent to obey their orders. The veteran North navigator was told he would have to serve as pilot under one of the two unseasoned captains already selected. It was a blow to his pride, but Barents was so determined to go that he accepted.

He wisely chose to serve with Jacob van Heemskerk. Young Jacob was an Amsterdam nobleman, a congenial comrade who bowed to Barents's superior experience, and with a spirit as dauntless as his own. He was later to command the Dutch naval fleet in an attack against the Spanish at Trafalgar, and though a cannon ball shot off his leg during the battle, he continued to encourage his men, and he retained his sword until he died. Little wonder that his monument in Amsterdam reads: "The man who ever steered his way through ice or iron."

The captain of the expedition's second ship, Jan Cornelius Ryp, was a cocky know-it-all. He began bickering with Barents about steering directions as soon as they had reached the Barents Sea in early June of 1596. De Veer discreetly mentions the "hard words" passed between the two officers; but the first mate largely devotes his own words of enchantment to the wonders to be seen as the voyagers glided closer to the Pole than any man before.

It was a surrealist world, where the fleecy ice floes looked now like white swans, now like lily pads, floating in emerald and jade waters; an eerie world of silence, except for seals that barked like dogs and walruses that roared like lions, sunbathing in a polar zoo under three blazing hot spotlights; the world of Edward Lear and his *Book of Nonsense.* There were indeed three suns hanging in the sky, for on June 4 they observed that "wonderful phenomenon in the heavens." Thus they were perhaps the first to record the reddish refracted images of the arctic sun, which scientists call parhelions and common seamen call sun dogs. De Veer saw two mock suns beautifully haloed in rainbows, and in the illustration later drawn by the Dutch artist, Levinus Hulsius, they are charmingly depicted as bearing angelic faces of cherubim.

The caption reads: "A wonder in the heavens, and how we caught a bear." De Veer thus couples the mock suns with one of his more lurid polar bear stories. Off an island nearby, the mariners in their rowboats gave chase to a swimming leviathan of a bear twelve feet tall. They battled with her for four hours with muskets, halberds and hatchets. But their quarry would not surrender her seemingly impregnable hide until "we cut her head in sunder with an axe." The illustration shows the bear crunching an oar in her teeth, while the sailors' muskets roar and the axes swing and the angelic suns smile down on them.

To commemorate the adventure, Barents named the island nearby "Bear Island," a name which it still holds today at close to 75 degrees latitude. The sailors further celebrated by climbing to the top of a snow mountain to gather burgomaster goose eggs and almost broke their necks tobogganing down Mount Misery on the seat of their pants. Barents scolded them for risking their lives, but took it as a good sport, and joined them in eating the succulent eggs.

On they sailed northward, past icebergs that loomed like Dutch cathedrals and over waters glinting as green as grass. On June 15, in misty and drizzling weather, they spotted a significant phenomenon, though they did not recognize it as such. "We saw a great thing floating in the sea, which we thought had been a ship. But passing along by it we perceived it to be a dead whale that stouncke monsterously."

Four days later, at roughly 80 degrees latitude, they sighted the land of the sawtoothed mountains. Eleven years later, Henry Hudson was to describe the cluster of islands as "a very ragged land, rising like haycocks." Willem Barents recorded in his log that it was a high and broken land, "consisting only of mountains and pointed hills; for which reason we gave it the name of Spitsbergen."

Although Spitsbergen was so close to the Pole, they were pleasantly surprised while charting its western coastline to discover that "there groweth leaves and grass." Dwarf willow poked out green tentacles from crevices in the rust-colored cliffs. On the shores of Amsterdam Island, which Barents considered very beautiful, one could admire the marsh grass flecked with purple Lapland rhododendrons and golden saxifrage

The original caption under this charming sketch by Dutch artist Levinus Hulsius read: "A wonder in the heavens, and how we caught a bear." The mock suns smiling down angelically on the melodramatic polar bear combat are refracted images of the Arctic sun, known to scientists as "parhelions" and called "sun dogs" by common seamen.

and peach-colored parryas. Most remarkable was the aviary of sea fowl. Millions of them darkened the sky and screeched their polar symphony. It was a concert of white whistling swans, peregrine falcons cackling their "Kak, Kak, Kak," old squaw ducks bagpiping their "Ow, Owdel, Ow" and De Veer's favorite, the big-bellied, white-collared barnacle geese, bassooning their "Rot, Rot, Rot." De Veer noted, "There was so great a number of birds that they flew against our sails," and the men plucked eggs from their nests by the dozens.

Barents tried to push still farther northward from this particular egg heaven, which he named Cape Bird, but thick ice barricaded his way, and the pilot turned back to Bear Island. There he got into a showdown argument with Captain Jan Cornelius Ryp over which path to pursue next. They parted company. Ryp returned home. Barents persevered alone. He made another dogged attempt to break through the ice barrier at the northernmost end of Novaya Zemlya. Instead it was the ice that broke him.

De Veer gives us a powerful picture of the crushing of their ship. Towards the end of August the currents came driving in harder and harder, the icebergs came slamming in bigger and bigger. And the swift clashing and congealing of the ice floes was unbelievable. They were like the dikes of the Zuider Zee piling on top of each other, like the salt mountains of Spain suddenly petrified, like "whole towns made of ice, with towers and bulwarks round about them." And with a groaning and shrieking of timbers, their poor ship was squeezed as if in a vise, her bow hoisted up four feet high as if in a jack, her tiller and rudders and lifeboat ripped to pieces, and her stem pinched and twisted over on her side as if in the grip of a giant wrench.

And so, on the evening of August 26, 1596, at 76 degrees latitude, on the northeast tip of Novaya Zemlya, beset in the bay prison which they ironically named Ice Haven, sixteen men and a boy were "forced, in great cold, poverty, misery and grief, to stay all that winter."

It wasn't all quite that grim. As De Veer later conceded, with his usual *élan*, "There was sometimes a holiday in the midst of our sorrows." After all, their ship was fairly well stocked with Dutch cheeses, casks of meal and oil for making porridge and pancakes, barrels of hardtack and brined beef, and hogsheads of wine and beer. There seemed to be plenty of driftwood on the beach for building a house. If all else failed, they could trap arctic foxes (whose meat once tasted proved "as dainty as venison unto us"). And, of course, the island abounded in walking polar bear steaks.

When ice crushed their ship on the northeast tip of Novaya Zemlya, the crew —
16 men and a cabin boy — cheerfully collected driftwood to build a winter home
off the bay that Barents named "Ice Haven." Their beloved leader entertained
them by playing a flute and reading aloud a history of China, which they had
tried to reach.

Barents attempted to make their winter hut as cozy as a bacillus in a Dutch cheese. A steam bath was fashioned out of a wine cask, seen at the right. But diarist De Veer claimed that despite a bonfire that blazed constantly in the centre of the shack, their washed shirts set to dry in front of the fire stiffened into knight's armor.

Indeed, while they were sledding supplies from the ship to the site where they were constructing a cabin, a prodigious bear stuck her snout into a tub of their beef. "She fared therewith as the dog did with the sausage," De Veer joked, citing the old Dutch proverb about the dog being soundly beaten for stealing a string of sausages. "For as she was snatching at the meat, she was shot into the head, wherewith she fell down dead. Then we ripped her belly open; and taking out her guts, we set her upon her forefeet, so that she might freeze as she stood."

By the end of September she had frozen solid into an icicled statue; and by then the northing novices began to feel that way themselves. A northeast blizzard blew, and thousands of smoky plumes of snow were gusting over the cemented and ice-lacquered drifts, and the knifing winds were so sharp a man could hardly breathe. It was so bitter, said De Veer, that the sailors had a hard time finishing the carpentry of their house. "When we put a nail into our mouths—as carpenters do when at work—ice would hang thereon when we took it out again."

By mid-October they were ready to move into their new home. It was a one-room rectangular hut about thirty-two feet long and twenty feet wide. The roof was a sail anchored down with shingle from the beach. A beer barrel with the bottom knocked out served as a chimney and landlubber's crow's nest. "Upon the top of the house," said De Veer, with light-hearted jocularity, "we placed a May Pole made of frozen snow."

Inside an attempt was made to make it as cozy as a bacillus in a Dutch cheese. Wooden sleeping bunks were arranged in a row along a wall. On the advice of the surgeon-barber a steam bath was fashioned out of a wine cask. From the ceiling hung a vast lamp fuelled with bear grease. On the frost-shattered ground in the centre of the shack a constant bonfire blazed. A big Dutch clock chimed away the hours.

Barents seems to have done wonders at keeping up the morale of his flock. We never once hear of his men's nerves rasping on one another, a virtual record in arctic wintering. With Dutch fastidiousness, the sailors were kept occupied washing their shirts regularly. They knitted fox trapping nets out of ropes, and used the captured fox tails for homemade caps and muffs. On "fair sunshine days" they exercised outside by catching a ball and playing golf—the golf course extending the two miles from the embayed ship to the house. They took turns going out to haul in firewood, on one excursion being amused by a polar bear who kept fetching the chunks of wood they aimed at her "as a dog useth to do at a stone that is cast at him." They were entertained as well by the

The foxes which scampered over the roof all winter were captured in traps and the fox tails used for homemade caps and muffs. Twelfth Night in January was celebrated with a lottery and game of charades, "and our gunner drew the winning ticket and was crowned King of Novaya Zemlya."

playing of Barents's six-hole beachwood flute. And one has a delightful picture of the pilot reading aloud to his simple mariners by the flickering light of the bearfat lamp *The Navigation or the Art of Sailing* by Pieter de Medina and *The History or Description of the Great Empire of China* by Juan Gonzales de Mendoza.

In short, it appears to be a picture of the Dutchmen making themselves as comfortably at home as the jolly peasant folk in one of Pieter Bruegel's sixteenth-century paintings.

Unhappily they soon found that the arctic elements cannot be domesticated that simply. By November 7 the reddish sliver of a sun vanished behind a mauve horizon. A fog-veiled moon peered out myopically. And icy winds glazed snowdrifts packed as high as their roof. It was so freezing that their clock stopped, and "we could hardly discern the day from the night. We thought that it was not day when it already *was* day."

They substituted the ship's hourglass to count the sands of time. But as the interminable winter night dragged on De Veer seemed to derive a perverse satisfaction out of measuring the intensity of the cold. It was as though the numbing chill was so ludicrous one could only laugh at it by gleefully drawing comparisons. Either that or De Veer was merely laying it on thick to give a vicarious thrill to the Dutch burghers reading his memoirs by their toasting hearthsides back home.

Apparently it was so cold that their spruce beer had the taste frozen out of it. It was so cold that their sherry sack had to be boiled free of ice and there was no trouble chilling it promptly to fit the demands of a wine connoisseur. It was so cold that the flintlocks froze in their muskets. It was so cold that their washed shirts set to dry in front of the fire stiffened into knight's armor. It was so cold that their slippers froze as hard as horns around their feet, and they shivered though wearing three pairs of pants and four pairs of stockings.

"It was so cold that as we put our feet to the fire, we burnt our stockings before we could feel the heat; and what is more, if we had not sooner smelt than felt them, we should have burnt them quite away ere we had known it. . . . And it was so extreme cold that as we sat close to the fire almost burning our shins at the foreside, we froze behind at our backsides; and were all frosted white, as the country peasants used to be as they come into the gates of the town in Holland with their sledges, after they have travelled all night."

Christmas Day was no joke. They lay in their bunks with hot stones at their feet, listening to the ice floes cracking at sea and the foxes scampering over the snow-covered roof. Yet somehow the Dutchmen contrived to make a joke out of their cheerless Yuletide. The sailors began debating whether the foot-pattering of the foxes was a good or evil omen.

"While we sat disputing why it should be an ill sign, some of our men made answer that it was an ill sign because we could not take them, to put them on the spit to roast them; for that would have been a *very* good sign for us."

Twelfth Night, on January 6, was celebrated with more festive merriment. They played games of charades, drank their best wine, ate pancakes with oil, and each sailor was given a captain's biscuit made of wheaten flour to dunk into his sherry.

"And so, fancying ourselves to be in our country and amongst our friends, it comforted us as well as if we had made a giant banquet in our own house. And we also held a lottery and played at being kings, and our gunner drew the winning ticket and was crowned King of Novaya Zemlya, which is at least eight hundred miles long and lyeth between two seas."

Their hilarity was dampened by a death, caused by the lack of fresh greens. Scurvy, that withering disease of the flesh, the gums and the teeth, claimed the life of one of the five who were to die of it on the expedition. They had a wretched time burying the dead man. They had to shovel a snow tunnel from the doorway, and the permafrost ground outside was like rock and the wind was an icy scythe. So the gravediggers took turns at their melancholy task, and with whitened knuckles and faces bloodied by frostbite, they finally dug a hole seven feet deep. Barents led them in reading prayers and singing psalms, and afterwards he tried to cheer them up by laying bets on when the sun would rise again.

"Whereupon our Master went to try if he could climb up through the chimney and so get out," wrote De Veer on January 27. "And while he was climbing one of our men went forth of the door to see if the Master were out or not, who, standing upon the snow, saw the sun, and called us all out. Wherewith we all went forth and saw the sun in his full roundness a little above the horizon. . . . Which made us all glad, and we gave God hearty thanks for His grace showed unto us, that that glorious light appeared unto us again."

By mid-April it was fair sunshine weather again, and they rejoiced to see the first eider duck diving in open blue water; most of the men were up and about, racing, catching a ball, and golfing to stretch their joints. They were even able to raise a chuckle about sharing the last of their beef supply: "It was still very good, and the last morsel tasted as well as the first. Only it had but one fault, which was that it would not last any longer."

The men were itching to be gone from there; and they wished to so inform their nominal captain, Jacob van Heemskerk. "But each was reluctant to make the skipper acquainted with it," says De Veer. "For he had given them to understand that he desired to wait until the end of June, which was the best of the summer."

Barents, though by now so stricken with scurvy that his men had to rig up a cot for him by the fire, still commanded their respect and affection. They decided to ask their "wise and well-experienced pilot" to mention their request to Captain Heemskerk. In light of the ego clashes with crew members that were to play havoc with Henry Hudson and other wintering commanders, De Veer here makes an interesting comment. It suggests a subtle rapport, based on confidence and courtesy, binding together the leader and his followers.

"Willem Barents held them off and quieted them," De Veer tells us. "And yet it was not done in a mutinous manner, but to take the best counsel with reason and good advice; for he heard all what they would say and they let themselves easily be talked over."

Jacob van Heemskerk was likewise equable yet firm. "He made answer that his own life was as dear unto him as any of ours unto us." He, too, did not wish to dwell there as a permanent burgher of Novaya Zemlya. But since the ship was too ice-battered, they would have to overhaul their two open rowboats and convert them into sailing skiffs seaworthy enough to risk an escape through the ice floes to Siberia. It seemed like an insane gamble. Yet though they were enfeebled with scurvy and exposure, everyone pitched into the task with a vigor; "for good will on the one side and hope on the other side increased our strength."

While they were busily working away, they had a farewell visit from a polar bear. It was as though she "had smelt that we would be gone and therefore desired to taste a piece of some of us." One sailor fired at her from his lookout in the beer barrel chimney; two others aimed their muskets at her from the door. With a bit of drollery heavily larded, one suspects, with hyperbole, De Veer claimed that a bullet passed clean through her body and went out again at her tail and her carcass was so tough that the bullet was as flat as a Dutch penny beaten with a hammer. Fortunately the bruin toppled over dead, once again "faring as the dog did with the sausage." The caption for the illustration reads: "How we shot a bear, wherefrom we got a good hundred pounds' weight of grease."

They stowed the grease, as well as their bundles of scarlet cloth, velvet, and trading trinkets for the Cathay infidels, into their two remodeled, high-gunwaled, square-sterned cigar boxes that were to serve as skiffs. Before leaving Barents performed a solemn ritual. He wrote a letter telling how they had come out of Holland to sail to the Kingdom of China, were forced to winter ten months in Novaya Zemlya, and were now attempting to head southward in two little open boats. "If any man chanced to come hither, they might know what had happened to us." Each man signed the document with a cross, and it was placed in a powder horn and hung in the chimney.

Then Barents and another ailing seaman, Nicholas Andrewson, were drawn on sleds and carried aboard the two leaky vessels almost as frail as themselves. And on June 13, 1597, with menacing floes and a hazardous sixteen hundred miles ahead of them, they cast off from "that wild, desert, irksome, and cold country."

Though his flesh was drooping and his bones ached, Barents sustained the men with his courage and good humor. Captain Jacob, who was in one boat, called out to his pilot in the other and asked how he did.

"Quite well, mate," said Barents cheerfully. "I still hope to be able to run before we get to Wardhuus!"

Yet as if he had a premonition that he would never see the northernmost tip of Novaya Zemlya again, Barents made a request of De Veer.

"Gerrit, are we about the Ice Point?" he asked. "If we be, then I pray you lift me up, for I must view it once again."

On June 17 it looked as though none of the men would ever see land again. Their boats were trapped in a fast-driving current and they were in danger of bashing into the whirling ice pancakes known as growlers.

"We were so sore pressed between flakes of ice that we thought verily the skiffs would burst in a hundred pieces," wrote De Veer. "Which made us look pitifully one upon the other, for good counsel was dear, and every minute we saw death before our eyes."

Captain Jacob asked for a volunteer to save the lives of the party. The man would have to leap from drifting growler to growler with a rope and tackle. Upon reaching the firm land ice he would then pull the boats ashore.

With an admirable show of bravery and modesty, and clutching at Dutch proverbs to justify himself, De Veer made his decision.

"No man, as in the tale of the mice, durst hang the bell about the cat's neck, fearing to be drowned," he considered. "Yet necessity required it to be done. And the most danger made us choose the least man. So as a drowned calf may safely be risked, and as the lightest man in the company, I took it upon me to carry the rope to the fast ice. And so creeping from one piece of driving ice to another, by God's help, I fastened the rope to a high hummock."

As soon as his shipmates were drawn to safety, he says, they hastily made beds of clothes on the ice for the sick men, and searched for sea fowl and eggs to nourish them. "And making account that we had escaped out of death's claws," De Veer adds, "it made us somewhat comfortable, and caused us to speak cheerfully one unto the other."

And yet death would not be cheated. Three days later, both invalids took a turn for the worse, and it was feared that Nicholas Andrewson could not long continue alive. When Barents heard that report, he turned to De Veer and said, "I think I shall not live long after him."

With a sense of tenderness, De Veer writes, "And yet we did not judge Willem Barents to be so sick. For we sat talking one with the other and spake of many things. And Willem Barents looked at my little chart, which I had made of our voyage, and we had some discussion about it.

"At last he laid away the chart and spake unto me, saying, 'Gerrit, give me something to drink.' And he had no sooner drank it but he was taken with so sudden a qualm that he turned his eyes in his head and died presently."

Thus on June 20, 1597, Willem Barents was buried on the shores of the icy sea named after him, and his shipmates mourned the death of their "chief guide and sole pilot on whom we reposed ourselves next to God."

On they struggled, "in the ice, over the ice, and through the sea," and they missed him terribly on their ghastly odyssey. Only twelve survivors of the original seventeen were left barely alive five weeks later when they reached the southern tip of Novaya Zemlya. There they were greeted by Russian fishermen whom they had entertained aboard their Dutch ship on a previous voyage. De Veer tells us that the Russians looked with pity at their gaunt, hollow-cheeked faces. "They were abashed and wondered at us, to remember that we were once so well furnished with a spendid great ship, provided with all things necessary, and then to see us so lean and bare."

Barents, the cabin boy and three others had perished by the time the twelve surviving crew members had completed a 1,600-mile journey in a couple of frail boats to the south end of Novaya Zemlya where they were rescued by Russian fishermen. They were welcomed in Holland's royal court like heroic ghosts, jauntily clad in foxtail caps.

They exchanged a few words in pidgin Russian.

"*Propal korabl?*—Is the ship lost?"

"*Korabl propal.*—The ship is lost."

In sign language the Russians indicated they had once drunk fine wine on the Dutch ship. What did the survivors have to drink now?

A Dutch sailor drew some melted ice water from the skiff and let the Russians taste it. The Russians spat it out. "*Nyet dobre!*—Not good!"

The Russians fetched them a round loaf of rye bread weighing about eight pounds and some roast fowl. But the Dutchmen sat by their fire to dip biscuits into boiled water and simply felt grateful for their company. So ravaged were their scurvy-sick gums and teeth they could eat nothing more solid.

They managed to swallow a little Russian vodka, but it was not until August 30 that they were able to rouse genuine Dutch cheer. It was then, at the Siberian fishing village of Kola, that they had a happy reunion. They were embraced by Jan Cornelius Ryp, master of the Dutch expedition's second ship, who had parted from them at Bear Island a year ago and had now returned to look for them.

"We received each other with great joy and exceeding gladness, as if either on both sides had seen each other rise from death to life again," says De Veer. "For we esteemed him, and he us, to be dead long since."

Ryp brought out barrels of potent Roswick beer and good Hollander gin, and they toasted one another with many a tankard of schnapps. A tumultuous welcome awaited them in Holland. Like heroic ghosts, jauntily clad in white foxtail caps, they were received at the royal court of Prince Maurice of Orange in The Hague. And as long as they lived the talespinners were asked by entranced listeners to "rehearse our voyages and adventures, both forwards and backwards."

The merchant burghers were most intrigued by the tale of the dead whale off Spitsbergen that "stouncke monsterously." That whiff led to the great whale rush of the 1600s. On the northwest tip of Spitsbergen, on the Amsterdam Island which Barents had considered so beautiful, the Dutch whalery of Smeerenburg, or Blubbertown, blossomed forth. And for several decades it stank monstrously of the grease and bones of thousands of dead whales. During its heyday the Dutch burghers shipped fifteen thousand whaling men to Blubbertown. It was an arctic boomtown ten degrees from the Pole. There were bunkhouses and bakeries (the baker blew a bugle when the buns came hot from the oven). There were churches and schnapps saloons. There was even a bordello well stocked with fleshy Rubenesque women.

And, of course, there was the Barents Sea that teemed with spouting wealth. These were the bowhead whales, their twin fountains of exhaled breath arching like blue plumes in the frosty air. They were called "right whales" because they were the right ones to harpoon for the most profit. A single slate-gray, sixty-foot-long bowhead might be wrapped in thirty tons of blubber. The blubber was peeled off like the skin of an orange, and after being boiled down in copper cauldrons, its rendered "train" oil fetched a good price for greasing wheels and lighting lamps. Equally valuable in the pre-plastics age was the ton or more of "baleen"—the some six hundred bristle-like plates of whalebone in the jaw of the bowhead. Tough, resilient baleen ultimately was worth as much as six dollars a pound because of the demand for corset stays to constrict the too fleshy curves of the Rubenesque women.

The Dutch made a fortune out of these floating money gushers—an estimated eighty million dollars before the Spitsbergen whales were entirely slaughtered by the end of the seventeenth century—and so the burghers had reason to bless the memory of Willem Barents.

The Barents story had another curious sequel. On September 7, 1871, while he was hunting for walrus on the northeast coast of Novaya Zemlya, Captain Elling Carlsen, skipper of the Norwegian sloop *Solid*, was forced by a driving snow storm to anchor in Ice Haven. There he found still standing, hermetically sealed in a thick coat of ice, Barents's driftwood wintering home. And inside, as though locked in cold storage for almost three hundred years, were the miraculously preserved relics of the expedition.

There stood the iron clock, its chimes stilled. There stood the wooden bunks, where the Dutchmen had once shivered with heated stones at their feet as they joked about the overhead thudding of foxes' feet. There was the note in the powder horn, just as Gerrit De Veer had described it.

There were other memorabilia more moving. There was the beechwood flute. There were the tin tankards long emptied of the chilled wine which the sailors had quaffed on Twelfth Night in salute to the mock King of Novaya Zemlya. And there were the small leather slippers of the cabin boy who had died in the cold.

There was a copper ink stand. Barents had stabbed a quill pen into its frozen ink while with numbed fingers he had painfully sketched a map of the islands the pilot had discovered en route to his illusory passage to Cathay.

There was a rusty iron seaman's chest. Frozen inside it was a touching assortment of trinkets Barents had brought to edify the pagan souls of Cathay. There were copper engravings of biblical scenes, such as the meeting of Esau with Jacob. There were prints of Dutch, Greek and Roman heroes, one entitled "The Defenders of Harlem," another, "Pallas, Juno and Venus in the presence of Paris." And there were tin medallions etched with symbolic pictures of Calvinist piety, one vignette showing a mother of mercy sheltering children, another of a saintly woman holding a cross and flaming chalice.

One tin medal seems to have had a special significance for Barents. On it he had scratched three inscriptions, one in Dutch and two in Latin, and they all dealt with the theme of time. He seems to have been obsessed with time. Would it never end on his seemingly endless polar wintering? In future time would his men's heroic endurance of the long arctic night be believed by posterity? As though to convince himself, he scratched around the margin of the medallion the poignant phrases: "*Abstrusam. Tenebris. Tempus. Me Educit. Tu Auras.*" ("Time, lead me out of the gloomy dark of the night into the light") and "*Veritas filia temporis*" ("Truth is the daughter of time") and finally, in the very centre of the medal, "Time that uplifts truth from the earth."

Although Barents sacrificed his life to prove it, his truth—that it was possible for European men to winter in the high Arctic—has happily proved to be an enduring truth. And history has enshrined imperishably his uplifting exploits. The original Ice Haven relics are still exhibited today in reconstructions of the Barents wintering home at both the National Museum in Amsterdam and the Dutch Naval Museum at The Hague. They are living memorials to the Dutchmen who dared icicles to hang in their beards. Their gaiety and their bravery in the face of the long polar dark have more than weathered the test of time, for such things are truly timeless.

Chapter 7

Mutiny on Hudson Bay

It is perhaps the best-known picture ever painted about the aftermath of a mutiny, and despite its sentimentality, the pathos of the scene is still powerful enough to break your heart. There is Henry Hudson, the noble old man with the long gray beard, cast adrift amid the ice floes in a small boat with his young son, Jack, and seven scurvy-sick men. They are left abandoned without food, without water, without clothing to protect them against the chill void of Hudson Bay.

The time is 1611, but the subjects seem frozen in a timeless limbo. The explorer sits at the tiller in his "motley" gown, vainly trying to steer the shallop through the bluish white maze of icebergs that loom around him like spectral wraiths. Cowering at his feet, thinly clad like a court page boy, lies Jack, his fingers reaching out for the warmth of his father's hand. Huddled beside them is the loyal crew member, Philip Staffe, the ship's carpenter who told the mutineers he would not be party to their villainy and instead chose "for the love of the Master to go down to the shallop."

What makes the picture so piteous is the look in Hudson's eyes. They are the eyes of a beaten man, totally dejected, staring into space with utter hopelessness.

It is an affecting scene, perhaps true in the sense that the artist has captured the mood of the melodrama, and yet it is a false one. The picture, which hangs in the Tate Gallery of London, is purely imaginative. The artist, the Honorable John Collier, painted it in the Victorian era some three hundred years after the event. It is a distortion, not only because no likeness of Henry Hudson is known to exist; but because it presents a one-dimensional portrait of the explorer's complex character.

One would like to remember Hudson as a paragon of virtue, the guiltless innocent done in by crafty villains. This is the black-and-white image which the painter and the historians of the Victorian age preferred to idealize. But a study of the facts today casts Hudson in a less noble light. He remains a sympathetic figure, but blemished with failings that make him appear more human to us.

His contemporary, William Shakespeare, who probed into the grays of the human heart so profoundly, portrayed a strikingly similar flawed hero in his *Tragedy Of King Lear*. Like that doomed old man, also driven to the point of insanity by his own follies, Hudson was both imperious and capricious; exasperatingly moody and indecisive; given to crankiness intermixed with gentle-forgiveness; a player of favorites; a poor judge of people; betrayed by the very favorites whose gratitude he so injudiciously sought.

His ultimate weakness was that he was a too-accommodating leader of men, vacillating when he should have been firm, placating when he should have been tough. In one of the few fragments of his personal journals that have been preserved, he remarks that the stormy seas, thanks to God, were "assuaged." He might have been speaking of his own philosophy; he was too intent on assuaging his mutinous crews, and in the end, they destroyed him.

And yet those journals also reveal that he could be considerate and kind, very determined and very brave in surmounting unflinchingly the calamities that Shakespeare called "sea sorrows." He seemed possessed by the intellectual curiosity of the impassioned discoverer, who does not necessarily want to reach a goal, but who is driven on and on, risking his life to see what fresh wonders he might find on the other side of the next iceberg. Perhaps he might discover—as he thought he did—a mermaid in the sea, or tropical heat near the Pole. He was the single-minded optimist, credulous with hope. No matter what the personal consequences, he was bent on solving geographical puzzles, or else, as he phrased it, "to give reason wherefore it will not be."

And it must not be forgotten that, despite being equipped with a single puny vessel on all four of his voyages, his navigational accomplishments were of a very high order. Hudson set a new record in arctic northing that was to stand for almost two centuries. He beat Willem Barents by penetrating the ice north of Spitsbergen to 80 degrees, 23 minutes latitude—roughly five hundred and seventy-five

The famous John Collier painting is an imagined depiction of Captain Henry Hudson with his son, Jack, and his loyal ship's carpenter, Philip Staffe, cast adrift with six scurvy-sick crew members in a shallop amid the ice floes of Hudson Bay. Of the thirteen mutineers who abandoned them, eight survived.

nautical miles from the Pole. Furthermore, he set new records in inland exploration of North America—delineating the great river of New York State that bears his name, as well as the great bay of Canada that is both his monument and his tomb.

Despite his achievements, scholars have been able to unearth surprisingly few facts about his early life. Historians used to cover up their ignorance with flowery phrases. They said he had blazed forth like a meteor out of obscurity, embarking on his four expeditions during the span from 1607 to 1610, and then had vanished just as mysteriously from the world's ken.

However, we now know more about him than that. He was born in London apparently of a distinguished sea merchant family. According to the Reverend Richard Hakluyt, the great Boswell of Elizabethan voyagers, Henry Hudson evidently had a grandfather of the same name who was a London alderman and a founder of the Muscovy Company of England. Young Henry must have served his sea-going apprenticeship with that company and by 1607 had risen to the rank of captain.

We also know that Henry Hudson was the father of three sons, Oliver, Jack and Richard. Furthermore, he was old enough to be grandfather of Oliver's daughter, Alice, and took time out between voyages to attend her christening in September of 1608. Henry's wife, Katherine, like the wives of many explorers, was a suffering but strong-minded woman. She later petitioned the directors of the company that had last hired her dead husband to the effect that she was left "very poor." Considering that Henry had "lost his life in the service of the Commonwealth," Katherine felt that the company was obliged to do something for her youngest son, Richard. The parsimonious merchants paid the youth five pounds for his "apparel and necessaries" and sent him first to Bantam in Java, and then to Japan and Bengal, to serve as a company factor.

Not satisfied with this, the widow Katherine demanded that she, too, be given a post in the East India trade. A provocative entry in the company's books reads, "Mrs. Hudson and her indigo." Apparently the extraordinary woman traveled all the way to Ahmedabad in India, stubbornly insisting on being engaged, with special privileges, in the remunerative commerce of her late husband's employers. And after a spirited dispute over the payment of freightage for her quilts, her dyes, and other trading goods, the company directors finally heaved a sigh of relief and closed the books with the phrase, "End of Mrs. Hudson's tiresome suit."

The merchants were no more generous with their risk capital when Henry Hudson embarked on his first expedition. On May Day, 1607, he set out from Gravesend on a mission to reach Cathay via an alleged short cut right over the North Pole. For this formidable jaunt the Muscovy Company equipped Captain Hudson with an ancient forty-ton bark named *Hopewell* and a crew of just eleven—one being the skipper's fourteen-year-old son, Jack, serving as cabin boy.

Vaulting the Pole was the quaint concept of the two leading geographic theorists of the day, the Reverends Peter Plancius of Holland and Samuel Purchas of England. Hudson, a devout Church of England man, seems to have been especially inspired by the Reverend Mr. Purchas's curious mixture of theology and geography. Although confessing that he had never ventured farther than two hundred miles from his birthplace of Thaxted in Essex, the armchair cosmographer drew upon Scriptures to certify that the North Pole was heaven and Cathay commerce over it would prove even heavenlier.

"That which I most grieve at," the clergyman sermonized the laggard stay-at-homes, "is the detention of further discovery of the Pole and beyond ... the desire of gain everywhere causing debate, and consequently loss of the best gain both in Earth and Heaven. Merchants might get the world and give us the world better, if Charity were their Needle; Grace their Compass; Heaven their Haven; and if they would take the height by observing the Sun of Righteousness in the Scripture-astrolabe."

And the Scripture-astrolabe showed that a northeast or northwest passage via the Pole could be accomplished with apostolic ease. For as one neared the Pole, argued the reverend divine, "that vast line at Circumference itself becomes (as the whole Earth to Heaven, and all earthly things to heavenly) no line any more, but a Point, but Nothing, but Vanitie."

And so Hudson steered boldly toward this "Point", this "Nothing", this "Vanitie". His boldness took him farther north up the east coast of Greenland than any explorer before. Unlike John Davis, who had shuddered at this Land of Desolation, Hudson felt there was a certain grandeur about its sugar-loaf mountains and castle-like crags. He remarked on the flying skeins of beautiful birds with "black backs and white bellies"—probably thick-billed murres—and at 73 degrees latitude the optimist named it the "Land of Hold With Hope". "This land was very temperate to our feelings," he noted, regretting that the dense mists and swirling ice pans would not let him satisfy his curiosity

Hudson Strait, the 450-mile long bottleneck leading out of the inland sea that is Hudson Bay, is a boiling maelstrom of currents and pulverizing ice pans in off-season. Mutiny began simmering when Hudson attempted entry in June 1610. Hudson would not give up his quest for the Northwest Passage, despite the battering floes. His imagination was intrigued by the "champagne land" on the Strait's southern shore; he named it "Desire Provoketh."

in investigating it further. "And, for aught that we could see, it is like to be a good land, and worth the seeing."

With Willem Barents's chart before him, he decided to probe northeastward and see if he could exceed the Dutchman's high record mark at Spitsbergen. Like Barents, he marveled at the glinting colors of the polar waters, now olive green, now azure blue; and the pointed mountains, which looked now like heaps of corn, now like haycocks; and the raucous clamor of the swooping sea fowl, especially the yellow-billed, red-footed snow geese and those guttural barnacle croakers which Hudson called "rot geese" and the myriads of long-tailed jaegers "with black backs and white bellies and long spear tails."

Close to 79 degrees latitude in early July it was "searching cold" and "this day we had our shrouds frozen." But by mid-July, past 80 degrees north latitude, on the northernmost tip of Spitsbergen, lemon-yellow poppies and golden saxifrage were blooming in swamps amid the snow. "Here we found it very hot." Indeed, when his men went ashore to collect specimens of greenery, deer antlers, and stones of the country, it was so hot they had to drink cool water from a mountain stream. Hudson was enchanted with this arctic Arcadia; he named it "Hakluyt's Headland" in memory of the blessed Archdeacon of Westminster who devoted his life to collecting explorers' journals.

His path blocked by "pestering ice," Hudson was forced to turn back. On the way home he stumbled upon a volcanic island northeast of Iceland which he named Hudson's Touches. Seven years later a Dutch whaler, Captain Jan Jacobsz May, claimed it on behalf of Holland and gave the place its present name of Jan Mayen Island. But by then the English merchants didn't care. They were more interested in laying claim to Whale Bay, a Spitsbergen inlet where Hudson found the whales so plentiful they wouldn't let a man do a little fishing in peace.

"In this bay," Hudson reported, "one of our company having a hook and line overboard to try for fish, a whale came under the keel of our ship and made her held. Yet, by God's mercy, we had no harm but the loss of the hook and three parts of the line."

English merchants thus felt they were entitled to compete with the Dutch for control of the Spitsbergen whale fisheries. So, though he had failed to sail over the top of the world, his Muscovy Company backers were sufficiently pleased to let Hudson attempt a second Cathay route in 1608. This time it was hoped that the *Hopewell* and her crew of fifteen would make the Northeast Passage, slicing through the Kara Sea ice barrier via straits either at the top or bottom of Novaya Zemlya.

Hudson on this trip was almost elegiac about the wonders he saw.

"We saw whales, porpoises, and the sea full of fowls," he exulted. "We heard bears roar on the ice, and we saw upon the ice an incredible number of seals. . . . The afternoon was clear sunshine, and so was all the night. . . Generally, all the land of Novaya Zemlya that yet we have seen is to a man's eye a pleasant land. . . . My party found it was very hot on the boggy shore, with young grass coming up an arrow shaft long, and they saw a herd of white deer, and they brought aboard some moss, flowers and green things that did there grow. . . . It being calm all this day, it pleased God at our need to give us a pretty gale. . . . And at the island where we rode lyeth a little rock, whereon were forty or fifty sea horses lying asleep, being all that it could hold, it being so full and little."

The most stunning marvel was the sight of a mermaid. Two of Hudson's mariners spotted the siren of the sea on the morning of June 15, a little north of 75 degrees latitude. They shouted to the rest of the crew below deck to come up and see her. "And by that time she was come closer to the ship's side, looking earnestly on the men." It was probably a harp seal. Yet Hudson recorded the event as ingenuously as modern science fiction buffs who swear they have witnessed Martians skimming aboard flying saucers.

"From the navel upward," he described the phenomenon, "her back and breasts were like a woman's, as they say that saw her. Her body was as big as one of us; her skin very white; and long hair hanging down behind, of colour black. In her going down they saw her tail, which was like the tail of a porpoise, and speckled like a mackerel."

The seductress was more enchanting than the malevolence the sea next thrust upon them: driving ice, squealing and rubbing against their nutshell of a ship, and "very fearful to look on." But Hudson had his men fend off the pack with beams and spars, and hooking his ship now onto one floe, and now onto another, he nimbly hopscotched his way out of peril. Yet ultimately the Kara Sea proved "so full of ice that you will hardly think it" and he admitted "with sorrow that our labour was in vain." The optimist turned homeward, vowing that "if the wind should friend us," he hoped on his next expedition to make a dash up the Northwest Passage "and to return as God should enable me."

But Hudson ended his log with an odd statement, unheard of from a sea captain. Before reaching England, he says, "I gave my company a certificate under my hand, of my free and willing return, without persuasion or force of any one of them."

In other words, reading between the lines, one suspects strongly that it was not the ice but an uprising of his insubordinate crew that forced him homeward. And one suspects further that the ringleader of the mutineers, to whom Hudson supinely yielded, was his first mate. This was a mysterious character named Robert Juet, an elderly, taunting mariner from Limehouse; and since he was to play so sinister a role in the Hudson tragedy, Juet needs some explaining.

Historians have never been able to rationalize satisfactorily the curious love-hate relationship between the two men. Though Juet had already proved to be a troublemaker, Hudson strangely persisted in taking him along as chief officer on his next two voyages. It was as though the sea captain were somehow fated to bear this incubus on his back to the fatal end.

Perhaps the most perceptive analysis was given by one of Hudson's biographers in the early 1900s, the American scholar, Thomas A. Janvier. According to Janvier, Juet had a psychological counterpart in one of the sea romances of Frederick Marryat, the nineteenth century sailor-novelist who wrote such moralistic tales as *Mr. Midshipman Easy*, *Masterman Ready*, and *Peter Simple*:

"It is my fancy that this 'ancient man' — as he is styled by one of his companions — was Hudson's evil genius; and I class him with the most finely conceived character in Marryat's most finely conceived romance: the pilot Schriften, in *The Phantom Ship*. Just as Schriften clung to the younger Van der Decken to thwart him, so Juet seems to have clung to Hudson to thwart him; and to take — in the last round between them — a leading part in compassing Hudson's death."

If Juet clung to Hudson, so did Hudson have the seemingly masochistic need to cling to Juet. For we find Captain Hudson bringing his second-in-command all the way to Amsterdam to accompany him on his third expedition of 1609.

Because the Muscovy Company now felt him to be an expensive luxury, Hudson had switched loyalties and offered his services to the Dutch East India Company. The mercantile burghers of Amsterdam, however, were just as frugal as the penny-pinching merchants of England. They paid Hudson a fee of eight hundred guilders (worth about sixty-five English pounds). His contract explicitly bound him to attempt only a northeast passage via the Kara Strait. If he did not return in a year, his wife, Katherine, would be compensated with the princely sum of two hundred guilders (about sixteen pounds). And he was to be equipped with a flimsy yacht of sixty tons, the *Half Moon*, as well as a mixed crew of sixteen Dutchmen and Englishmen — riffraff who appear to have been the dockyard dregs of both countries.

As soon as the *Half Moon* reached the pitching ice off Novaya Zemlya, we are told by Dutch historians, a mutiny broke out. The unruly men refused pointblank to risk their necks in a northeast passage. Hudson meekly temporized and mollified. He suggested two alternative northwest passage routes. They might try penetrating the Furious Overfall on the west side of Davis Strait mentioned by Captain John Davis. Or they might explore a second entry into North America at roughly 40 degrees latitude which he had heard about from his friend, the renowned Captain John Smith of Pocahontas fame, who had three years previously established an English colony in Virginia. Grumbling, the crew accepted the latter compromise.

Robert Juet, who kept the only surviving journal, makes no mention of the mutiny, which he himself undoubtedly led. His log omits entirely any of the black dealings which occurred during that fortnight between May 5 and May 19. But the entries that he did make about the *Half Moon's* drunken and bloody procession up the Hudson River as far as modern Albany reflect darkly upon his own character and that of Henry Hudson.

One gathers that Hudson and his crew had no scruples whatsoever about debauching the Indians. In exchange for gifts of Indian maize and tobacco, the *Half Moon* mariners introduced fire water to the natives, dressed them in red coats out of sheer horseplay, and then stood back to watch their intoxicated guests reel about helplessly. Juet tells us that one "savage," liquored up by Hudson with four or five glasses, was rowed ashore, where the drunken innocent then "leapt and danced." Another shipboard party was so notorious that its tradition lingered on for two hundred years, the Mohicans and Delawares referring to the awesome binge as "place at which we were drunk." Juet describes the orgy thus:

"Our Master and his mate determined to try some of the chief men of the country, whether they had any treachery in them. So they took them down into the cabin and gave them so much wine and aqua vitae that they were all merry. And one of them had his wife with them, who sat so modestly as any of our country women would do in a strange place. In the end one of them was drunk . . . and that was strange to them: for they could not tell how to take it."

Besides introducing them to hooch (our modern short form of the Indian term, *hoochenoo*), the white interlopers were quick to originate the axiom: "The only good Indian is a dead Indian." Making the assumption that the peaceful Indians were as ruthless as themselves, Juet writes of a pillaging raid made by his piratical crew: "Then we manned

Hudson and his mutineering mate, Robert Juet, debauched the Indians with "hoochenoo" as the 60-ton yacht, The Half Moon, *sailed drunkenly up the Hudson River as far as modern Albany, N.Y. The explorers slaughtered six Indians off present Coney Island. After swapping a few knives and trinkets for a rich haul of Indian beaver peltries near the site of today's Manhattan, Juet recorded: "This is a very pleasant place to build a town on." Hudson's other namesake was the great bay of Canada that is both his monument and his tomb. New research reveals he was like Lear, flawed with human frailties.*

our boat and skiff with twelve men and muskets, and two stone pieces or murderers, and drove the savages from their houses, and took the spoil from them, as they would have done of us."

The savagery of the palefaces was displayed most barbarously while the *Half Moon* was anchored near the present site of Coney Island. An Indian climbed through the cabin window and tried to pilfer Juet's pillow, a couple of his shirts, and two cartridge belts. The first mate killed him with a single vengeful shot through the breast. The cook sliced off another Indian's arm with a butchering stroke of the sword. And at least a half dozen natives in canoes were slaughtered like so many clay pigeons being popped off at a carnival shooting gallery in modern Coney Island.

"I shot a cannon at them and killed two of them," Juet writes with callous dispassion. "Yet they manned another canoe which came to meet us. So I shot at it also with a falcon, and shot it through, and killed one of them. Then our men with their muskets killed three or four more of them. . . ."

Yet it would be unfair to say the expedition was entirely taken up with mayhem and *hoochenoo*. In the few fragments of a log we have from Henry Hudson, the skipper presents a smiling picture of the New World and its people. "It is as pleasant a land as we need tread upon," he says rapturously of its tall oaks and chestnut trees, so different from the treeless Arctic. It was fruitful with blue plums and red vines, teeming with sturgeon and oysters. And the native people, though "they have a great propensity to steal, appear to be a friendly people."

When he landed at one Indian village in the present resort area in the Catskill Mountains, the tribesmen greeted him with songs and their chieftain threw a magnificent clambake for him. Reed mats were spread out in an oakbark lodge and the paleface guest was feasted with roast dog, Indian corn, pigeons and pumpkins and hot clams, and he was invited to sleep there overnight.

"These natives are a very good people," said Hudson. "For when they saw that I would not remain, they supposed that I was afraid of their bows, and taking the arrows, they broke them in pieces, and threw them into the fire."

Even Juet was captivated. "The land is very sweet," he rhapsodized. There were goodly grapes and rose bushes, "and very sweet smells came from them." Despite his automatic distrust, he confessed the people could be "very loving." The women garlanded the sailors with beads of wampum shells, and casting a lecherous eye on the dusky young maidens of sixteen, Juet had to admit they "behaved themselves very modestly."

The first mate also cast a shrewd eye of appraisal on the real estate. Sailing past the greenish white cliffs of today's New Jersey Palisades, "we saw a very good piece of ground." The other side of the river, he notes, "is called *Mannahata*"—apparently after the Manhattan Indian tribe. And after swapping a few knives and trinkets for a rich haul of Indian beaver peltry, Juet jots down about the potential trading centre, "This is a very pleasant place to build a town on."

The town of New Amsterdam which the Dutch built on Manhattan Island was ultimately, of course, to become New York. But Hudson did not reap any rewards from his discovery. On his way home he had to quell another mutiny. Again Juet omits any reference to the uprising. Amusingly enough, though, he does mention how the ship's cat terrified the superstitious mariners: "This night our cat ran crying from one side of the ship to the other, looking overboard, which made us to wonder; but we saw nothing."

When the *Half Moon* arrived in Dartmouth on November 7, Hudson gives us a hint of the dissension aboard in a note he sent to his Dutch employers. He was game to make another northwest passage attempt closer to the Pole, but he wanted six or seven of his crew exchanged for others more docile. The English merchants put a quick stop to that. They had him arrested and accused him of enriching a pack of Dutch foreigners. He would be permitted to embark on a new expedition to the Furious Overfall which had thwarted John Davis, but it would have to be done for his own country's commercial gain.

And so on April 17, 1610, with the backing of a syndicate of wealthy English merchants headed by Sir Dudley Digges and Sir John Wolstenholme, Henry Hudson sailed the fifty-five-ton *Discovery* down the river Thames on his last ill-starred voyage of discovery.

Only eight of the twenty-three discoverers aboard were fated to see England again. They were an oddly assorted ragtag-and-bobtail of a crew. Perhaps none was more odd than the scribe who saved his neck from the gallows by leaving to posterity a highly biased record of the tragic events. He bore the improbable name of Abacuk Prickett. A onetime haberdasher, he had become a manservant to the expedition's patron, Sir Dudley Digges, and his master had sent along the valet to keep an eye on his investment. Prickett was a servile, Uriah Heep-ish sort of puritan, who covered up his suspect behavior with treacly quotations from Holy Writ. His unctuous hypocrisy reminds one of King Lear's revelation: "See how yond justice rails upon yond simple thief. . . . change places, and, handy-dandy, which is the justice, which is the thief?"

Prickett railed largely at another odd passenger aboard the Ship of Fools. This was Henry Greene, who in company with first mate Robert Juet, was to become a ringleader of the final infamous mutiny. Again Shakespeare, in his *Tragedy Of King Lear*, summed up Henry Greene in a phrase: "The prince of darkness is a gentleman." Greene was a clever, well-educated young gentleman from a respectable family in Kent. He was gifted at writing, a bit of a snob, something of a dueller, and evidently an atheist. He shocked the Scripture-quoting Prickett with his assertion that when it came to religion he was a clean sheet of paper whereon Prickett could write as he pleased. Greene also seems to have been a hell-raising wastrel, who squandered his money on bawds in taverns. His own mother, we are told, would trust him with no more than four pounds, so he could buy a new suit appropriate to wear on the expedition. Hudson had taken a fancy to the charming ne'er-do-well, given him meat, drink and lodgings at his London home, and had promised to find his protégé a place in Prince Henry's regiment of guards after the voyage was over.

Hudson appears to have sneaked Greene aboard ship at Gravesend, without the knowledge of the ship owners, and this show of favoritism seems to have galled other officers of the crew. Their smoldering resentment broke out soon after the *Discovery* touched Iceland. They bathed in a hot spring at Lousy Bay, where "the water was so hot it would scald a fowl," and Prickett read baneful augury in the sight of erupting Mount Hecla, "which cast out much fire, a sign of foul weather to come."

The mutinous fire on ice began blazing with a furious fight between Henry Greene and the ship's surgeon. Hudson unwisely condoned the wild behavior of his young protégé. Old Juet, sensing that the captain had rejected him for a new favorite, took out his venom in a drunken tirade. The first mate charged that Hudson's new pet had been taken on as a stool pigeon to "crack his credit" with the captain. Furthermore, Juet muttered about the crew's need to keep swords and muskets ready in their cabins for the bloody manslaughter looming ahead. Not content with that, in the hearing of his skipper, the first mate threatened to turn the head of the ship homeward from the action.

Hudson was at first enraged, for he vowed that he would leave his old shipmate beached on Lousy Bay. Then he was placating, for we are told that he eventually "pacified" Juet, "hoping of amendment."

With these seeds of jealousy and rancor planted, Hudson steered his unhappy ship toward the hellish riptides known then as the Furious

Overfall and better known today as the mouth of Hudson Strait. His men were thrown into a sick funk by the spectacle, and little wonder.

The strait is a bottleneck, a hundred miles wide and four hundred and fifty miles long, boiling with currents. It is the funnel outlet of North America's biggest inland sea. This is Hudson Bay, which is six hundred and fifty miles wide and eight hundred and fifty miles long—a mammoth milk bottle containing two hundred and ninety-four thousand square miles of frozen salt water. The bay and strait are relatively ice-free and navigable no more than three months of the year, from mid-July until October. But the *Discovery* tried to enter the strait on June 25. At that time the bottleneck is an uncorked fury—a maelstrom of churning, pulverizing ice pans escaping from the bay into the open sea.

Hudson himself was dismayed by the sight of somersaulting bergs in the "great and whirling" turbulent tides. He later confessed he felt he "should never have got out of this ice but there have perished." Buffeted by floating ice islands, he tacked desperately in the strait's gateway between the sentinel cliffs on the banks of Baffin Island to the north and Labrador's Torngat Mountains to the south. With a twinge of wavering indecision, he democratically showed the crew his chart and took a vote whether they should proceed any further, yea or nay.

"Whereupon some were of one mind and some of another," we are told, "some wishing themselves at home and some not caring where, so they were out of the ice."

One crew member swore that if he had a hundred pounds, he'd give ninety pounds of it to be back in England. But Philip Staffe, the stout-hearted ship's carpenter from Ipswich, differed. "If he had a hundred, he'd not give ten pounds upon such condition, but would think it to be as good money as ever he had, and to bring it as well home."

Hudson slithered and lurched on blindly through a hammering storm and coiling mists and marblelike waters. On July 8 his resolution was strengthened as he skirted a bay on the strait's southern shores. This region of north Quebec today bears the romantic name of Ungava, Eskimo for "Far Away"; and Hudson evidently sighted its Akpatok Island, Eskimo for "Place Where Auk Birds Are Caught." It was a high, haycock land powdered with snow, but populous with ptarmigan and polar bears, and somehow it caught Hudson's imagination. He saw it as a "champagne land" and named it "Desire Provoketh," and his curiosity was provoked to search on westward. No matter if he was being drawn to his own damnation, the obsessed discoverer was prepared to damn the consequences.

On he sailed. Past wrinkled brown mountains of "riven rocks and plashes of water." Past a startled polar bear who "cast her head between her hind legs and then dived under the ice." Past rippling whirlpools and rustling cascades. Past icebergs parading by like a procession of opaline pagodas from Cipango.

At last he reached the end of the Strait, and made a left turn, and triumphantly, records Hudson, "we put through the narrow passage." For it was here the *Discovery* sailed between two lofty headlands, basaltic cliffs lancing two thousand feet high, which guard entry into the burnished blue waters of Hudson Bay.

"The head of this entrance on the south side I named Cape Wolstenholme, and the head on the northwester shore I called Cape Digges," wrote Hudson on August 3, 1610. "Then I observed and found the ship at noon in 61 degrees, 20 minutes, and a sea to the westward. . . . "

His journal there breaks off, and it is the last entry we have from his surviving fragment of a log, the remainder of which was destroyed by the mutineers. Yet one can well imagine, as a contemporary says, that Hudson felt "proudly confident that he had won" the Passage to Cathay. Surely that was the open Pacific Ocean he saw beckoning invitingly westward and southward.

Hudson was so impatient to go on that he wouldn't let his crew members delay to pick up fresh meat they had uncovered at Cape Digges. Prickett, whose dubious journal we must now rely on, had taken a boatload of mariners ashore to the cliffs of Digges Island. There they had found Eskimo stone cairns stored like a butcher shop with plentiful "fowls hanged by their necks"—possibly the long-necked, chestnut-colored birds named after the explorer's bay, Hudsonian godwits.

The valet tells us he tried to persuade Master Hudson to stay there for a couple of days. The ship was provisioned for just six months, and they could replenish their dwindling pantry by looting the Eskimo poultry larders. "But by no means would he stay." The Master recklessly ordered the crew to push on. "So we left the fowl," says Prickett with obvious resentment," "and lost our way" poking fruitlessly for three months down the east coast of Hudson Bay "in a labyrinth without end."

It must have been a frustrating disappointment for Hudson. There he was groping through the coastal mists for a glimpse of the glinting gold roofs of Japan and hoping to smell the sweet fragrance of the balm-bearing spice islands. Instead he cruised by the bald pre-cambrian rock sites of such Eskimo villages as *Ivugivik*, meaning "Place of the Piling up of Ice," and perhaps pushed past that loveliest-sounding of Eskimo names, *Povungnituk*, which bears the unlovely translation of "Place of the Stinking Caribou."

By September Hudson was growing desperate. He was boxed in a blind alley at the very bottom of Hudson Bay—the shallow cul-de-sac now known as James Bay. His officers were in a sullen, lowering mood. They taunted their skipper as he beat back and forth uncertainly, north and south, east and west, in a futile attempt to find his dreamed-of thoroughfare. And Robert Juet jeered at the Master's vain "hope to see Bantam in Java by Candlemas."

Hudson's nerves, already frayed, snapped at this sarcastic jest. He held an open mutiny trial. All the allegations of Juet's past "abuses and slanders" were raked over. It resulted in Juet being stripped of his rank and his pay. Replacing him as first mate was a mariner "who had showed himself honestly respecting the good of the action." This was Robert Bylot, an able but ambiguous pilot, a shadowy mixture of fidelity and treason. While he was about it, Hudson also demoted the boatswain and elevated to that position a rough, brawny hooligan named William Wilson.

With characteristic capriciousness, Hudson assuaged the former favorites he had just deposed. "If the offenders yet behaved themselves henceforth honestly," he promised them, he "would be a means for their good and forget injuries."

But sulking Robert Juet could neither forget nor forgive being ridiculed like a castoff lover, and we are told he "nursed his hatred like a red-eyed ferret in the hutch of his dark soul."

According to Prickett, Hudson's temper and irritability soon grew strained to the point of irrationality. By November 1 the *Discovery* was beset by ice beside the dun-colored rocks and tidal mudflats at the mouth of the Rupert River. And by November 10 they were frozen in for the winter. They found themselves, at about 51 degrees north latitude, beached in the subarctic bleakness in the southeast pocket of James Bay.

Even today it seems a haunted place. The silence of the bay is pierced by the plaintive cry of the red-throated loons, as though they are protesting their fate. And strewn all around the frost-shattered ground are granite ridges, looking like upended tombstones. It is just south of the tree line, where stunted black spruce and jackpine verge into tundra. The trees are tilted, leaning now one way, now another, like a drunken dwarf forest, their branches bald on the north side, because their leaves have been shorn clean by the cutting winds.

193

They spent a dreadful winter there, racked by cold and scurvy and fractious querulousness. Hudson first alienated his sole officer who appears to have been genuinely loyal to him, Philip Staffe. After a seemingly senseless long delay, Hudson ordered the ship's carpenter to cut down trees and build a house ashore.

"The carpenter told him that the snow and frost were such as he neither could nor would go in hand with such work," says Prickett. "Which when our Master heard, he ferreted him out of the cabin to strike him, calling him by many foul names and threatening to hang him. The carpenter told him that he knew what belonged to his place better than himself, and that he was no house carpenter. So this passed, and the house was after made with much labour, but to no end."

Hudson next made the more crucial mistake of picking a quarrel with that hell-raising gentleman, Henry Greene. The ship's gunner having died of scurvy, Hudson had promised to let Greene have the dead man's gaberdine cloak. But Greene, apparently out of sheer mischief, went out hunting for ptarmigan with the Ipswich carpenter who had just fallen out of favor with Hudson. On their return, Hudson was so peeved that he retaliated by bestowing the gaberdine gown instead upon his current favorite, Robert Bylot, newly elevated to first mate.

Greene immediately challenged Hudson for breaking his promise. We are told that Hudson exploded into a fury and reviled his onetime protégé with words of disgrace. Hudson told the profligate that "all his friends would not trust him with twenty shillings, and therefore why should he? As for wages, he had none, nor none should have, if he did not please him well."

With malevolence, Henry Greene joined the estranged Robert Juet in whispering words of revenge against their erratic Master. And there must have been a touch of madness there, in the frosty air at the edge of the Bay, for soon Hudson was playing his reckless game of favorites again. He demoted first mate Robert Bylot and enthroned instead an ignoramus named John King.

"To speak of all the troubles of this cold winter," says Prickett, "would be tedious." It was a kind of hornet's nest on ice, so freezing that Prickett was crippled lame and another seaman had the nails frozen off his toes. "Herod's daughter," the mariners' nickname for scurvy, broke out. Until conifer buds dispelled the sickness, their gums blackened and the jawbones rotted around their teeth. Sheer hunger drove them into eating frogs and moss, "than which," says Prickett, with the distaste of a gentleman's gentleman accustomed to serving Sir Dudley Digges malmsey wine and English roast beef, "I take the powder of a post to be much better."

Their hopes rose in spring with the coming of a few migratory birds and the first Indian or Eskimo they'd seen. Hudson gave the shy native a knife, mirror and buttons. With enticing signs the captain promised the visitor more if he would return with provisions.

The native came back the next day pulling a sled heaped with two beaver skins and two deer skins. He returned the gifts which Hudson had given him and proceeded to barter. Sad to say, white man's greed— the same greed which later induced the Hudson's Bay Company to set up the Rupert's House trading post at almost that very spot—bedeviled Henry Hudson, its first overly avaricious fur trader.

"The Master showed him a hatchet, for which he would have given the Master one of his deer skins," says Prickett of Hudson's hard bargaining. "But our Master would have them both; and so he had, although not willingly. After many signs of his people to the north and to the south, and that after so many sleeps he would come again, he went his way, but never came back any more."

Having thus scared off a potential food provider, Hudson ventured out in the shallop alone in a last desperate attempt to acquire meat from the other native tribesmen. He came back nine days later reporting failure. The natives had actually set fire to the woods when they saw him coming.

He returned to find his crew in literal terror of starvation. Their fishing netted them no more than fourscore small trout, "a poor relief for so many hungry bellies." And apparently they had provisions left for only two more weeks. We are told that Hudson distributed to his men their remaining rations of a pound of bread each and divided five cheeses among them. "And he wept when he gave it to them."

His men were not moved by his tears. If Prickett's testimony is to be believed, Hudson was not entirely blameless for the ensuing outburst of anarchy and pent-up grievances. For by mid-June, when he had the *Discovery* in the open water of James Bay, the explorer seems to have cracked up emotionally. The stresses of privation and the trials of taming a recalcitrant crew came close to unhinging his mind.

First he had the cabin boy break open the sea chests of the crew to search for hidden bread. It was said that the boy delivered to the Master thirty loaves in a bag. This was a foolhardy risk to take with men like Juet, who had already murdered purloining Indians for rummaging through his personal belongings.

Secondly it was claimed that Hudson himself had been hoarding reserves of provisions. The mutineers unanimously charged in Admiralty Court later that the captain had cut a secret scuttle from the hold to his cabin, and there he had stored his private supply: two hundred ship's biscuits, a peck of meal, cheeses, a keg of beer and aqua vitae brandy. Allegedly he summoned his favorites to his cabin and doled out food and drink to keep up the strength of the privileged few. If true, this was inexcusable, for a shipmaster to play God with his men and choose who was to starve and who was to live.

But finally, to cite Shakespeare, it was something "more fell than anguish, hunger, or the sea" that stirred the simmering malcontents into open rebellion. After a winter's soliloquy, Hudson's insatiable curiosity was not yet stilled, and it was this mania that his puzzled men could neither understand nor tolerate. The dreamer was apparently determined to continue searching for the Northwest Passage, even if it meant leaving some of his men behind. The Reverend Samuel Purchas, his sympathetic geography tutor, who had all the evidence before him, unwittingly drops a damning phrase in his summary of the tragedy. The parson tells us that a few days after Hudson had his ship becalmed in a James Bay ice field, "their victuals being almost spent, and he, out of his despair, *letting fall some words of setting some on shore*, the conspirators . . . entered his cabin in the night." The italics are not his, but the chilling significance of what he revealed has been overlooked by Hudson's apologists.

And yet, for all his failings, Hudson might well have exclaimed with King Lear, "I am a man more sinn'd against than sinning!" For the explorer suffered the ultimate anguish of being forsaken by the very ingrates upon whom he had lavished the greatest kindness.

There were three Judases who were the principal ringleaders of the mutiny. There was Henry Greene, the scapegrace daredevil of the conspiracy, who said he "would rather be hanged at home than starved abroad." There was Robert Juet, sly in his deviousness and brooding with vindictiveness, who "swore plainly he would justify this deed when he came home." And there was the muscle of the revolt, William Wilson, who would fain be a pirate rather than an elevated boatswain, and who was tigerish to get on with the bloody action "while it was hot."

On Saturday night, June 21, 1611, the unholy trio crept stealthily into Abacuk Prickett's cabin and the cabal made the lackey privy to their plot. They intended to cast the Master, his favorites, and the feeblest members of the crew into the shallop and let them shift for themselves.

"For there they lay," said the intriguers, "the Master not caring to go one way or other; and they had not eaten anything these three days; and therefore were resolute either to mend or end; and what they had begun, they would go through with it or die."

Prickett claims he tried to dissuade them. They were married men, with wives and children, and for the sake of their loved ones how could they commit so vile a crime in the sight of God? He would not sanction any mischief that reeked of blood and revenge. Eventually he managed to salve his conscience; for he joined four other conspirators in swearing an oath on the Bible that their scheme was designed for the "good of the action, with no harm to no man." It was a sanctimonious pretext; for Prickett tells us in the next breath that a prime mover of the oath-taking was the atheistic Henry Greene, who flew into a rage swearing to "cut his throat," of any man who might impede their nefarious plan.

"If there be no remedy," Prickett consoled himself piously, "the will of God be done."

Prickett urged them to wait for three days or two days before they perpetrated the deed. But William Wilson would not wait, and jested sardonically to Henry Greene about the valet's qualms, "He is in his old song, still patient."

Prickett seems to have swallowed his qualms at least partially. "I hoped," we hear him muttering, "that some one or other would give some notice . . . to the Master." Yet the valet, with elastic morality, did not think to risk his own skin by giving that warning to the Master. So it is manifest that Prickett thus became a silent accessory to the crime. Reviewing the evil doings later, Prickett's contemporary, Captain Luke Foxe, who was also to explore Hudson Bay, made the incisive indictment: "Well, *Prickett*, I am in great doubt of thy fidelity to Master *Hudson!*"

In his journal Prickett sets the scene for the skulduggery as though it were a melodrama out of the Old Testament. "It was dark," he writes, "and they in a readiness to put this deed of darkness in execution. I called to Henry Greene and Wilson, and prayed them not to go in hand with it in the dark, but to stay till morning. Now, every man, I hoped, would go to his rest. But wickedness sleepeth not. For Henry Greene keepeth the Master company all night and others are as watchful as he."

When dawn broke over the shimmering ice field on Sunday morning, Henry Hudson stepped out of his cabin. Waiting for him were William Wilson and two confederates. The thugs pounced on the captain and pinioned his arms behind him with rope.

What did they mean? asked Hudson.

He should know what they meant, said Wilson, when he was cast in the shallop.

While Hudson was struggling with his captors, Robert Juet went below to settle a grudge. He wanted to seize personally Hudson's current favorite, who had superseded both himself and Robert Bylot as first mate. This was the former quartermaster, John King, who could neither write nor read, and it galled Juet that yet "the Master loved him and made him his mate." John King put up a fight for his life. He drew out his sword and almost killed Juet; but other conspirators overpowered him and hurled him down into the shallop.

One by one the other victims, "the poor, the sick, the lame men," were pulled out of their cabins and dragged along the deck and heaved into the small sailing boat that was tied to the ship's stern. "To most of them," the testimony was later read in British Admiralty Court, "it was utterly unknown who should go, or who tarry, but as affection or rage did guide them in that fury that were authors and executors of that plot."

One crew member, Thomas Woodhouse, described as a student of mathematics, was thrust out of the ship into the shallop weeping. He vainly implored the executioners to take his keys and share his goods if only they would let him stay aboard.

Two treacherous seamen, Arnold Lodlo and Michael Butt, were themselves implicated in double treachery. Both were fellow mutineers who mocked at Hudson's favorites, John King and the captain's cabin-boy son, Jack, for their knavery. In a sudden reversal of whims, Henry Greene decided to jettison his two henchmen, and "with much ado" the pair of knaves were dumped kicking and screaming beside the victims they had just tormented.

Out of that horror emerged one hero with honor. Philip Staffe, the Ipswich carpenter, had once been threatened with a flogging by the Master for balking at building a house on a snowbank. But when it came to murder on ice, he had a conscience and loyalty that told him where a Christian's duty stood.

The mutineers entreated him to stay. They had need of his strength and his skills.

Let them be hanged, he said. He would not stay in the ship unless they forced him. Out of love for the Master, he chose "rather to commit himself to God's mercy in the forlorn shallop than with such villains to accept of likelier hopes."

They bade him go then, for they would not stay him.

"I will," said he, "so I may have my chest with me, and all that is in it."

Silently the traitors passed down to the good carpenter from Ipswich his chest of tools, and in recognition of an honest man, gave him as well a fowling piece, a little meal, and an iron pot.

His wrists bound behind his back, clad only in a motley morning gown, Hudson went down to his doom with a final stunned awareness of betrayal by those who he had once befriended. It was later charged in British Admiralty Court that the ringleaders had auctioned off before the mast the very clothes of their captain; and although he denied it, Robert Bylot, the suspiciously noncommital criminal accomplice, was accused of stealing Hudson's finger ring.

As the mutineers led the captain down the hatch, says Prickett, "The Master called to me. I came out of my cabin as well as I could to the hatchway to speak to him. There on my knees I besought them for the love of God to remember themselves, and to do as they would be done unto. They bade me keep myself well, and get me into my cabin, not suffering the Master to speak with me."

The lamed Prickett then crawled over to his cabin window, and as they flung Hudson into the shallop, he heard the Master shout at him, "It is that villain, Juet, that hath undone us!"

"Nay," cried out Prickett, "it is that villain, Henry Greene," and Prickett adds, "and I spake it not softly."

The mutineers quickly got the ship under way, towed the little shallop until they neared the edge of the ice, and then cut it adrift. And so they sailed northward, leaving behind their shipmates, the Master and his son and seven men, marooned "without food, drink, fire, clothing or any necessaries, maliciously abandoned to their death."

Now that the deed was done, in the phrase of one of Hudson's biographers, Llewelyn Powys, a "paroxysm of licence" gripped the mutineers. Within a half hour they ransacked every inch of the *Discovery* like robbers who have slain the goodman of the house. They grabbed at clothes in the lockers, looted belongings in sea chests, wrangled over whether Robert Juet or Robert Bylot was to serve as chief pilot and, of course, they gobbled up the food and liquor secreted in the captain's cabin as well as the remaining provisions discovered in the hold—a vessel of meal, two firkins of butter, a half bushel of peas, twenty-seven pieces of brined pork.

While they fought over the spoils, a blood-chilling cry arose. The shallop was in sight, and like some skeletal nemesis, was following them.

"Hudson abandoned" was the caption for this melodramatic boy's book illustration of the Victorian era which presented the explorer as a heroic victim. The records show, however, that Hudson was a capricious leader who displayed extreme favoritism and was ready to abandon some of his men ashore.

Whereupon, Prickett tells us, "they let fall the mainsail, and out with their topsail, and fly as from an enemy."

One can only surmise how Hudson must have felt, a forsaken figure in his gown of many colors, standing and staring as his last hope of survival vanished amid the blue mists and white ice fields of his vast uncharted bay. Perhaps like mad Lear, cast away on the blasted heath with his fool, he may have cried out to the heavens to inflict justice on his persecutors:

A plague upon you, murderers, traitors all!

And indeed terrible retribution struck down the guiltiest of the betrayers. The thirteen aboard the *Discovery* spent five weeks fumbling blindly, like frightened children in the dark, in the direction of Hudson Strait. They were smitten by "stout gales of wind" and ripping rocks and clutching ice "into the which we ran from thin to thick, till we could go no further for ice."

And all the while they quarreled among themselves for their depleted rations of food. Prickett tells us that the godless Henry Greene, who had assumed the role of Master, gradually became satanic in his hunger. "He began (very subtly) to draw me to take upon me to search for those things which he himself had stolen. And he accused me of a matter no less than treason amongst us: that I had deceived the company of thirty cakes of bread."

With his fund of phrases from Scriptures, one wonders why the glibly pietistic valet saw no parallel with the thirty pieces of silver.

At length, towards the end of July, they sighted the sea fowl screaming and wheeling over the lancing cliffs of Digges Island, and there a kind of poetic justice caught up with some of them. Prickett went ashore with a boatload of mutineers to do some trading with a band of Eskimos. The kayakers welcomed them with friendly dancing and leaping, showed them how to snare birds, and offered the Englishmen walrus tusks for barter. But Henry Greene, brandishing such knickknacks as mirrors, jew's harps and bells, seems to have alienated the native traders; for "he swore they should have nothing till he had venison."

The upshot was a savage Eskimo onslaught. Henry Greene, yelling "Coragio!", laid about him with his truncheon, says Prickett; but the duellist was slain outright by a shower of arrows. Prickett himself, after grappling a knife away from an Eskimo, ("God enabling me"), slit his assailant's throat with a Scottish dirk; but God, alas, didn't enable the valet to escape until "I received a cruel wound in my back." William Wilson had his "bowels cut"; and that tigerish boatswain, who had been so hot for bloody action, died bloodily "swearing and cursing in most fearful manner." Altogether four mutineers were slain gruesomely, and their shipmates had so little regard for their one-time ringleader, Henry Greene, that they dumped that gentleman atheist's corpse from the rowboat into the sea without burial rites.

Robert Juet suffered the slower and more agonizing death of scurvy and starvation. After they had eaten the sea fowl they had caught at Digges Island, the mutineers expiated their sins on a famishing diet of seaweed fried in candle grease, and feathers and bones consumed with vinegar. Five weeks later, when the *Discovery* rolled and bucketed into an Irish seaport, its untended sails flapping aimlessly in the wind like a scarecrow, only one man, Robert Bylot, had strength enough to lie upon the helm to steer. The other seven scurvy-sick survivors were strewn about the deck like bony ghouls. And Robert Juet, after a futile attempt to escape the gallows by directing the ship to Newfoundland, had finally "died of mere want." As Parson Samuel Purchas sermonized in summary, "Everywhere can Divine Justice find executioners."

Yet in the end mercantile cupidity was stronger than divine justice. The Masters of Trinity House examined the eight surviving mutineers and judged "they all deserve to be hanged." But the High Court of the Admiralty, evidently with an avaricious eye on the potential British commerce that the parasites might produce, waited an unseemly seven years and then declared them guiltless of murder or treason. Indeed, the merchants were so greedy for gain that Robert Bylot and Abacuck Prickett were hired almost immediately to steer the *Discovery* on an unsuccessful expedition, in 1612, to exploit the Northwest Passage to the Indies supposedly lying beyond "Hudson, his Bay." And the evidence suggests that Bylot, as pilot, made no attempt whatsoever to search for Master Hudson at the bottom of his Bay.

The moral of the Hudson story, if there is any, was probably best suggested by Shakespeare. The dramatist tells us of the mariner who watched the sharks destroy their prey and asked, "Master, I marvel how the fishes live in the sea?" And his Master answered, "Why, as men do a-land; the great ones eat up the little ones."

The fate of Henry Hudson, his son Jack, and the seven castaway seamen remains a mystery to this day. At their British Admiralty trial, the mutineers testified that the *Discovery* had eventually "lost sight of them and never heard of them since." Explorer Thomas James, after whom the very bottom of the Bay is named, himself spent a dreadful winter there twenty years after the mutiny; he said he found wooden stakes driven into the ground which may have been sharpened by the iron tools of Hudson's carpenter. The evidence is not conclusive, but it may be so.

All one can do is cite Shakespeare again, and conclude that the heroic yet tragically flawed figure wrought his own ruin; and that the dreamer almost wilfully chose as his destiny to:

Lie where the light foam of the sea may beat
Thy gravestone daily.

And so consumed by curiosity and beset by his ego-driven sea sorrows, Henry Hudson, like other obsessed explorers who followed in his footsteps, lost his life discovering that the illusory Polar Passage was, after all, "but a Point, but Nothing, but Vanitie."

Chapter 8

Astronomer of the Midnight Sun

"*Wednesday, the eighth of July, 1612.* In the morning I perceived the sun and the moon, both very fair above the horizon.... I purposed to find out the longitude of that place.... Most part of this day I spent finding the meridian line; which I did upon an island near the sea....

"This finding of the longitude, I confess, is somewhat difficult.... Some will say this kind of working is not for mariners, because they are not acquainted with working out propositions by the table of sines, and an instrument is not precise enough....

"Yet I know some of the better sort, who are able to work this and the like propositions exactly.... And how necessary it is that the longitude of places should be known I leave to the judgment of all skilfull mariners and others that are learned in mathematicks."

With this opening entry in his journal—carefully recorded while he was piloting the English ship *Patience* through ice floes up the west coast of Greenland—William Baffin strides with seven-league boots onto the centre stage of Arctic exploration.

"The ablest, the prince of Arctic navigators." This was how a later explorer, Captain Sherard Osborn, ranked him. And so William Baffin undoubtedly was. But the prince of scientific navigators—the pilot-astronomer who came nearer to solving the riddle of the Northwest Passage than any discoverer in the Renaissance age—was almost cheated by history. He had to wait two centuries before receiving his belated recognition.

It was an ironic twist of fate. For, as befitting a true Renaissance man, the scope of his feats was truly magnificent. His geographic accomplishments alone were breathtaking. He piloted that battered old bark of Henry Hudson's, the *Discovery*, high up in Baffin Bay—more than three hundred miles past the record northing established by John Davis—and reached a latitude in those icy waters named after him that was to stand unequaled until the nineteenth century. There, at close to 78 degrees, he discovered Smith Sound: the gateway to the North Pole. Then he probed southwestward until he came upon the entrance to another channel immediately north of that other Arctic monument bearing his name, Baffin Island. There, at close to 74 degrees, he discovered Lancaster Sound: the only feasible gateway leading to the Northwest Passage. To the English-speaking world in a later day, those two liquid avenues, Lancaster Sound and Smith Sound, were to become as renowned as Fleet Street and Wall Street.

In his day William Baffin was not content with rewriting geography. The Renaissance man was also a virtuoso in nautical astronomy, far ahead of his time in charting the changing map of the heavens. While his shipmates were playing football on ice, he loved to set up his wooden, wedge-shaped astronomer's quadrant—four feet in semi-radius, he tells us, with a plumb line falling across a scale of degrees—and sight his beloved instrument at sun, star, or moon. For the art of "celestiall observations," as he called it, was the mathematical seaman's joy and "felicitie." As a result he scored a galaxy of firsts while scanning the polar sky.

He was the first explorer on record to describe a complete lunar observation at sea. He was the first English navigator to figure out his observations for longitude while under way, using a highly original system for checking his time calculations against a modern almanac. He was the first to sail so close to the north magnetic pole and, naturally, the keen observer was the first to measure the extraordinary variations of his compass there. His magnetic needle swung "above five points or 56 degrees," which filled him full of wonder, "increasing and decreasing so sudden and swift . . . a thing almost incredible and matchless in all the world."

Indeed no detail was too minute to escape the all-encompassing attention of those sharp binocular eyes and that devouring curiosity of his. He measured everything, whether it was the refraction of the polar sun or the moon pull on the arctic tides; the size of an Eskimo kayak ("twenty feet long, in form of a weaver's shuttle"); or the size of an iceberg ("240 feet high above the water"); the exact shape of a muskox hoofprint or the precise location of the star gleaming so brightly in the centre of the Great Bear's tail.

He was, in short, exalted by the orderly logic and purity of numbers. Only demonstrated facts and verifiable figures, he felt, would help discoverers comprehend the heretofore veiled mysteries of the universe.

"It is an easy thing to make a man believe that which he desireth," as he once expressed his philosophy. "Yet what we have promised (as to bring certainty and a true description) truth will make manifest."

There spoke a true scientist. Yet his scientific skill was all the more remarkable because he was a self-educated scholar. Moreover, he had to rise above the rigid caste system of his time. We have no contemporary portrait of him, and know little of his past, except that he was evidently a Londoner-born, of humble origin. The Reverend Samuel Purchas—the geographer who botched the job when compiling his truncated journals and maps and thus almost robbed Baffin of his place in history—gives us a single scant clue about the explorer's background. With a trace of condescension, the parson anthologist introduced him as: "Master Baffin, that learned-unlearned mariner and mathematician, who, wanting of words, so really employed himself to those industries."

If Baffin was unlucky enough to have been born poor, he was lucky to have acquired his learning in the right period for a pilot fired with the spirit of scientific inquiry. By the second decade of the 1600s, when King James of England was shaking up the theological world with his revisions of the Bible, the scientific world was undergoing a similar shakeup.

Dutch opticians started manufacturing cheap new telescopes. Thus was revealed a host of new stars and vagabond planets and valleys of the moon hitherto concealed from the naked eye. Intellectual astronomers, like the Italian Galileo Galilei and the German Johannes Kepler, were challenging the Talmudic certainties of the horoscope-casting cosmographers. Thus was thrown into a spin antique mythology about the tropical poles and the music of the heavenly spheres and the sun revolving like a cosmic ferris wheel around man's fixed universe, the earth. In England, enlightened navigational mathematicians took up the questioning and the scepticism. They agreed with John Donne, the English poet laureate of science, that the "new philosophy calls all in doubt":

The sun is lost, and th' earth, and no man's wit
Can well direct him where to look for it.

Mercantile shippers, too, were undergoing a painful sea change in their nautical thinking. Though still tight-fisted with their money, the skinflints were gradually realizing that a new breed of pilot, versed in astronomy and geometry, had to be trained. The day was past for the ignorant salt-sea skipper, who had a smattering of arithmetic and counted with an abacus or his fingers. The illiterate couldn't cope with the new logarithm tables and astronomy almanacs. Neither could he handle the improved instruments being devised. Among the inventions, for example, were a complicated traverse board for calculating distances and a series of knotted ropes tied to a log for measuring a ship's speed (hence the nautical terms, "knot" and "log").

Schools for unlearned mariners were launched by two of England's more astute merchant princes, and it is highly likely that William Baffin was their brightest student. One was launched by Sir Thomas Smith, the investor in all five of Baffin's Arctic voyages, after whom the explorer named Smith Sound. Smith was a shrewd, trowel-bearded financier, a leading light of the Muscovy Company who in 1600 was elected the first governor of the English East India Company. Lectures on navigation were delivered both at his house and on the public platform by the mathematical astronomers Edward Wright and Thomas Hood. At his first public lecture at Leadenhall, Professor Hood was so elated at the prospect of teaching common seamen that the don danced on the platform with a cry of, "Yeah, I triumph, indeed I leap for joy!"

The second academy was founded in 1598 by Sir Thomas Gresham. Also a backer of Cathay expeditions, Gresham was head of the Royal Exchange and author of Gresham's Law, which maintained that in the circulation of currency bad money drove out good money. Gresham put his good money into Gresham College of London. It proposed to teach scientific navigation to unlettered sailors who sought to master the streamlined "sea chariots of England." The first professor of geometry was the illustrious Henry Briggs. He was the astronomer-geographer who later inspired another precocious pupil, Captain Luke (North-West) Foxe, and had a cluster of Hudson Bay islands named in his honor, "Briggs His Mathematicks." Though he was the author of *Arithmetica Logarithmica*, Professor Briggs was radical enough not to read his Gresham public lectures in Latin, as he did while instructing at Oxford University. Instead he taught in plain English for the benefit of plain-speaking seamen.

The learned-unlearned pilot, William Baffin, responded to the plain talk. He was the embodiment of the solid, practical unpretentious student of science. True, he occasionally liked to show off his erudition a little, like the bright boy in school. When setting down a column of longitude in his chart, he allowed himself to boast it was "not usual in Journals." And after using his protractor to help draw a superb map in red and green colors, he couldn't resist adding with transparent false modesty about his voyage up Hudson Strait, "I hope I have not much erred from the truth, coming nearer than some which have been employed that way before."

It was likewise true that, although he enjoyed hearing his favorite shipmate quote from Virgil's classical *Aeneid*, Baffin was not given to poetry. His hero was John Davis. He admired his precursor because that meticulously scientific pilot had brought the language and the instruments of the "most wonderful precise certainty" to Arctic navigation. "I take the plain highway in relating the particulars," was Baffin's motto, "without using any refined phrases or eloquent speeches."

If Baffin was indeed Parson Purchas's pilot "wanting of words," the words expressing his yearning and his questing were brilliantly articulated for him by his contemporary, John Donne. The English poet's imagination seems to have been kindled by Baffin's polar voyages. Even his love sonnets are laced with metaphors linking passion with the new maps and telescopes and new-rigged ships of discovery seeking "myne and spice" in the New World; his imagery is intoxicated with references to explorations which "search out the secret parts of the India," the "all-ey'd firmament" and the "star-full Northerne Pole."

It is almost as though Donne were addressing Baffin personally when he poses the questions, like a Greek chorus, "Is not thy sacred hunger of science yet satisfy'd?" and "Hast thou courageous fire to thaw the ice of frozen North discoveries?"

On his first northern voyage, in 1612, Baffin had plenty of courageous fire, but he tempered it with cool objectivity. The "young Arts-man," as a fellow mariner then described Baffin, had embarked on a strange mission. He was piloting the one-hundred-and-forty-ton *Patience* and her sixty-ton consort, the *Heart's Ease*, on an English expedition in search of fabled silver mines on the west coast of Greenland.

His skipper on this wild-goose chase was a rapacious old salt from Hull, a stormy-voiced, hard-a-weather Yorkshireman named James Hall. King Christian IV, the Sailor King of Denmark, had already dispatched Hall on three voyages to Greenland. The intention originally was to find the lost Viking colonies of Eric the Red and possibly discover the passage to the spiceries of Cathay. But Hall, like Frobisher before him, had been waylaid by shining mountains which supposedly contained precious metal. The Danes kept sponsoring Hall on his fruitless silver hunt, until the going got too tough. Hall was thwarted by mutinous crews, impenetrable ice, and—most hazardous of all—hostile Eskimos. His crews had kidnapped five Eskimos and brutally killed at least two of them. It was small wonder then that the natives had beat off his ships with a hail of rocks from slingshots.

Hall was undeterred by this stony reception. The Yorkshireman had persuaded a syndicate of English merchant adventurers—headed by Sir Thomas Smith and another director of the East India Company, Sir James Lancaster—to back him on a new attempt to locate Greenland's El Dorado of silver. It was Baffin's first trip to the land of the perpetual summer sun and the flame-colored auroras flickering over the sugar-loaf mountains. The pilot-astronomer made the most of the celestial fireworks display.

Baffin let his shipmates have their "good sport" watching their mastiff dogs do battle with a couple of captured seals aboard ship. He considered it more fun to take methodical observations of the sun and the moon fighting it out for supremacy in the bloodshot morning sky. In his very first journal entry, written while the *Patience* was moored near the modern Greenland town of Sukkertoppen (Danish for sugar loaf), we find him experimenting ingeniously with a longitude reckoning based on the relative positions of the heavenly bodies.

In calculating the score, he sounds rather like a schoolmasterish referee presiding over a cosmic boxing match. "There may be some small error," he says of his longitude, which was, in fact, a trifle off. "But if it be carefully looked unto, and exactly wrought, there will be no great error, if your almanac ephemerides be true."

A little later, in another fjord, he measured the variation of his compass. With a touch of prideful pedantry, he found it to be 13 degrees, 22 minutes, "contrary to the observations of others in this place. And if any do doubt of the truth thereof, they may with a little pains prove it."

He exhibited the same academic curiosity about all phases of what John Donne called:

> *That unripe side of earth, that heavy clime*
> *That gives us man up now, like Adam's time*
> *Before he ate....*

To Baffin the west coast of Greenland, with its Stone Age peaks and lunar, dreamlike valleys, was "an exceeding high land ... almost nothing but mountains, which are wonderful high as far as we could perceive. There are some rocks in these mountains which are exceeding pure stone, finer and whiter than alabaster. And some are of one colour, and some of another, and all glistering, as though they were of rich value; but indeed they are not worth anything."

One may be sure this blunt conclusion was not based on mere guesswork. For along with James Carlisle, the ship's goldsmith, Baffin carefully inspected the mica quartz shining like rock candy in the alpine gneiss. Scientific tests proved that the imagined silver treasure was nothing but a pipe dream.

Baffin continued his inspection, turning from geology to botany. On the north sides of the valleys, though their slopes were often covered with snow, he was delighted to find rocks wearing a lacy mourning veil of black lichen. He unearthed angelica, whose tender young stalks were as sweet and brittle as celery; green stonecrop poking their delicate yellow flowers through the carapace of snow; and spidery branches of the black crowberry or *Empetrum nigrum,* which "runneth along the ground like three-leaved grass in England." And on the south side of a steep cliff, the amateur botanist detected a true rarity—a grove of dwarf birch, "some six or seven feet high, like a coppice in England that had been some two or three years cut."

His zoological notes were equally painstaking. Though he didn't see the shaggy monsters, he took the trouble of measuring a muskox hoofprint, "which we supposed to be of some great elk; the foot was as big as any ox foot." He did, however, scrutinize very closely the packs of blue arctic foxes and the wolflike Eskimo dogs. For he records the fact, "One thing is very strange, I thought; the penises of both dogs and foxes are bone."

His observations of the Greenland Eskimos were as clinically detached as an anthropologist's. Like a good man of science, he scrupulously avoids preconceptions and moralizing prejudice. He was, of course, wary of possible Eskimo animosity. For he was attached to a foolish crew that recklessly tried to kidnap another native on this trip. Nevertheless, he made a sincere attempt to comprehend the Eskimos' point of view and their culture.

The kidnap outrage occurred in Godthaab (that is, Good Hope) Fjord. It was the same pleasant rendezvous where John Davis had entertained the Eskimos with flute playing and hornpipe dancing and kind conversation. Apparently the Eskimos remembered these previous courtesies. The kayakers welcomed the white newcomers with the identical friendly cries of *Yliaoute!* (which Baffin translated as, "I mean no harm!").

But while the natives were bartering sealskins for iron nails, a sailor named James Pullay made the mistake of indeed meaning harm. He seized an Eskimo trader and yanked the captive into the ship's longboat. A fellow kayaker promptly hurled a spear and Pullay was fatally wounded. The enraged crew hauled the captured Eskimo aboard the *Heart's Ease* with the intention of kidnapping him back to England.

A delegation of two tribal elders paddled to the ship and pleaded for the innocent prisoner's deliverance. Captain James Hall, fearing a general Eskimo assault, grudgingly agreed to let him go.

"To requite the injury done," we are told, "our General gave unto him a knife, a seeing glass, and a yellow and red cotton coat. Yet he, with a frowning look, desiring to be gone from us, leapt overboard, and the other two did help him ashore. And when he was ashore, the savages cut off the coat our Master gave him, from his back, so little did they regard it."

News of this encounter—a new kidnap attempt and the pointed snub as a rejoinder—swiftly passed up the coast. "For when we came near any island," we are informed, flotillas of menacing kayakers "did throw stones at us with their slings."

Eskimo revenge aimed at Captain James Hall reached a dramatic climax on the morning of July 22. Retribution came in an exotic setting just north of the Arctic Circle. The Englishmen sailed into the spacious harbor of Holsteinsborg. Named after Danish Count Holstein, it is today a busy halibut-and-cod-packing settlement, with a population of some two thousand native Greenlanders. But the fjord itself probably hasn't changed much over the centuries.

Baffin would have piloted his ships through purple mists into what first appears spookily like the mouth of some carniverous dragon; its teeth are the iced gneiss crags biting hundreds of feet high into a scarab-green sky. Baffin tells us he anchored on the south beach. There he would have smelled the faint scent of red willow. He would have seen blue harebells and yellow crowfoot and balls of white cotton sedge lifting their heads over quaking chocolate bogs. He would have heard the querulous screams of arctic terns and parrotlike puffins and pure white ivory gulls whirring overhead by the thousands.

The greeting accorded to his captain, Baffin records with calm dispassion:

"About nine or ten of the clock, the savages came to barter with us,

William Baffin and his mate Robert Fotherby collaborated in these delightful primer sketches of whaling in Spitsbergen.

"Whoso doth strike the first harping iron into him, it is his whale if his iron hold," Baffin described harpooners' rivalry.

Like peeling an orange, the whale's blubber was ripped off "in square-like pieces, 3 or 4 feet long, with a great cutting knife."

The whale oil was rendered into barrels and the English Muscovy Company's mark was stamped on bundles of whale bone.

The men labored around the clock hip-deep in stinking grease, with time out only "to eat their meat—refuse blubber called 'fritters'."

It was like child's play to lance walruses, which lay on the beach in herds of up to 500, "grunting much like hogs."

being about forty of them, and continued about an hour and a half. At which time our Master, James Hall, being in the boat, a savage with his dart stroke him a deadly wound upon the right side. . . .

"We all mused that he should strike the Master, and offer no harm to any of the rest of us. Unless it were that they knew him since he was last there with the Danes. For out of that river they carried away five of the people, whereof never any returned again; and in the next river they killed a great number. And it would seem that he who killed him was either brother or some near kinsman to some of them that were carried away. For he did it very resolutely, and came within four yards of him."

And yet, although the Master died next morning, "being very penitent for all his former offences," Baffin does not blame the Eskimos. "For ought we could see," he adds, with understanding, "the people are very kind one to another, and ready to revenge any wrong offered to them."

Unlike his shipmates, Baffin refused to condemn the natives as barbarians, if the facts proved otherwise. "Diverse of our men were of opinion they were man-eaters, and would have devoured us, if they could have caught us," he writes. "But I do not think they would. For if they had been so minded, they might at one time have caught our cook, and two others with him, as they were filling of water at an island a great way from our ship."

His reportorial objectivity extends to the Eskimos' most esoteric customs. He is not interested in speculation, but simply in collecting all the details and getting them right. Nothing much escapes the dragnet of his avidly inquisitive mind. He notes, for example, their burial rites. The Eskimo hunter is entombed in a stone cairn high on a hill, buried with his best bow and arrows and sealing spears and sometimes his favorite sleigh dog.

He describes how the women tattoo their faces with black beauty marks: "The skin being raised with some sharp instrument when they are young, and black colour put therein, that by no means it will be gotten forth."

He marvels at their navigational skill with kayaks: "In these boats they will row so swiftly that it is almost incredible; for no ship in the world is able to keep way with them, although she have never so good a gale of wind. And yet they use but one oar, which enables them at an instant to go backward and forward as they please."

He can even appreciate the logic of why, in a land where metal was rare, they would pilfer the white man's rustiest iron nail. Understandably, he says, "they do as much esteem it as we Christians do gold and silver."

On Baffin's return to England, Sir Thomas Smith was disappointed when the esteemed silver ore was proven dross. However, Baffin more than compensated the mercantile gamblers for their investment on his next two expeditions. In 1613 and 1614 he piloted two whale-hunting fleets up to the frozen northeast nose of Spitsbergen to establish monopoly trade and discovery rights on behalf of the English Muscovy Company.

It was a dingdong scrimmage between English and Dutch whalers, not without its periods of comedy. The Muscovy Company falsely claimed that Henry Hudson had been first to scent out the blubbery riches of Spitsbergen in 1607. So their whalers brandished a royal decree proclaiming English sovereignty over what they high-handedly renamed King James His Newland. Any foreign interloper impudent enough to enter His Majesty's blubber preserve was a poacher. The trespasser's mizzenmast would be shot down with a cannon ball if he didn't hand over half his whale catch. The Dutch East India Company claimed prior discovery by Willem Barents in 1596. Their whalers flaunted a similar proclamation issued by Prince Maurice of Orange. And the Dutch "wagoners of the sea" were escorted by men-of-war ready to fire cannon balls to make *their* claim stick.

The rather pompous nationalistic contest had a couple of embarrassing complications. The Dutch were just gaining their sea legs in Spitsbergen waters. So they were compelled to hire English pilots on the sly to steer their sea wagoners. This bit of unsportsmanship induced the English to cry foul play. They condemned the turncoat "runnagados" for lack of true British patriotism. Even more humiliating, neither the Dutch nor the English knew how to catch a whale. So both sides in the blubber war were reduced to hiring those born whalers, the Basque harpooners from the Spanish Bay of Biscay.

On Baffin's first whaling jaunt of 1613 we learn that his fleet of seven ships employed no fewer than two dozen Basque "whale stickers." Baffin served as chief pilot aboard the two-hundred-and-sixty-ton admiral ship, the *Tiger*. That name pretty well described Benjamin Joseph, fleet admiral on both voyages. Captain Joseph was a crusty old shellback from London, bristling for plunder. He threatened to fight every alien whaling ship that didn't bow to his supremacy by the time the sand had run out of his hourglass.

Baffin tells us amusedly how Captain Joseph got into a hot

Sir Thomas Smith was the financier who sponsored all five of Baffin's Arctic voyages. He was a leading investor in the English Muscovy Company, founder of a school that taught astronomy to seamen. In his honor Baffin named Smith Sound, the gateway to the North Pole.

argument with the skipper of a foreign ship, the *Rochelle*: "It was because of a whale which was in strife between *his* Biscayans and *ours*. Then, for some peremptory speeches, two of the *Rochellers* were ducked at our yard arm, the one on the one side, and the other on the other."

A more agreeable shipmate on Baffin's two journeys to Spitsbergen was Robert Fotherby. Baffin's fellow recorder and master's mate, Fotherby was a young Lincolnshireman with a warm and generous nature akin to Baffin's. They were close chums. Fotherby accompanied Baffin on many a survey trip, "being helpful the one to the other"; on one trip each rescued the other from a near-drowning in icy waters. Together they corkscrewed their twin shallops through crooking fjords, in "drizzling snow and hummocking seas," as high as 80 degrees north latitude. Together they tramped up to the peaks of the needlelike mountains and the absinthe-green tongues of glaciers for the sheer pleasure of exploring untrod territory.

Wherever they went, they took formal possession by planting a wooden cross with a King James sixpence nailed to it. When the Dutch removed the sixpence and substituted the emblem of Prince Maurice of Orange, Baffin and Fotherby knew how to handle the vandals' jiggerypokery. They swiftly tore down the damnable Hollander emblem and hammered to the cross King James's coat of arms, *cast in lead.*

Together the young adventurers enjoyed botanizing, analyzing the red algae which created the apparent scarlet snow of Red Beach, and examining the brownish earth of treeless Spitsbergen, which seemed so devoid of greenery except for "a certain straggling grass with a bluish flower, much like young heath or ling, which grows upon moory ground in north England." Together they caught arctic fox cubs, "which we made as tame and familiar as spaniel whelps." And together they lanced walruses, which lay on the beach in herds of up to five hundred, "grunting much like hogs, and sometimes creeping and tumbling one over the other."

Fotherby was a literate fellow, who must have entertained Baffin considerably with his knowledge of classical literature. On one notable hunting excursion, their greyhound, mastiff and water spaniel struggled through knee-deep snow to help them bag three reindeer bucks. "Poor rascals," Fotherby describes the scrawny deer, "yet very good meat, as we presently made trial and tasted." Then the astonishing seaman bursts into Latin verse. Well provided with hunter's sauce, namely keen appetites, jokes Fotherby, they devoured the roast venison around the campfire, much like Virgil's Aeneas and his companions in the epic poem:

Then Achates saw a spark flickering against flintstone
And he nurtured the flames with moss
(For no leaves fall where no trees bloom)
And his comrades slice and skewer trembling morsels of meat on the spit,
And thus with bellies fed we renew our vigor.

Fotherby must have endeared himself to Baffin because of their mutual scientific curiosity. On another excursion up a glacier, they were surprised to hear a stream of rushing snow water evidently flowing far below in the bottom of a huge fissure in the ice. "For better satisfaction," says Fotherby, "I broke down some pieces of ice with a staff I had in my hand. Which, in their falling, made a noise on each side, much like a piece of glass thrown down the well within Dover Castle. Whereby we did estimate the thickness or height of this ice to be thirty fathoms."

Fotherby shared Baffin's interest in mapmaking and drawing, too. The master's mate produced seven water color sketches, charming cartoons really. One illustration depicts polar bears, deer and foxes scampering up and down the Spitsbergen mountains as if the creatures were skylarking. The other line drawings, coupled with Baffin's notes and Fotherby's journal, furnish us with a graphic picture of the early whaling industry.

The poet John Donne may have created flashier images. In his later verses, which use the arctic whale as a metaphor, Donne soars into a spiritual ecstasy about the power of the "flail-finn'd Thresher." The gargantua has a "gulf-like throat" that sucks in oceans, his ribs are ivory pillars, his brazen tail blunts steel, and wherever he went:

He spouted rivers up, as if he meant
To joyne our seas with seas above the firmament.

All very picturesque. But one feels that the description of whaling presented by Fotherby-cum-Baffin, though cruder, brims with greater on-the-spot authenticity:

"The whale is a fish, or sea beast, of a huge bignesse, about 60 feet long and 18 feet thick," the discourse begins. "His head seems to be one third part of his whole quantity. His finnes (which we call whale bone in England) do grow within his spacious mouth; and he also has two swimming finnes. . . . His eyes are not much bigger than the eyes of an ox. His body is in fashion round. His broad spreading tail is of a rough and solid substance. Therefore it is used to make chopping blocks upon which to chop the whale's fat (which we call blubber)."

We are told that when the whale surfaces, his gigantic body sometimes leaping right out of the sea, he usually spouts eight or nine times before his bulbous head ducks under again. His two gushing streams of water can be seen six to nine miles away, and he "doth blow through his S-shaped spout holes fiercely, roaring like a wind which bloweth into a cave, or like an organ pipe."

"There he white waters!" cry the Basque whale-stickers, and they scud out in their little shallops through the freezing spray and around the blue-green ice hummocks to surround him.

"The order of the Biscayans," notes Baffin, "is that whoso doth strike the first harping iron into him, it is his whale if his iron hold." Consequently there was intense rivalry, so that a Biscayan could boast that he had laid his shallop onto the velvety dark prize—"wood to blackskin" was the common term.

"So soon as they come within stroke of the whale," we learn further, "the harpooneer stands up ready in the head of the boat. He darts the harping iron out of both his hands, striking the quarry near the swimming finne to pierce into his entrails. Wherewith the stricken whale descends to the bottom of the water. And the men in the shallop do weir out 40, 50, or 60 fathoms of rope — yea, sometimes 100 or more.

"But when wounded, he is like to wrest the lance out of the striker's hand; so sometimes two men are fain to pluck it out, though but one man did easily thrust it in. And having received his deadly wound, then casteth he forth blood where formerly he spouted water. And now will he frisk and strike with his tail very forcefully. And in convulsions he is sometimes hitting the shallop and splitting her asunder, sometimes also maiming or killing some of the men. And before dying, when he most commonly turneth his belly uppermost, he may drag a split shallop three or four miles from the place where he was first stricken with the harping iron."

It must have been a murderous trade. Baffin stoically observes that six whale-hunters were lost in one shallop, and another was slain in a boat "overwhelmed by too much haste in following the whale, after the harping iron was in him."

It was certainly a sweated industry. Except on the Sabbath, the men worked around the clock rendering the whale oil into barrels and stamping the company mark on bundles of whalebone. Hip-deep in stinking grease and blood, they labored in shifts. "For when some slept, others wrought. Our men received no intermission from work and sleep, but only time to eat their meat—the refuse blubber called 'fritters,'

A wounded whale sometimes leaped right out of the sea, thrashing and plunging. Baffin observed that six whale-hunters were lost in one overturned shallop and another killed "by too much haste."

whereof they had sufficient. Besides, some were allowed aqua vitae at each four hours' end."

After the rich cargoes were stowed, there was a little time for "gamming." A "gam" was the recreation period when whaling ships flying the same colors exchanged sociable visits in the fjords and the harpooneers swapped yarns about their catch. Some crew members, Baffin says, had archery contests on the ice or played stool ball—a form of football still popular in some Sussex villages. Baffin himself preferred the intellectual exercise of scanning the puzzling, sub-aqueous, milky light of the Arctic heavens.

Homeward-bound, he tells us, the night being crisp and clear, "I had very good opportunity to find the sun's refraction." He calculated it to be 26 degrees. "But I suppose the refraction is more or less according as the air is thick or clear, which I leave for better scholars to discuss," he adds modestly. "But this I thought good to note, for the better help of such as do profess this study."

It was an understatement, for measuring the sun's refraction was an extraordinarily advanced piece of scholarship. John Donne, who seems to have had such an affinity with Baffin, expressed the sense of triumph the pilot-astronomer must have felt:

> *Mysteries are like the Sun, dazzling, yet plain to all eyes....*
> *Man hath weav'd out a net, and this net throwne*
> *Upon the Heavens, and now they are his owne.*

Baffin had ample opportunity to study polar riddles on his next two expeditions. Sir Thomas Smith's optimistically titled syndicate—the Company of the Merchants of London, Discoverers of the Northwest Passage—wanted the pilot to make the company's name come literally true. In dogged pursuit of that lodestar, however, Baffin was to discover the truth of another Donne verse:

> *On a huge hill,*
> *Cragged and steep, Truth stands, and he that will*
> *Reach her, about must, and about must go.*

On his voyage of 1615, the merchants seemed bent on handicapping Baffin. He was equipped with a crew of just fourteen men and two boys. As if to compensate for the piffling size of his crew, the merchants promised a reward of triple wages if his mariners delivered the Passage.

His ship was Henry Hudson's ice-scarred old rattletrap, the *Discovery*. The fifty-five-ton veteran had already blunted her bluff bows in four failed attempts to reach fabled Cathay at the end of Hudson Strait. Robert Bylot, the silent mutineer who allegedly stole the gold ring off Henry Hudson's finger, had been pilot on three of those voyages. Now Bylot was to serve as Master on the *Discovery's* fresh ice assault.

Pilot Baffin, who refers to himself as "his mate and associate," passes no judgment on Bylot's shadowy past. He simply calls him "a man well experienced those ways, having been employed the three former voyages." Yet reading between the lines of Baffin's journal, one feels that the relationship between Master and Pilot was as tightly strained as the creaky oaken bark that Baffin wrestled down the Strait. Baffin gauges, for example, the movements of the arctic tides with his usual impeccable accuracy, only to be contradicted by his Master. We keep hearing the refrain, "although our Master was confident to the contrary" or "although Our Master was persuaded otherwise."

The squelching must have riled Baffin, for Bylot's inferior seamanship was demonstrated at virtually the beginning of the expedition. On May 17, while they were dodging the huge, mushroom-shaped bergs off Greenland's Cape Farewell, Baffin had to submit to poor guidance. Bylot advised him to steer across the almost solid ice pack of Davis Strait and then make a ridiculously early start at penetrating Hudson Strait.

"Our Master asked my opinion concerning the putting into the ice," remarks Baffin. "I could not much say against his opinion. . . . He knew the manner of this ice better than myself. So presently we resolved to put into the ice."

It was a dreadful crossing. The *Discovery* cleaved through sleety and squally gales, through clammy fogs and clinging snow, through "much ice lying in long drifts and ledges." By God's assistance, says Baffin, they managed to sight on May 27th the high hill of Resolution Island, the craggy parapet guarding entry to the riptides of Hudson Strait. "That night we moored our ship to a piece of ice, with much snow freezing on our shrouds and tackle."

From his past experience, one would have expected Bylot to realize it was far too soon in the season to bash through the ice-pestered Strait. Until July it was like a seething punch bowl, with the pans and the floes whirling around like giant chunks of ungrated nutmeg. But Bylot made the mistake of not waiting.

On June 2 we can almost hear Baffin gritting his teeth as he records their gropings along the north side of the Strait. "To write of our often mooring to ice," he says, "taking in of sails, and fast enclosing, would prove but tedious to the reader, as it was troublesome to us."

It was not all tedium. He cruised past the hilly, oddly shaped islands, which later navigators named "Saddleback" and "Virgin's Paps," and he enjoyed the discoverer's prerogative of handing out his own descriptive names. On his beautifully executed map, he painted a flag emblazoned with a red cross to denote each spot where he landed. His first landing in the Strait was at one of the many clusters of islets fringing the snow-peaked, windswept cliffs of south Baffin Island.

He named the cluster the Savage Isles. Evidently it was because he was greeted by about forty wolfish Eskimo dogs howling savagely in front of a deserted village of sealskin tents. There was certainly nothing savage about the Eskimos. After climbing to the top of a hill, Baffin hallooed at fourteen of them who were paddling a umiak about a musket-shot away.

"I called unto them (using some words of Greenlandish speech), making signs of friendship. They did the like to us. But seeing them to be fearful of us, and we not willing to trust them, I made another sign to them. I showed them a knife and other small things, which I left on the top of the hill, and returned down to their tents again."

There Baffin gained the distinction of becoming one of the first art critics and collectors of Eskimo carvings. In one tent he found a leather bag. It contained little images of Eskimo hunters and a figurine of a woman with a child at her back. He took possession of the sculpture. He left knives and beads and other baubles in payment.

Baffin then paid tribute to the design of some Canadian Eskimo artifacts he found. He praised their bone-shod sleighs and their dog collars. These furnishings he ranked "very fitting." But the connoisseur felt some of their other creations weren't quite up to scratch. They couldn't compare with what he had seen handicrafted in Greenland.

"They are not so neat and artificial, seeming to be more rude and uncivil," he wrote with esthetic disapproval.

(Ironically, at the end of the Strait, Baffin was to pass by the present site of Baffin Island's Cape Dorset. This is the Eskimo settlement whose exquisite Eskimo prints and handicrafts have today made Baffin's namesake island world-famous.)

The pilot-astronomer was on safer grounds at his next landing. Stinging winds and pounding ice cakes forced him to anchor on a jutting Baffin Island cape. He named it "Point Fair Ness," because the foul weather suddenly turned fair, though the ice did not. "We were so fast closed up with ice that we couldn't well dip a pail of water." While ice-locked eight days, the crew played football.

"Seeing I have begun to speak of exercise, I think it not amiss to relate one day's exercise of my own," the dedicated scientist writes with endearing coyness. "The weather being fair, upon the 21st day of June I saw both the sun and moon very clear. Then, thinking it a fit time to be doing something to employ myself upon, I fitted my instruments to take both the almicanter and azimuth of the sun, and also of the moon."

Baffin thus became the first navigator to calculate his longitude at sea by taking a complete lunar observation. It was a superlative feat of nautical astronomy. It moved Sir Clements Markham, the British Admiralty historian, to laud him in 1921 as "undoubtedly a genius." It awed Sir William Edward Parry, the English explorer, who anchored at the same Point Fair Ness in 1821. Despite crude instruments, the lack of a yet-to-be invented sextant, and chancy observations made on a plunging deck, Baffin's longitude reckoning of 74 degrees, 30 minutes, Parry reported, was "not a degree to the westward of the truth." Out of respect for "this able and indefatigable" trailblazer in Arctic astronomy, Parry named Arctic Canada's biggest island "Baffin Island."

The trailblazer clawed his way to the northerly end of the Strait, and off the southwest corner of Baffin Island, he was almost crushed to death on a rocky little island aptly named by himself. On July 1st, 1615, Baffin titled it "Mill Island." "By reason of the great extremity and grinding of the ice," said the explorer, "as this night we had proof thereof."

That night Baffin felt the *Discovery's* shuddering deck timbers screech in agony under the crunch of whirlpool and icepack. Fangs of ice, he says, "came driving from the southeast floodtide with such swiftness that the ice overwent our ship.... But God, which is still stronger than either rocks, ice, eddy, or stream, preserved us."

This narrow escape, accompanied by the shattering of several ship timbers, merely hardened Baffin's mulish resolve. It also led to a near showdown with Bylot. By mid-July, the *Discovery* had punched her northerly way through snarling winds and thickening ice up the northeast coast of Southampton Island as far as Frozen Strait. Named after the third Earl of Southampton, the sprawling island might be likened to a double-headed cork. It partly plugs up the neck of juglike Hudson Bay to the south and the entrance of Foxe Basin to the north. Names were awarded to two points on the cork, with Baffin planting his

FALL OF AN ICEBERG.

On his historic expedition in 1616, Baffin dodged around Baffin Bay's most treacherous deathtrap. It was later officially named Melville Bay and known to whalers as Bergy Hole, because it was a spawning ground of wicked icebergs. Baffin probed up to 78 degrees north latitude—a record high northing in those ice-strewn waters unequalled until the 19th century.

red-cross landing flag at each spot. One was named "Cape Comfort" (because it offered comforting hope of the Northwest Passage). The other Baffin named "Seahorse Point" (because of the aggressive walruses lurking there).

On July 17, Baffin was so eager to pursue exploration that the usually cool-headed navigator seems to have virtually lost his temper with the dilatory Bylot. Off Seahorse Point, reports Baffin, "Our Master asked our opinion whether it were better for us to seek out some harbour hereabout to see if we could kill any of those seahorses we saw."

"My answer," Baffin snapped back, "was that, seeing we are bound for discovery, it would not be our best way to spend any time in search of these seahorses. . . . If we should kill some few of them, they would not be worth the time we should spend."

Bylot accepted the sharp rebuke meekly, as though Baffin were the captain and he himself the ship chauffeur.

"When I had spoke," says Baffin, "our Master said he was also of that mind."

When they arrived back in England seven weeks later, having been checkmated by the "foul and dirty ice" of Frozen Strait, there was no doubt who was boss. It was Baffin who supplied the merchant backers with the best-mapped survey thus far of the tides and geographic features of both Hudson Strait and the waters north of Hudson Bay leading to Foxe Basin. And it was Baffin who was accepted as spokesman of the expedition. His report realistically cast doubt on the feasibility of a northwest passage via the Hudson Strait route unless it were "some creek or inlet." Instead he urged his patrons to let him take a stab at searching those seeming open, blue waters north of Davis Strait which had so intrigued his idol, Captain John Davis.

The merchants took him up on the challenge. And so, on March 26, 1616, with seventeen men aboard her, the cranky old bucket *Discovery* rattled out of the port of Gravesend on her most momentous adventure of discovery.

Though Bylot was listed as nominal Master, we hear no more of him giving orders in Pilot Baffin's chronicle. "We live in an age the poets term an iron age," Baffin jotted down. And on this expedition his determination to bring back conclusive evidence of a possible Cathay passage was iron-tough.

As his ship bowled along through hissing spray up the west coast of Greenland, he had little time to socialize with the Eskimos, unless it was absolutely necessary. He passed by villagers who stood on rocks "wondering and gazing at us" and he paused briefly on May 14 to hand out gift pieces of iron to six salmon-fishing kayakers. "Supposing we had intended to come to anchor, they were very joyful," Baffin says. "But when they saw us stand off from shore, they followed us a while. Then they went away, discontented to our seeming."

On the last day of May he spotted Sanderson's Hope. This was the shining granite beacon near modern Upernavik marking the most northerly point reached by Davis. There Davis Strait broadens out into the vast blue body of water, some eight hundred miles long and three hundred miles wide, that now bears the name of Baffin Bay.

Under a dazzling disc of a sun Baffin pushed north that evening into the unknown. He doubtlessly did his own gazing and wondering at what a later explorer, the American Elisha Kent Kane, described as gorgeously gleaming bergy bits of ice, "one great resplendency of gemwork, blazing carbuncles, and rubies and molten gold." Baffin was a bit more restrained. "Much ice," he refers to the bergy bits. They pestered him and stalled him in the Upernavik Islands. Baffin named one cluster the "Women's Islands" because there he spent a pleasant interlude with female companions: two tattooed old women, two young maidens, and a mother with her child at her back.

They were hitchhikers, so to speak, hoping for a lift to another island to meet their menfolk. Baffin obliged them. He gave them necklaces and nails, accepted their gifts of seal blubber, and invited them to hop aboard.

"The poor women were very diligent to carry the blubber to the waterside to put into our casks," he observes sympathetically. "And when they were aboard, they much wondered to see our ship and furniture. We gave them of our meat, which they tasting, would not eat." He could not understand their distaste; for when he dropped them off at their village, he remarked in his notebook: "The inhabitants are very poor, living chiefly on the flesh of seals, dried, which they eat raw."

By June 10, Baffin was more concerned about his own survival. Nosing the *Discovery* westward, he smacked into the massive middle icepack of Baffin Bay. Bergy bits may be as big as a raft. But the middle icepack is like a floating continent. Driven by wind and tide, its glacial jumble jams the Bay, almost reaching right across from Greenland to Baffin Island. Once entangled in its tentacles, said Elisha Kent Kane, a navigator must wriggle backward and forward, "like a China fish seeking an outlet from a glass jar." Venturesome whalers later tried to squirm through its network of channels. If they were wise, they cautiously skirted around the middle pack's outer fringes, hoping they could "sneak by the ice when it wasn't looking."

Baffin took the latter course of hugging the northwest coastline of Greenland. Occasionally he attempted a westward dash through an opening in the middle pack. "But this attempt was soon quailed," he says. "For the more ice we went through, the thicker it was, till we could see no place to put in the ship's head."

He kept retreating back to the shoreline and threading north. Onward he sailed past marvelous sights. Past Horn Sound, which he so named because of the bounty of narwhal and walrus tusks he obtained from bartering Eskimos. Past schools of flopping whales and blizzards of screaming auks. Past grotesque porphyry spires, looming through the mists, and later to be named the "Crimson Cliffs" and the "Horse's Head" and the "Devil's Thumb."

On Midsummer Day, with "our shrouds, ropes and sails so frozen we could scarce handle them," he dodged around Baffin Bay's most treacherous death trap. This was Melville Bay, named two centuries later after the First Lord of the British Admiralty. "Bergy Hole," whalers named it more trenchantly, because it was a cesspool of wicked bergs.

By the fourth of July, Baffin had worked his way to Thule, the Greenland fjord where a United States military base now stands. Baffin named it "Sir John Wolstenholme Sound" after one of his backers. The ice-free sea in the area, known to whalers as the "North Water," was a heart-lifting sight. "It revived our hope of a Passage," wrote Baffin.

His hopes were soon dashed. A violent storm raged. It ripped off the *Discovery's* foresail. It blew away her anchor and cable. And, in John Donne's phrase, "as the winds blew, waves like a rowling trench before them threw."

Yet northward the little *Discovery* stumbled on, lurching and heaving in a green-gray sea, her slanting deck candied with ice, her canvas frozen stiff as vellum. At last, on July 5, 1616, Baffin reached the very portal to the North Pole. He sighted two soaring cliff headlands, Cape Isabella and Cape Alexander, which like twin thrusting sword blades guard entry into what he proudly named "Sir Thomas Smith's Sound."

Not until 1853 was this record highwater mark in that longitude bettered by Elisha Kent Kane. "They have been until now the Arctic Pillars of Hercules," Kane wrote reverently, as his American naval ship *Advance* sailed past the twin sentinel capes, towering fifteen hundred feet high into a yellow sky. "They look down on us as if they challenged our right to pass."

Baffin couldn't penetrate much beyond the two pillars, because the alleyway was blocked by "a great bank of ice." Nevertheless, the scientist was thrilled to sail so close to the ever-shifting north magnetic pole (in recent years located at roughly 75 degrees north latitude). Baffin recorded that his newly discovered sound, which "runneth to the north of 78 degrees, is admirable in one respect, because in it is the greatest variation of the compass of any part of the world known."

Baffin was soon thwarted again. Poking southwestward, he reached what seemed to be a wide, ice-locked harbor immediately north of the purplish Iron Mountains of Baffin Island. Little did he know that he was so heartbreakingly close to the magical gateway that opened into the Northwest Passage. On July 12, 1616, he named it after another patron, "Sir James Lancaster's Sound." "Here our hope of passage began to be less," wrote Baffin, "for from this Sound to the southward we had a ledge of ice between the shore and us. . . ."

Apart from the pestering ice, he was worried because his cook had died and his scurvy-sick crew members were so weak they could hardly pull a rope. A loving compassion for his shipmates, he felt, must override "our great desire to perform the discovery." So, in a valiant display of both comradeship and icemanship, the great heart abandoned further exploration and crossed Baffin Bay again, masterfully maneuvering around the ragged edges of the middle ice pack in a deathlock struggle "to get some refreshing for our men."

He made it to Sukkertoppen, the sugar-loaf oasis of southwest Greenland, where, green as grass, he had started recording the first of his polar voyages four years ago. There he now prepared scurvy grass boiled in beer for his sailors, and he fed them salads of fresh green sorrel as well. "And with the blessing of God, all our men within eight or nine days' space were in perfect health, and so continued till our arrival in England."

His report to his mercantile backers was far from rosy. "In a word," he declared with spearlike directness, "there is no passage nor hope of passage north of Davis Strait." He didn't blame Captain John Davis; for immediately north of Sanderson's Hope, "the sea is open, and of an unsearchable depth, and of a good colour. . . . Yet we having coasted all, or near all the circumference thereof, found it to be no other than a great bay."

Still he wasn't discouraged. He consoled the merchants with news of the untapped whale and narwhal riches to be harvested in his bay. As for himself, he felt that "time hath not been spent in vain. . . . And I dare boldly say (without boasting) that more good discovery hath not in shorter time been done since the action was attempted."

As with John Davis, the discovery dream engrossed Baffin to the end. He told the English East India Company that he was determined to get seafaring employment and "search the Passage from Japan, by the coast of Asia, any way he could." His Cathay obsession, and his wanderlust, are evoked in several of John Donne's lines:

Dreamer, thou art,
Think'st thou fantastique that thou hast a part
In the East Indian fleet, because thou hast
A little spice or amber in thy taste?
Because thou art not frozen, art thou warme?
If thou beest borne to strange sights,
Things invisible to see,
Ride ten thousand days and nights,
Till age snow white hairs on thee
To live in one land is captivitie.

And so for the next six years, aboard an English East Indiaman in the spice trade, Baffin piloted fleets to the sunlit waters of India and Arabia, Africa and Persia. In 1619, after he had served as master's mate aboard the *Anne Royal* on a surveying expedition, we hear of him being granted "a gratuity for his pains and good art in drawing out certain plots of the coast of Persia and the Red Sea."

On his last voyage he served as Master of the *London* in a fleet of five East India ships assigned to attack the Portuguese-held fort of Ormuz in the Persian Gulf. There the pilot-astronomer met his death gazing at the sun with his beloved scientific instruments in his hand. On January 23rd, 1622, he went ashore to observe the height and distance of the castle wall. "As he was trying his mathematical projects and conclusions," we are told, "he received a shot from the castle into his belly. Wherewith he gave three leaps and died immediately."

In his sonnet, *The Will*, John Donne bequeathed him a fitting epitaph:

My constancie I to the planets give

Baffin had need of that poetic legacy. For the rest of his money-grubbing contemporaries treated his memory most shabbily.

Following Baffin's death, we learn for the first time that the explorer had left a widow behind. Mrs. Baffin, it seems, had the gall to demand the eight hundred pounds which the East India Company owed to her late husband for his outstanding services. The stingy merchants squabbled over payment of that money for three years. The dispute landed in the courts, with arbitrators being called in to help settle the impasse. In January, 1628, the "troublesome, impatient woman" was finally awarded five hundred pounds; and in closing the books the Company added the gratuitous slur that the pilot's widow, now apparently deaf, old and remarried "had made an unequal choice of a man not the best governed."

More mean and miserly was the mercantile sycophant who compiled explorers' journals, the Reverend Samuel Purchas. Not only did the dunderhead suffer from a frosty superciliousness which looked down upon the mute and unlearned Baffin; the theoretical arctic geographer was afflicted as well with mental snowblindness and a freezing of the purse strings. In his four-volume anthology of 1625, *Purchas His Pilgrims*, the parson did not see fit to include Baffin's detailed maps and tabulated logs of his journeys. In the eyes of Purchas, they were "somewhat troublesome and too costly to insert." Instead the bungler published only a very abbreviated version of Baffin's last, and most significant, Arctic findings. As a result of this mischief, Baffin was discredited; for the next two centuries his newly discovered bay and its offshoot sounds were thought to be a hoax.

Baffin's cometlike feats were clouded over as late as 1812. That year a London atlas was published entitled *The Possibility of Approaching the North Pole*. It bore a circumpolar map inscribed with a dotted line and the doubting legend: "Baffin's Bay, according to the relation of W. Baffin in 1616, but not now believed."

In 1818, Sir John Barrow, the Second Secretary of the British Admiralty, was more insulting than that. In his *Chronological History of Voyages into the Arctic Regions*, Barrow's map left a space entirely blank north of Davis Strait. Moreover, the eminent Arctic authority slandered Baffin's character posthumously. The pilot-astronomer, whose reports had always been lucid and exact models of scientific precision, was now denigrated. According to Barrow, he was a "slovenly, vague, indefinite and unsatisfactory" stargazer who saw mirages under the midnight sun. "Indeed, from the multitude of whales, which he describes to choke up those Sounds," Barrow mocked acidly, "they were perhaps nothing more than openings between huge icebergs."

Happily, in that same year of 1818, Sir John Ross, on a voyage of exploration for the British Admiralty, rediscovered Baffin Bay. And he authenticated the "remarkable accuracy" of all that Baffin had observed—including the latitude of the sounds and the multitude of whales that choked them. Ross felt it was shocking that Baffin had been robbed of fame during his lifetime, had his discoveries expunged from maps, and his epochal bay "treated as a phantom of the imagination." Ross said he derived sweet "pleasure from the reflection that I have placed in a fair light before the public the merits of a worthy and able Navigator." In the sometimes sour annals of Arctic exploration it was a generous redeeming of an undeservedly tarnished reputation.

In his commentary on Baffin's voyages Parson Purchas had written: "Poets are not always the best oracles." He was wrong, in this case, just as he was wrong in his evaluation of the "learned-unlearned mariner and mathematician." In the end John Donne had proved to be the best of contemporary oracles. It took a poet to discern that among pale satellites an ardent amateur scientist could shine like a shooting star. And it took a Renaissance poet to sum up for posterity the illuminating qualities of the prince of Arctic pilot-astronomers:

> *The passage of the West or East would thaw,*
> *And open wide their easie liquid jawe*
> *To all our ships, could a Promethean art*
> *Either unto the Northerne Pole impart*
> *The fire of these inflaming eyes, or of this*
> *loving heart.*

Chapter 9

The Foxe-James
Yacht Race to Cathay

There were gentlemen and there were seamen in the navy of King Charles. But the seamen were not gentlemen, and the gentlemen were not seamen.

MACAULAY'S HISTORY OF ENGLAND

I t was the first week of May in 1631, and like greyhounds straining at the leash, two graceful, square-rigged, yachtlike oaken barks prepared to lunge out from two different English seaports. They were embarking on the craziest competition in the annals of Arctic exploration.

Both ships were equally matched, each roughly seventy tons. Each was manned by a crew of twenty-two, greenhorns all in polar seafaring. Each proudly bore a regal name. One was the *Charles* named after England's reigning monarch soon to be beheaded by the Puritans, King Charles I; the other *Henrietta Maria*, after his Queen. Each carried an identical letter from the crown addressed to the Emperor of Japan, on the grandiose assumption that the long-dead Kublai Khan could read English. And each mail carrier hoped to be first to deliver the royal message via that unknown postal route, the Northwest Passage.

The great race to Cathay was on, and the prize sought was a veritable Grail. For the rival seaports of London and Bristol it was the trade monopoly in silks and spices and orient gems. For the competing captains in command it was glory and immortality and the sheer adventure of winning the sporting event of the century.

No two yachtsmen could be more unlike than Thomas James,

captain of the Bristolian merchants' *Henrietta Maria*, and Luke (North-West) Foxe, skipper of the London-backed *Charles*. They were as dissimilar as Don Quixote and Sancho Panza. In the wonderful way that life imitates art, they were virtual caricatures of the two chivalric travelers that sprang from the imagination of the seventeenth-century satirist, Miguel de Cervantes. In a sense, too, they symbolized dramatically the conflict then arising in the Royal Navy between the "gentleman" and the "tarpaulin" schools of sea captains.

But they were, of course, neither caricatures nor symbols. They were complex individuals, each with his complementary warts and virtues.

Thomas James was a wealthy, high-minded, puritanical Welshman, a barrister-at-law of the Inner Temple related to the mayor of Bristol. His portrait appears on the vague map he drew of Hudson Bay (which he explored concurrently with Foxe) and of its southerly James Bay (where James spent an excruciating winter). The portrait reveals a forty-year-old bachelor in a fussily embroidered court collar. James has a pointed beard and moustache, thinning long hair carefully combed over a high forehead, and rather dreamy, widely spaced eyes. His features seem indecisive, and so is the motto beneath his picture. It reads: "Some has a time." We don't know if it suggests he has plenty of leisure time, or whether it means he was biding his time for expected fame.

During the time we come to know him, he emerges as a bookish and ascetic idealist, ready to compose a poem or to pray in the midst of the most harrowing experience. He was a dilettante sailor, woefully accident-prone, although he was equipped with such expensive instruments as a quadrant made of pear wood and was said to be well schooled in the science of navigational mathematics. He appears to have been a gentle and self-effacing courtier, modest to a fault about "my unworthy self." Yet, contradictorily, his contemporaries said he was a good raconteur; and later on, when he was hired by the British Admiralty to chase channel pirates, the ungentle commander of the *Ninth Whelp of the Lion* was commended for his daring attack which had "lately crushed a small pirate in the egge."

Behind his polish, James may have had a snobbish streak in him. After the race, Foxe gibed at his opponent for being a "Gentleman of quality" who hadn't done "as much as I, being a man of meaner Rank in his conceit; and I have heard since that his ambition hath abused my worth and name." But this accusation smacks of a rival's spleen. James, of course, was too gentlemanly to reply. He had a reputation to maintain

"Some has a time" was the motto of Captain Thomas James, who competed with Captain Luke Foxe in the race to Cathay via Hudson Bay. They were the odd couple of exploration: James the bookish Don Quixote and Foxe the earthy Sancho Panza.

"of being a very civil man in his conversation." He was also totally humorless; utterly romantic; yet endearingly naive; and was evidently loved by all his men. In the mawkish tradition of his day, court poetry was written on his return lauding him for his piety and heralding him as a "Heroicke Soule."

One pictures James, in short, as Don Quixote tilting at icicled windmills with a book of verse in one hand and the Bible in the other.

North-West Foxe, as he nicknamed himself, was a different stamp of man. He was an earthy, pragmatic, hardheaded Yorkshireman, a self-educated salt from Kingston-upon-Hull. Regrettably no portrait accompanies the beautifully detailed map he drew delineating his cruise around Hudson Bay and places north of the Bay that now bear his name: Foxe Channel, Foxe Basin, and Foxe Peninsula on the west coast of Baffin Island. Instead of a self-portrait Foxe drew on his map a quaint sketch of his punning emblem: a fox racing off with a stolen goose. However, we do know that he was forty-five at the time of the Cathay race. He was still deeply in love with his wife, Anne, whom he had married eighteen years before. And from his journal one imagines him to be a bearded channel pilot with a rolling gait out of Gilbert and Sullivan's *Pirates of Penzance* and a tanned, nutcracker face well toughened from his former travels to the Mediterranean and Baltic Seas.

He was a proud man full of *panache*. He was proud of being the son of a master mariner. He was proud of being bred with the salt tang of the sea in his nostrils. He was proud of having acquired his nautical skill and his scientific tutelage the hard way, like the self-made pilot-astronomer he most admired, explorer William Baffin. He disdained the lofty humility of Captain James, who claimed to have undertaken the Northwest Passage exploration only because his courtier friends had so importuned him. Foxe confessed unblushingly "I had been itching after it" since he had been a beardless younker of twenty.

No doubt Foxe could be bumptious and cross-grained and arrogant. No doubt he often tongue-lashed his men. Yet his bark was worse than his bite; he sometimes displayed an unexpected sensitivity hidden underneath his grumpy façade; and he was endowed with a ribald vulgarian humor that was refreshingly free of the posing assumed by other Arctic explorers. In a characteristic pungent simile, he could urge his crew to race the *Charles* through a path in melting ice floes like "the mackerel men at London, who must hasten to market before the fish stink."

Foxe was, in short, Sancho Panza with both feet firmly planted on deck and determined to steer his mulish ship right over the North Pole if need be, come hell or high water.

Apart from their tenacity and bravery, which they shared equally, the two explorers had one other thing in common. Both Northwest Passage racers were destined to be blackmarked by the doyen of arctic scorekeepers, Sir John Barrow.

Two centuries later, in his *Chronological History of Voyages into the Arctic Regions,* the Second Secretary of the British Admiralty was scathing in his sarcasm. Barrow inveighed against James for being a navigational fumbler of the most inept sort. Furthermore, sneered the eminent Arctic authority, James's journal was a litany of "lamentation and weeping and great mourning; it is one continued strain of difficulties and dangers and complainings."

This was manifestly unfair. To be sure, James may have been an unlucky and absent-minded amateur yachtsman. But the book he wrote, *The Strange and Dangerous Voyage of Captain Thomas James,* cannot be dismissed as a whining Job's diary. It has remained one of the classics of Arctic literature, a best-seller that went through numerous editions well on into the nineteenth century.

What Barrow overlooked was that James was an accomplished storyteller. Naturally, he exaggerated; after all, he was a lawyer by profession. In recounting his many hairbreadth escapes from the very "jaws of death" he piled horror upon horror, like a barrister presenting his case before a jury. He was never merely buffeted by ice. In the tradition of all great talespinners he took poetic licence and was "much tormented, pestered and beaten with the ice, many pieces being higher than our top masthead." And the polar wind never just blew. It was personified as "Satan's malice"; it lacerated the *Henrietta Maria* with "his old anger and fury, tearing violence and uttermost malice."

Moreover, Barrow neglected to consider that James was a Welshman; he had the Welsh flair for musical rhetoric. When James strums his dirge of woes, he is the true Welsh minstrel or bard, and his lyrical prose almost scans like poetry. He begins his narrative:

"Many a storm, and rock, and mist, and wind, and tide, and sea, and mount of ice, have I, in this discovery encountered; many a despair and death had almost overwhelmed me."

No wonder his fellow poet, Samuel Taylor Coleridge, was thrilled when studying James's journal in the Bristol library more than a century later. In *The Road to Xanadu,* the modern literary critic, John Livingston Lowes, has shown how the exploits of Captain James inspired some of the finest lines in Coleridge's *Rime of the Ancient Mariner.*

Barrow was likewise unjustly nasty in his attack upon Foxe. The British Admiralty historian conceded that Foxe was " a keen, shrewd Yorkshireman, and evidently a man of considerable talent. . . ." Then came the sting in the tail: "But he was conceited beyond measure; and the style of his journal is so uncouth and the jargon so obscure and comical, as in many places to be scarcely intelligible."

If Foxe appeared conceited, it was humanly understandable. It was the veneer of a self-educated man. He was supremely confident of his seamanship. Yet he was on the defensive when competing with a master in the uncharted seas of belles-lettres. Foxe admits as much in an apologia to his book, *North-West Foxe.* He begged readers to pass over the deformities of his narrative; he acknowledged it was as roughhewn as shipwright's timber. His excuse was that he was no "aery or aetherial" scholar—taking a facetious dig at the effete James. Nor could he afford to hire a ghostwriter to add literary touches to his language of the sea.

"Whereupon, not knowing otherwise how to proceed," he says, "I was enforced, with such Tackling, Cordage and Raftage as I had, to Rigge and Tackle this ship myself. I hope she will sail the better in this Trimme if you be pleased to conduct her."

Yet he had no need to apologize. *North-West Foxe* stands out as an unpolished gem among polar diaries. For all its knotty grammar and homely puns, the prose is alive and kicking on every page. And when making hard-won observations about the sea, Foxe has a flavorsome tang that excels the super-refined James's style.

"To keep a warm cabin and lie in sheets is the most ignoble part of a seaman," writes Foxe. "But to endure and suffer a hard cabin, cold and salt meat, broken sleeps, mouldy bread, dead beer, wet clothes, want of fire. . . . So doth Experience show Art how to see without spectacles."

Foxe merits credit, too, for being a pioneer Arctic historian. He gleaned from seamen still living and from Hakluyt's reports every scrap of information available about some fifteen Cathay expeditions that had attempted what Foxe called "the Search." His research led him to hope that the Northwest Passage must lie in one of those "creeks or inlets" that William Baffin had not touched in the pilot-astronomer's Hudson Bay survey of 1615.

Specifically Foxe hoped to find the magical pathway somewhere near the mouth of the modern Churchill River on the western rim of Hudson Bay. It seemed an odd choice, for two previous explorers had gone through terrible privations while wintering in that region. Yet, such are the delusions of the obsessed, each trailblazer felt that he had

Sir Thomas Button, British precursor to Foxe and James, was the first to delineate the western shoreline of Hudson Bay. In 1612, he was also the first European to set foot on the modern Canadian province of Manitoba and to stick his neck into the rocky entrance of Port Churchill, which was mistakenly thought to be the gateway to Cathay. Button nosed as far north as 65 degrees latitude, which he named Button's "Ne Ultra"—Latin for "Go No Farther." Foxe delighted in renaming it "Ut Ultra" (meaning "Go Farther") and, indeed, poked up as far north as 66 degrees, 47 minutes latitude into Foxe Basin.

stumbled upon the very threshhold of discovery. All that was required was one more step into the unknown.

One was a British admiral, retired penniless with his seven children and his debts to obscurity in Cardiff. Foxe took the trouble of interviewing him personally and thus resurrected his genuine achievements from history's oblivion. He was Sir Thomas Button, a valiant Welshman. His portrait reveals him resplendent in a white silk sash tied around his chest gorget of metal; he is clutching what appears to be a pistol in one hand and the polar region of the globe in the other.

Button warrants recognition for having discovered in 1612 most of the western shoreline of Hudson Bay just as Henry Hudson in 1610-1611 had discovered its eastern coast. The first European to set foot on the modern province of Manitoba, Button wintered at what is now Port Nelson; he named it after his sailing master of the *Discovery*, Francis Nelson, who died there. Button buried five other sailors slain in a fight with Eskimos after his crew had stupidly killed with a musket shot an Eskimo kayaker at Digges Island at the entrance to Hudson Bay. Button himself almost perished, and many of his scurvy-racked crew did die wretchedly that winter at the estuary of the Nelson River.

"God a mercy," Button told Foxe, "I had not above eight sound men."

But Button continued exploring. He was the first to stick his neck into the rocky entrance to Canada's present grain shipping port of Churchill. (Button named it "Hubart's Hope" after his Hull pilot, Josias Hubart.) Button persisted in probing some six hundred miles along the western coast of Hudson Bay until he reached as far north as 65 degrees latitude. There, just west of the Bay's top cork of Southampton Island, he was frustrated by an icelocked inlet named by Button *Ne Ultra*. (This was Latin for "Go no farther" which Luke Foxe was to rename *Ut Ultra*, meaning "Go farther.")

Button returned to England with his crew diminished and his second ship *Resolution* abandoned in the bleak wastes of the Bay. Yet despite "unknown coasts, hideous storms, and dark and long continued mists," the Welshman urged Foxe to follow in his footsteps. "I do confidently believe there to be a passage," said Button, demented with his dream, "as I do there is one between Calais and Dover or between Holy Head and Ireland."

Obsessed with the same mania was a second admiral-to-be, this one a gallant Dane named Jens Munk. In an epic 1619 wintering at Port Churchill (Munk named it "Devil's Cape of Nova Dania"), the forty-year-old Danish explorer agonized as scurvy slashed like a scythe through his crew of sixty-five men.

He saw his sailors die "with great pains in the loins, as if a thousand knives were thrust through them." He smelled the sickly stench of festering corpses, and he was too weak to drag their bodies overboard, "and I was like a wild and lonely bird." He wrote out his will, "because I was myself then quite miserable and abandoned by all the world"; and he requested "If any Christian men should happen to come here, that they will bury in the earth my poor body, together with the others which are found here."

By sucking the roots of greenery, Munk and two shipmates somehow managed to survive. Yet when the trio limped home to Copenhagen a year later aboard the bedraggled *Lamprey*, Jens Munk, like Button, continued to harbor his dream. That was to come back to the Bay and seek the Passage again beyond the beckoning mouth of the Churchill River.

After these failures, the prospect of whipping up enthusiasm for another Cathay attempt seemed slim. Luckily Foxe had rooting for him that distinguished cheerleader, Henry Briggs. A fellow Yorkshireman, Professor Briggs was the innovator of logarithms who gave instruction in astronomy at Oxford University; he also taught navigational mathematics to unlettered pilots like Foxe at Gresham College in London. He was the same Northwest Passage advocate who had offered encouragement to William Baffin. Though on his deathbed, the good professor pulled strings for Foxe. He gained the financial backing of London merchants, headed by Sir John Wolstenholme; he won the patronage of the court through his connections with King Charles's ambassador, Sir Thomas Roe.

The merchants of Bristol got wind of the London enterprise, and immediately sought similar court sanction for their expedition to be undertaken by Thomas James. His Majesty granted private audiences to both captains, and he handed each contestant the identical letter to be delivered to the Great Khan of Cathay. But this by no means diminished the growing spirit of rivalry.

Apparently James was miffed because the King had loaned Foxe the use of the British Admiralty's cast-off *Charles*. "Best ship in the world," Foxe gloated publicly. Though she actually proved to be a rotting, unseaworthy craft, ready to be scrapped in the Navy's boneyard, James took umbrage that *he* hadn't received a royal yacht. He rather haughtily asked that both expeditions be combined; and, evidently

Danish explorer Jens Munk spent a ghastly winter in Port Churchill, indicated by this woodcut which illustrated the account of his 1619 voyage into Hudson Bay. Scurvy wracked his crew of 65 men and he watched them die "with great pains in the loins, as if a thousand knives were thrust through them." Sole survivors were Munk, an old man and a boy. The Dane was received shabbily on returning to Copenhagen. Denmark's "Sailor King", Christian IV, imprisoned him for leaving a ship behind. Munk's wife had been unfaithful during his absence and divorced him. The obsessed Munk yearned to return to the Bay.

because of his higher social status, James ought to be named supreme admiral.

"That he might go in the higher place," Foxe riposted with rare understatement, "was denied."

James retaliated that the Bristolians had allowed him to choose personally a "well-conditioned, strong ship" beyond compare. She had been victualled by a baker, brewer and butcher who "truly proved themselves Masters in their Arts." And he had stocked the *Henrietta Maria* with a chest full of the "best and choicest mathematical books that could be got for money in England."

Tongue in cheek, Foxe replied that he didn't know whether his baker, brewer and butcher were hoity-toity artists. All he knew was that he'd been provisioned for eighteen months with excellent fat beef, strong beer, admirable sack wine and aqua vitae brandy, good wheaten bread with butter and cheese, and the best potions and purging pills. As for navigational literature, he wouldn't have the leisure time for reading, preferring not to be like the Dutch skipper forced to run to his chest full of books to learn how to steer his wagoner of the sea.

When it came to selecting their complement of twenty men and two cabin boys each, neither could claim superiority. James made a curious admission. "I utterly refused," he said, sailors experienced in "northerly icy seas for some private reasons unnecessary here to relate. Keeping thus the power in my own hands, I had all the men to acknowledge immediate dependence upon myself alone." Critics have suggested, perhaps unfairly, that he took this foolish tack because the thin-skinned amateur didn't want to betray his lack of icemanship before his crew.

Foxe was more practical. He intentionally tried to recruit mariners who had weathered "those frost-biting voyages," so that "by their counsel I might better have shunned the ice." But he was disappointed when unable to sign on a single veteran of northern expeditions. Instead his backers high-handedly picked his crew for him. They added to his hardship by saddling him with an inefficient shipmaster and master's mate, evidently a pair of indolent, boozing smart alecks from the East India Company. Foxe's running feud with these two discordant officers supplied, as we shall see, a kind of semi-comic obligato that kept disrupting his otherwise relatively harmonious voyage.

From the very beginning of the race we catch an entertaining glimpse of the personalities and skills of the rival captains. James seemed to have a gloomy outlook from the outset. He cast off from Bristol on the breezy afternoon of May 3, 1631, after his crew had kneeled in prayer and had been exhorted by a preacher into the ways of brotherly love. But no sooner had the *Henrietta Maria* slipped down between the high banks of the Severn Channel that evening when the breeze changed to a high wind whistling fretfully through her rigging. "The wind opposed itself so strongly against us," James lamented, "that we were driven to bear up and come to an anchor at Lundie Rode, where we remained until May 8th in the morning."

The first lap of the race was to Greenland's Cape Farewell; and by the time James reached it a month later, cutting through wallowing green-gray troughs and blustery storms and "thick, foul weather," catastrophes began to pile up on him. Shards of ice crushed his shallop to shreds. His men labored day and night to stave off the slamming bergs, but their poles all snapped like carrot tops.

On a gale-lashed June 6, amid "a stinking fog and the sea very black," James sounds his lugubrious incantation: "All this day we did beat and were beaten fearfully amongst the ice.... We were enclosed amongst great pieces as high as our poop, and some of the sharp, blue corners of them did reach quite under us. . . ."

Foxe, on the contrary, sounds as exhilarated as if he was going on a gala jaunt in a regatta. "I set sail from Deptford on the Thames," he records exuberantly on May 5, "and coming by Greenwich, where then the Court lay, I discharged my ordnance twice, being seven cannon in number."

After this salute to her regal namesake, the *Charles* skimmed through hissing spume with delightful ease, the wind humming her gentle song in the rigging. Off Scotland, to be sure, Foxe privately curses his patrons for supplying him with a decrepit ship; for "I broke my mainyard in the midst, it being half rotten before." But apart from this slight mishap, he rejoiced in weather that was hot and winds that were fair and the sight of whales lolling in a quiet sea.

On June 3, as he neared Greenland, he was a bit taken aback: "This fulsome ugly morning presented the foulest child that the whole voyage brought forth, with such variety and changes of the elements, air and water, as if all had conspired to make our destiny fatal."

But six days later he is chronicling cheerfully: "Fair weather; the sea so smooth as if it had made ready to have been bowled upon."

Instead of trembling at the bergs off Cape Farewell, he admires their splendor: "In the evening we espied an island of floating ice, like unto a church, with a steeple upon the one end, and as high as our main topmast head."

And in a reversal of roles, Foxe takes to poetry when he sees a school of black, globe-headed pilot whales playing follow-the-leader and skipping in the frothy wake of his ship. The grampusses, as he calls them, remind Foxe of a scene out of *Britannia's Pastorals* written by William Browne; the poem is about the mythical sea nymph goddess, Thetis, mother of Achilles. Foxe sentimentally quotes the passage: "The Tritons wafted Thetis along the British shores." Then he adds in his diary: "So well in this sea those fishes followed their leader."

Unfortunately these idyllic fantasies were rudely interrupted. Captain Foxe had the first of his leadership squabbles with his pusillanimous officers. The master's mate, whom Foxe names either Yourin, Hurin or Urin, was evidently a grumbling, lazy, "saucy growler"; the sailing master, whom Foxe doesn't even deign to name, warranted a more vituperative description. "I do hold him the most arrogant bullkase that ever went or came as Master this way, and the most faint-heartedest man," Foxe confides to his private log. "His very men, to the Cook, take notice thereof and laugh. Three or four things he is good for: To make us believe he doth take a great deal of pains in calculation. Eating and sleeping is the other."

In their initial hot argument, Foxe wanted to steer more northerly. But the "ambitious Master" countermanded his order and took a northwesterly course. "Which I bore withall," Foxe temporarily resigned himself, "there being more danger to the voyage in crossing a proud fellow than could ensue in that direction."

The second lap was across Davis Strait to the furious riptides and ice whirlpools guarding entry to Hudson Strait. Both racers were appalled by the sight, but naturally James made it seem more spine-chilling. Coleridge's yarnspinning mariner with the glittering, hypnotic eye here echoed some of James's most haunting phrases:

And now there came both mist and snow,
And it grew wondrous cold,
And ice, mast-high, came floating by,
As green as emerald.

And through the drifts the snowy clifts
Did send a dismal sheen:
Nor shapes of men nor beasts we ken —
The ice was all between.

The ice was here, the ice was there,

The ice was all around:
It cracked and growled, and roared and howled,
Like noises in a swound!

On June 18, in the misty dawn of 4 A.M., James tells us he sighted the ghostly humpbacks of Resolution Island at the gateway of Hudson Strait. It was so piercing cold that it almost shattered his compass. Freezing fog clung to his ship's sails and rigging, and she was ice-sheathed as if in coat of mail. With a "hollow and hideous noise," the whirling sea flung ice monsters at James, and they thrashed and flailed and ground and tore at his bruised ship.

His men hooked grappling anchors to a battering ram of a berg ("which was our buckler") and they sought to cleave a path around the hungry rocks and hemming ice hummocks betwixt them and the shore.

At length, after pushing off ice floes with axes, iron crowbars and their shoulders, the crew used cable and tackle to pull the *Henrietta Maria* into a cove. And with her three skimpy masts thrusting like broomsticks out of the towering bergs around her, "the ship lay as if she had lain in a bed of ice."

James took his men up to the highest hill on Resolution Island, and erected a stone beacon, and put a cross upon it, and named the cove "Harbor of God's Providence." "Then was our sorrow turned to joy," writes James, "and we all fell on our knees, praising God for His mercy in so miraculous a deliverance."

On June 23, Foxe cruised by Resolution Island and saw smoke curling from the bonfire his rival had lit on the hilltop. The Yorkshireman hastened on. He observed acidly that only a nincompoop loiterer would risk being gashed by hidden rocks and besetting ice in harbor there. Instead Foxe pushed headlong into Hudson Strait, seeking what he called sea room.

It was too early in the season, though, and he didn't find much elbow space. "We had many stout blows," he noted, "and the wind bloweth hard by puffs." Still he made a masterful effort "to thread-needle up the channel . . . shooting shuttles in the old loom." It was his colorful locution for threading through narrow lanes of water between shifting masses of ice, and constantly tacking backwards and forwards, like the shuttle of a loom.

As he zigzagged up the Strait, Foxe introduced some marvelously fresh phrases to Arctic lore. His major contribution was to be perhaps the first to make an accurate distinction between two kinds of ice.

The perils faced by James and Foxe when charting the top and bottom of Hudson Bay were melodramatically illustrated in British books. James contributed to the hyberbole: The "great rowling sea ... over-racked us so that we were like Jonas in the whale's belly." His wintering in James Bay, though, was excrutiating.

"Mashed or flake ice," as he termed it, was the floe, field or pack ice, owing its origin to the freezing of salt water. The second type he named "mountainous ice," meaning icebergs torn from polar glaciers, and these giants, of course, were fresh water ice.

It was the "frigitating" flake ice that kept stalling and pestering him in the Strait. But unlike James, Foxe took the battering as well as the "thick rain, soft sleet, and warm fog" with good cheer. "No men ever before entered this passage with so good weather, and of such long continuance; for it is so hot on some days as in Scotland," he exulted. "The west wind only is sharp, making our noses run like alembic stills." Some days, he observed, the orange sun was so fiery that it "maketh both ice and boiling tar to run."

Here Foxe's journal entries about the elements assume a beauty of their own. "This morning the sun licked up the fog's dew as soon as he began to rise and made a shining day of it," he writes. "The evening sun kissed Thetis in our sight; and at the same instant the rainbow sun dogs made an appearance, I think to canopy them abed." "This delicate morning," begins another entry, "the sun rose clear, and so continued all this cold virgin day." And again: "The sun unveiled himself through Vapour Land, and the south wind drave away the vapours." And in still another entry: "This evening the sun set clear; the air breathed gently from the east; and we lay quietly all night amongst the ice."

He gives us a vivid picture of the aurora borealis flickering and darting across the sky during the Arctic "white night" while the sun dipped briefly below the horizon. To Foxe the northern lights were "henbeams" or "pretty dancers," and they flashed like "strange comets in the air, bloody and gem yellow" and sometimes "like the flame that cometh forth out of the mouth of a hot oven." He can even muster appreciation for the game that his obstreperous sailing master killed and "kindly bestowed" upon his messmates. The fish-smelling black guillemots Foxe benevolently accepted as "strong and good pottage." A young polar bear, when boiled, didn't "taste bad at all, like beef," though admittedly, when roasted, "it tasted oily and ramish."

Ramish meant goatlike, and that term summed up the intermittent butting that went on between Foxe and his two skittish officers. "We are all upon good terms, drinking one to another," Foxe reported one day. "God hold it."

But the next day the sailing master was openly insolent and the master's mate was supporting his impertinence. "I fear a mutiny or hindrance to the voyage," Foxe jotted in his journal. He found the rest of the crew willing workers, but his two officers kept stirring up trouble and urging him to turn back.

"But, while life lasted, I would have the voyage proceeded," wrote Foxe. "Nor did I care for their growling or grumbling. . . . I am engaged in Honor (which is the most precious of all to man in things of this life), having the eyes of the Court and Commonwealth fixed upon me in expectation. . . . And what a shame it would be for us to go home and pass along the streets to be pointed at, as we were worthy to be."

One feels sorry for Foxe as he tries to cheer on his sailors, despite his interior anxieties and his quarrelsome officers. Stalled in the ice, he confides to his unpublished diary. "We lie here in greater danger than I dare make shew of. God, for his mercy's sake, set us at liberty."

Meanwhile, tobacco, hard liquor, and lazing in the cabin were the sole preoccupations of his dronelike officers. When the sailing master grew peevish at being summoned to stand watch, says Foxe, "I told the rest the matter was not great, for children did so when they are awaked out of their sleep." A bit later Foxe observes cooly, "Not one word passed between him and me. Nor have we drank one to the other since he told me he cared not for me. *It spareth drink well.*"

The friction apparently grew worse towards mid-July. The sailing master, serving his midnight watch, attempted to turn the ship about. "Well, I would not trust him, and therefore stayed up to conduct the ship for two hour glasses," Foxe noted. "Going into my cabin to ease myself, being weary with watching and wet, I fell asleep. . . . He bore to the leeward four glasses, just as at our entering into the Strait he had done before, and also would have done again, but I would not suffer it."

On July 13, when they were gripped by ice at the end of the Strait, Foxe's anguish was truly touching: "God, for thy' Mercy's sake, send what thou knowest we stand in need of; for, if it thus hold, it will break my heart. I have no comfort of one or the other. Nor doth any man bear a part of the care with me. We lie fast here; he eats and drinks and is well pleased to sleep two suns. That this noble voyage should be lost for want of fitting associates!"

Three days later the *Charles* was free of the ice and pushing northwestward on the third lap of the race across the top of Hudson Bay. Foxe felt a little contrite. "Well, let speeches pass," he remarked blithely. "So long as I am sailing, I bless God and care not."

Thomas James aboard the *Henrietta Maria* reached the end of the Strait just as his rival was spurting out of it. It had been a rough lap for James. The fog was so thick that James could not see a pistol shot ahead.

James inspired Coleridge's Rime of the Ancient Mariner, *thus illustrated.*

The steel plates of his ship were all bruised and broken, her knees spoiled and torn. And the vindictive sea had so brutally "over-racked us that we were like Jonas in the whale's belly."

His tribulations were by no means over. On July 27, the weather cleared for the first time. James gazed out at the burnished blue waters of Hudson Bay and found himself stuck in the ice for the next four days.

"I measured some pieces, which I found to be one thousand of my paces long," he wrote dolefully. "Notwithstanding we put abroad all the sail . . . the ship stirred no more than if she had been in a dry dock."

His frustration was evoked a century and a half later in Coleridge's famous lines attributed to the Ancient Mariner:

All in a hot and copper sky,
The bloody Sun, at noon,
Right up above the mast did stand,
No bigger than the Moon.

Day after day, day after day,
We stuck, nor breath nor motion;
As idle as a painted ship
Upon a painted ocean.

Water, water, every where,
And all the boards did shrink;
Water, water, every where,
Nor any drop to drink.

Well, in real life, it was not quite that dry for James. As his sailors began to murmur, thinking they were trapped there permanently in the icepack, James tells us, "I comforted and encouraged them the best I could; and to put away these cogitations, we drank a health to his Majesty on the ice—not one man in the ship, and she still under all her sails."

Eventually, after much prayer and heaving with the shoulders, his men prised the *Henrietta Maria* free from the hugging floes. Then, taking a short cut, James took a southwesterly course and steered directly across Hudson Bay to today's Port Churchill, Manitoba. "Hubart's Hope," as Sir Thomas Button had named it, proved to be a disappointment. "This was the very place where the Passage should be," remarked James. But after penetrating about fifty-five miles into the seemingly landlocked bay, James was forced to make a bitter jest about it. Hubart's Hope, he said, was hopeless.

James turned southward dejectedly. On August 16, after losing his anchors, he cautiously skirted the sandy red, puddle-ish estuary of the Nelson River. By coincidence Foxe was on that very day anchored in the muddy harbor of Port Nelson. But James almost wrecked his ship on a jutting rock in the area, and he didn't tarry. Instead he struck out eastward, bent on investigating the hitherto unexplored coastline stretching from Port Nelson to James Bay.

On August 26, he paused off a bank of low, flat marshland, and the Welshman ceremoniously proclaimed it the "New Principality of South Wales," and celebrated the occasion with a jollification. "We drank a health in the best liquor we had to Prince Charles, his Highness, whom God preserve."

Unfortunately God failed to preserve James from further catastrophes. The winds did "snuffle and blow," and he kept losing his grappling anchors, and snow and hail made the late August weather "as cold as at any time I have felt in England." Then one squally evening a rope got snarled in the cable as his sailors were walking the capstan and eight of them were seriously injured. The gunner, "an honest and a diligent man," had his leg mangled to the bone. He wept with pain. The surgeon amputated the poor fellow's leg at the gartering place and dressed the others that were sorely bruised. "After which," says James, "we comforted each other as well as we could."

James received cold comfort from his next encounter. On August 29, by extraordinary coincidence, the *Henrietta Maria* met the *Charles* on the last lap of their Cathay race in the vast, unexplored spaces of southeastern Hudson Bay.

"I saluted him according to the manner of the sea, and received the like of him," recorded James. "Captain Foxe and his friends came aboard of me, where I entertained them in the best manner I could."

The rival captains made quite a night of it, not parting until dawn next morning, while each opponent tried to pry secrets from the other. Foxe played the better poker game. He adroitly obscured all that had happened to him thus far ("for every man will report the best of his own actions"), and one must consult his diary to determine what had actually occurred.

On slipping out of Hudson Strait, Foxe had made a dash northwest of the Bay, determined to exceed Button's *Ne Ultra*. He had a grand time pinning names on new places he discovered. Somewhere west of the

Bay's top cork of Southampton Island, his men landed on an islet. In honor of his court patron, Foxe named it Sir "Thomas Roe's Welcome"—an appellation since given to the entire strait, Roe's Welcome Sound.

There his men were welcomed by a spooky "sepulchre" of five hundred Eskimo graves. Since the Eskimos customarily placed their dead in a flexed position, bent at pelvis and knees, Foxe assumed the corpses were midgets four feet tall. "They seem to be people of small stature," he remarked. "God send me better for my adventures than these!"

Coasting southward, he anchored at modern Marble Island; its white quartzite cliffs were feathered with sea fowl. His crew bagged a couple of snowy-plumaged whistling swans as well as an apparent whooping crane. The crane's long, writhing, pin-feathered neck must have appeared as outlandish to Foxe as Tenniel's modern drawing of the preposterous game of croquet played in *Alice In Wonderland.* Foxe reckoned it was an arctic ostrich. The ship hunting hound also brought a caribou to bay. Foxe was disappointed because the quartermaster failed to shoot the quarry. "It may be," Foxe remarks drolly, "he took compassion when he saw the deer shed tears."

At another islet, just south of the present Eskimo settlement at Rankin Inlet, Foxe's sailing master did himself proud. He captured a dun-colored fox and brought it aboard ship alive. The feuders must have patched up a temporary truce; for Foxe observed benignly, "The Master told me he had named the island Dunne Foxe Island, after my own name and the foxe's colour, which I liked well."

"Dunne Foxe Island" it remains today. Regrettably, though, geographers have erased from the map the waggish name that Foxe gave to a cluster of nearby islands. He called them, in memory of his deceased logarithms tutor, "Briggs His Mathematicks."

When he sailed into Churchill Bay, Foxe had great fun punning with the name "Hubart's Hope." "Hubart makes me hope," he said, while skimming past resinous, balsam-scented dwarf woods, gaily studded with yellow daisies and haylike grass. Then he was harassed by battalions of needling marsh mosquitoes. "I do yet hope well, or else I say Hubart was an ass." Then, disgustedly, when his passage was blocked by rocky shoals: "I could see the bottom of Vainly Hoped Hubart."

The woods seemed to thicken with scrub fir and spruce as he poked into Port Nelson. His men had a picnic gathering strawberries and blackberries. Everybody was a little saddened when they discovered relics of Button's unhappy wintering there twenty years before. But Foxe's *joie de vivre* was soon restored. Simultaneously with James, he sailed eastward from Port Nelson to begin original exploration of the unknown southern shore of the Bay.

It was beautiful weather. The bluey white beluga whales were flopping in the Bay like "pork fish." And the sun was so pleasantly warm that Foxe wished the farmers of England could enjoy a climate as nice for harvesting their crops. It put him in mind of his native Yorkshire, and he named the undiscovered shores "New Yorkshire."

The sight of wild geese winging southward also made him feel homesick. On August 23, after saying his prayers, he makes a tender reference to his wife, Anne: "The ship is anchored, the watch is set, a mark set upon the lead line, and sleep, like a thief, doth slyly steal upon me. My wife is now upon her second sleep, being in bed, as I suppose, about five hours. Good night."

Six days later, though, the grouchy side of his nature was on exhibition. For it was then Luke Foxe encountered his opponent, Thomas James.

The clash of their conflicting egos is exposed wonderfully well in their journals: James playing the role of the uppity barrister, Foxe being plain bitchy.

Dinner was served between decks of the *Henrietta Maria*, evidently because James's big cabin was not large enough to hold all his guests. Between courses of wine and partridge, foam-flecked waves washed over the decks and drenched everybody. The ship drew so much bilge water, Foxe jested, that the diners wouldn't have needed sauce if they'd been served roast mutton. It led him to wonder if James's meal ought to be impounded amongst the ice, where it might be "kept from putrefication by the piercing air; or in open sea, to be kept sweet by being thus daily pickled."

Pursuing the same vein of raw humor, he wisecracked that the *Henrietta Maria* was imbibing her liquor as generously as the diners; "for her nose was no sooner out of the pitcher but her bill, like the duck's, was in it again." Neither was his host's scholarly conversation to Foxe's taste. "The Gentleman could discourse of Art," was Foxe's lemony comment, "but he was no Seaman."

Apparently James wasn't impressed by his guest either. "He told me how himself had been in Port Nelson, and had made but a cursory discovery hitherto," James wrote of Foxe with glacial condescension,"and that he had not been aland, nor had not many times seen the land."

Foxe laughed at James for flying his flag in such choppy waters. James replied with hauteur: he was on his way to the Emperor of Japan on behalf of His Majesty, and he wouldn't think of striking his flag on such a lofty mission.

"Keep it up then," quoth Foxe. "But you are out of the way to Japon, for this is not it."

James then tried to persuade Foxe to winter with him in the Bay. Cold weather was drawing near and Button had taken up his winter quarters the fourteenth of that very month.

Foxe turned him down flatly. "I was not come to do so much as another man," Foxe boasted, "but more than any, as I had already done."

When Foxe finally returned to his ship in the morning, he inscribed in his journal, "This seventeen hours was the worst spent of any time of my discovery." The meeting had given him but one satisfaction. He relished the fact that when both ships stood off into the sea, the *Charles* "went faster than the *Mary*."

The two ships then raced for the southeastern-most point of Hudson Bay proper. Foxe reached the cliffed cape first, on September 2, and named it "Wolstenholme's *Ultimum Vale*." "For," Foxe announced wryly, "I do believe Sir John Wolstenholme will not lay out any more monies in search of this Bay."

James arrived there a day later. He named it after his ship and his Queen, "Cape Henrietta Maria"—the name still in use today. Then James swung southward into James Bay for the soul-shrivelling wintering that tested his piety and his poesy to the utmost.

Foxe meanwhile worked his way northward. He was resolved to make a last desperate attempt to do some original exploration in what came to be known as the Foxe Basin northeast of Hudson Bay. Before attaining "Foxe His Farthest" (close to the Arctic Circle at about 66 degrees, 47 minutes latitude) he had a pretty grim time of it. Icicles sheathed his rigging. Snow, sleet and cold converted his tubs of salt brine into frozen cannon balls. And when he wasn't being impeded by bergs in swelling seas, he was wrangling with his officers.

"The Master came not to prayers nor dinner this day," he scribbled one foul day. "The one is a greater miracle than the other." In satirical commemoration of his dozing master, he named a cluster of islets the "Sleepers."

Yet for all his bluster, Foxe was essentially a kind-hearted man. The next morning we hear him commiserating, "The Master is not in health, for which I am very sorry." He has compassion for his men, who were "pitifully wet," shivering in the freezing fog, and he issues them extra rations of brandy. "This working in cold, without hope of passage, doth quite discourage them. Nor, indeed, can we long hold out. Therefore I thank God for my own health, being enforced to look to both watches."

Then scurvy broke out, and half his crew were racked with pain. On September 22, Foxe knew he had to give up "the Search." Because of "the weakness of our persons, the long nights, the cold dark weather with the decayed moon," he regretfully gave orders to steer home.

The news revived his drooping men. "The Master is up again," Foxe noted, and he twitted him with the old proverb, "The hackney will drive best homewards."

That lazy good-for-nothing, the master's mate, appeared to have recovered, too. Though "all wamble" from drinking too much sack, the tipsy fellow successfully steered the *Charles* through the grinding floes in a narrow passage off Mill Island at the west end of Hudson Strait. Foxe paid him tribute by giving the passage the name it still bears today, "Hurin Throughlet."

But the Northwest Passage itself eluded him. When Foxe arrived in England on October 31, with his entire crew safe and sound, the Yorkshireman conceded that the Passage remained undiscovered. It was as hard to find as "a needle in a bottle of hay."

Yet despite having accomplished more original exploration than James, Foxe was criticized viciously and unjustly for not staying on to winter like his rival. His patron, Sir Thomas Roe, excoriated Foxe in scalding language.

"I never knew men to seek a Northwest Passage on a northeast shore," mocked Roe. "So will our hopes now rest upon Captain James, who is resolved to lose his life or return with more honour. . . . He shall hath gained infinite reputation to have taken this resolution, not to come home like a sluggard and say, '*A lion roars or was in his way.*'"

Back in James Bay, Captain Thomas James was praying. It was no roaring lion that tormented him. It was a rock in "a great rowling sea" that gashed the *Henrietta Maria* and almost caused her death's wound. It was a crazed storm that "did nothing but snow and blow" and flung away his shallop. And it was the moaning of his gunner, the poor man with the amputated leg, who finally died in his cabin, so chilled that his plaster cast was frozen at his wound and trying to ease his last misery by sipping a bottle of sack wine that James had given him.

So on a desolate island he named "Charlton," after Prince Charles, in the bottom pocket of the bay bearing his own name, James got down on his knees and composed what he called a "ragged and teared Rime":

Oh, my poor soule, why doest thou grieve to see
So many deaths muster to murther me?
Look to thy selfe; regard not me; for I
Must doe (for what I came), performe, or die. . . .

It would be easy to lampoon James in his slough of Despond. He was given to attitudinizing. He was addicted to hyperbole. He was a sad-sack, scoutmasterish camper, who made one mistake after another. Yet he was so sweet-natured towards what he called "my loving companions" that one forgives him for his excesses and his blunderings.

Four of his shipmates were to die during that nightmarish wintering on Charlton Island. They perished either of the cold or of scurvy, and James makes you feel every ache and pain that they suffered.

The weather was so bitter, he says, that his leaky, partially submerged ship looked like one big floating icicle. His men looked like walking chandeliers of ice, their beards so hoary they didn't recognize one another. Their noses, cheeks and fingers froze as white as paper. They couldn't see because their eyelashes were frozen stiff. They couldn't walk because the frost raised blisters on their poorly shod feet as big as walnuts.

It was so slashingly cold, says James, "I caused the surgeon to cut the hairs of my head short, and to shave away all the hair of my face; for that it was become intolerable, and that it would be frozen so great with icicles. The like did all the rest, and we fitted ourselves to work."

They worked away at building three wintering shacks: a "mansion" for the officers, a workshop for the "subordinate crew," and a shed for storing the woefully few ptarmigan and caribou they shot. Though weather-proofed with spare sails, the huts provided little warmth. Icy stalactites hung from the ceiling. Hoar frost shrouded the beds. Wine, vinegar and oil froze as hard as wood and had to be cut with a hatchet. The turpentine-ish branches of evergreen firewood gave off a terrible choking smoke and made the occupants feel like a platoon of chimney-sweeps.

When scurvy struck, the mansion was converted into a sickbay; two-thirds of the crew were laid up with sore mouths, blackened loose teeth, and dagger stabs in the joints. The sickest men could not turn themselves in bed, says James, and had to be tended like infants. Others, not as badly crippled, managed to crawl through the snow on hands and knees to fetch firewood.

"Our surgeon (as diligent and sweet-conditioned a man as ever I saw) would be up betimes in the mornings," reports James. "And, whilst he did pick their teeth and cut away the dead flesh from their gums, they would bathe their own thighs, knees and legs.... It was a maxim amongst us that if anyone kept his bed two days, he would rise no more. This made every man to strive to keep up for life."

By mid-April, the sailing master and two others asked permission to sleep aboard ship. James gave his consent. "For indeed they had lain very discommodiously all winter with sick bed fellows, as I myself had done, every one in that kind taking their fortunes. By lying aboard, they avoided hearing the miserable groanings and lamentations of the sick men all night, enduring (poor soules) intolerable torment."

Spring brought green vetches and sorrel grass, whose juices mixed with beer and cider, alleviated the scurvy. And May Day Eve was celebrated with a dance, which helped relieve the men from being "struck down all in a dump." His merrymaking sailors, says James, "made a good fire, and chose Ladies, and did ceremoniously wear their names in our caps, endeavouring to revive ourselves by any means."

But hot weather, alas, also brought what James called the "hot glooms": bloodthirsty mosquitoes. "We tore an old ship's flag in pieces, and made us bags of it to put our heads in; but it was no fortification against them. They would find ways and means to sting us, so that our faces were swollen hard out in pumples."

The hottest of the glooms was brought about by James's own mismanagement. On the warm evening of June 25, James climbed up the tallest tree on Charlton Island and ordered a sailor to set fire to a small evergreen below. His object was to arouse an answering signal from any friendly Indians who might be lurking in the neighboring islands. The biggest island in James Bay is named *Akimiski*, which is Indian for: "It looks like a long, black smoke." Conceivably the name is based on the misadventure of Captain James. The non-conservationist was Canada's first white camper to recklessly touch off a forest fire.

The tinder-dry birch, balsam and firs immediately exploded into flames. James leaped down from his tree and ran for his life, the blaze crackling hard at his heels, as he put it, like a train of powder. The holocaust raged all night and next day, and in a trice, burned down to the ground Charlton's little town of three shacks. Luckily no lives were lost, and valuables had already been stowed aboard the repaired and pumped-out *Henrietta Maria.* The Indians wisely stayed away from the white man's foolishness.

On July 1, James prepared to cast off from his primeval island. First he performed an absurd yet somehow touching ceremony. With colors flying and kettledrum beating, the ragged survivors trooped to a high sandy hill where a wooden cross had been raised. The cross marked the burial place of the dead. On it, as a symbol of having taken possession of the island, James had affixed pictures of the King and Queen, a shilling and a sixpence, the royal arms, and the arms of the city of Bristol.

Prayers were said for their dead shipmates. Then, leaning his arm on one of the tombstones, James recited some poetry he had written. "Though perchance they may procure laughter in the wiser sort," he later said self-consciously of his lachrymose verses, "they yet moved my young and tender-hearted companions at the time with some compassion."

His most significant lines reflect the tremendous stress that James, the romantic idealist, placed on honor and glory:

We that survive perchance may end our days
In some employment meriting no praise,
And in a dung-hill rot; when no man names
The memory of us, but to your shames.
They have outlived this feare, and their brave ends
Will ever be an honour to their friends. . .

Almost four months later, on October 22, 1632, the battered *Henrietta Maria* staggered into Bristol. "Being all here arrived, we went all to church," said James, "and gave God thanks for His preservation of us."

Three years later Thomas James and Luke Foxe were dead. Again by extraordinary coincidence the two captains met death within a few weeks of each other in 1635.

Which yachtsman had won the great Cathay race? Neither of them did. Both died disappointed men, for neither had won the prize of the Northwest Passage. Yet at least they died knowing that each had pushed back the geographic mists a little farther. Each had left large footprints on hitherto untrod beaches of Hudson Bay. And each inspired other north-wanderers to continue "the Search."

Luke Foxe had the last word. "Although we all have sometimes stumbled, yet we may be excused, considering the long and strange journey we had to go: and, who followeth, doth but persevere by our example," he concluded. "My pen and self now is grown weary; and, hoping some other brave Spirit will enter the Lists and attempt the Enterprise, I rest."

Thirty-five years later brave spirits did indeed enter the lists to found the Company of Adventurers of England Trading into Hudson's Bay, known today as the Hudson's Bay Company. For guidance the fur-trade adventurers turned to those pioneering classics, *North-West Foxe* and *The Strange and Dangerous Voyage of Captain Thomas James.*

Chapter 10

Fur-Trade Caesars in the Savage Country

One day in the year 1666 King Charles II, the pleasure-loving monarch of Restoration England, granted an audience at Oxford to two renegade fur traders from New France. As the King listened enthralled to the pair of vagabond French Canadians, he was so charmed that he temporarily forgot about the Great Plague of London, his tennis matches with his dear cousin Prince Rupert, and even about his many mistresses.

They were certainly plausible rogues, this Monsieur Radishes and Monsieur Gooseberries. They told such thrilling stories that your hair stood on end and your eyes glittered with greed. It was greed for the fortune in beaver furs waiting to be plucked from the Indians in the New World.

The more eloquent of the two, Pierre-Esprit Radisson, who claimed to have lived with the Iroquois since the age of fifteen, made it all seem romantically simple. Meanwhile his brother-in-law, Médard Chouart, Sieur des Groseilliers, a former lay assistant to Jesuit missionaries among the Huron Indians, convincingly embroidered with corroborative details.

Radisson's yarn-spinning was so fantastical that King Charles had him write the narrative down. One may be sure his tale lost nothing in the respinning. It seems that the Galahad in buckskin had led fur-hunting expeditions out of Quebec as far west as the undiscovered "shores of that sweet sea," possibly Lake Superior, and as far north as the "Bay of the North," which may have been James Bay.

Though his knowledge of geography may have been hazy, Radisson's insight into human avarice was obviously not. When he first set out from Ville Marie de Montreal with canoe loads of cheap trading trinkets, he knew he would have no trouble recruiting fellow *coureurs de bois.* "For where there is lucre," said Radisson, "there are people enough to be had."

Arrived among the Crees, he tossed gunpowder into the fire to tame the barbarous people. And he smiled to think, "The wildman durst not speake, because we weare demi-gods."

The Indians were afraid to guide his party into alien territory. So the white god beat their strongest warrior with a beaver skin and taunted, "For my part, I will venture, choosing to die like a man than live like a beggar." Then the shamed tribesmen carried the palefaces aloft on their shoulders, "like a couple of cocks in a banquett," and Radisson rejoiced. "We weare Cesars," he cried, "being nobody to contradict us!"

Exploiting the nation of "poor, barbarous, wildmen," who wandered near the frozen sea of "sugar candy," was ridiculously easy. "They are of a good nature, and not great whore masters," said Radisson, "and are more satisfied than any others that I knewed. . . . The men are fools, but diligent about their work. . . . They are the best huntsmen of all America. . . . They clothe themselves all over with beaver skins. . . . We weare well beloved, and they could not tell what to give us, and they weare so overjoyed that we promised to come again with ships."

What most impressed King Charles was Radisson's claim that his argosies had brought back to Quebec some six hundred thousand pounds of beaver pelts. If Radisson wasn't lying, that was indeed "heavenly manna . . . no fibbe." For felted beaver hats were then the fashion rage of European dandies, and London hatters couldn't keep up with the demand.

In two royal ships, the *Eaglet* and the *Nonsuch,* the King sent the pair of fortune hunters off to Hudson Bay. The *Eaglet* was turned back by storms. But the sturdy, low-waisted, forty-three-ton ketch, *Nonsuch,* lived up to her name. She bucked the ice of Hudson Strait and managed to make it to the region of Thomas James's Charlton Island in the southeast pocket of James Bay. A log fort was built at the mouth of the Rupert River. No fewer than three hundred bartering Indians came to taste their ale and their beer. Without losing a man, the winterers returned with a lucrative haul of the silkiest prime beaver.

As a result, on May 2, 1670, King Charles II granted to his tennis partner, his "dear and entirely beloved cousin," Prince Rupert, a trading monopoly over almost half a continent. Without consulting the Indian or French inhabitants, he signed away more than one and a half million square miles drained by Hudson Bay. The "true and absolute Lords and Proprietors" of the loosely defined Rupertsland were eighteen mercantile investors. They were incorporated under the name of the "Governor and Company of Adventurers of England Trading Into Hudson's Bay."

This cumbersome title became more familiarly known as the Hudson's Bay Company; its initials H.B.C. sometimes later derisively interpreted as meaning "Here Before Christ" or "Here Before Canada"; and its Latin motto, *Pro pelle cutem*—"A skin of goods for a skin of furs"—translated to read, "We skin you as you try to skin us."

Radisson, the co-founder of the company, found this last witticism most apt. As a reward for his services, the "Honourable Company" presented him with a hogshead of claret. Later, when he was down in his luck and pleading for a job, the aging adventurer was refused a post as its London warehouse keeper. He ultimately died a poverty-stricken and embittered old man of seventy-four, honored by the Honourable Company with a half-pension of fifty pounds per annum.

The Honourable Company was severely criticized—not for its lack of charity but its lack of enterprise. Parliamentary critics claimed that the terms of the royal charter implied that the Company would seek out a northwest passage to the Western Sea. Yet for almost a century its employees remained stuck in their forts which were dotted, like horseshoe nails, around the lower rim of Hudson Bay. At an alleged 2,000 per cent profit, critics claimed, the feudalistic landlords found it more lucrative to let its H.B.C. clerks serve as veritable store clerks. Supposedly they did nothing but hand out trading goods to any fur-bearing customers who chanced to pass by.

H.B.C. historian Douglas Mackay made the interesting observation that it wasn't moral scruples that prevented the Honourable Company from chaining Indians into slavery. After all, it wasn't until the 1830s that Britain ceased trafficking in "black ivory"—African Negroes shipped to slave plantations in the British West Indies and the American South. In Rupertsland, though, chaining the natives would not work economically. Indians required freedom to trap beaver. Furthermore, the English and Scottish peasants imported to the Bay factories generally tended to be incurious humble servants. With a few notable exceptions (like bold Henry Kelsey and Anthony Henday), they were reluctant to leave their forts and live off the land like their aboriginal customers. As one Company detractor remarked, the lackadaisical sluggards were more interested in sleeping beside their sea of furs than searching for the Western Sea.

Two daring, inquisitive fur-trade explorers broke out of this mold. Each roved northward to make important Arctic discoveries. And each, in his own way, came to grips with what the first wilderness Caesar, Pierre-Esprit Radisson, called the Wildmen of *Le Pays Sauvage*—literally "The Savage Country."

Samuel Hearne, the first white man to gaze upon the North American Arctic Ocean, was an unlikely Caesar. He was mild-mannered, patient, tolerant, a fastidious teetotaller, a self-taught artist, a lover of birds and animals, a reciter of nature poetry. He was the sort of zealous hiker who thought nothing of snowshoeing through the Savage Country for months, content as long as his packsack was loaded with a razor, cake of soap and a good supply of books.

Thus sparsely equipped, he spent the years from 1769 to 1772 cheerfully exploring by foot some five thousand miles of one of the most forbidding regions on the cap of the continent. This was the bald rock and treeless tundra northwest of Hudson Bay. Much of it is now called Keewatin District, an Indian term meaning "North Wind." Hearne named it the "Barren Ground." He discovered as well the Coppermine River, which winds for more than five hundred miles like a cold green serpent until its fangs bite into Coronation Gulf off the central coast of the Canadian Arctic Ocean.

Hearne was just twenty-four when he first set out on his trek from the stone gateway of Fort Prince of Wales, the H.B.C. trading post at the mouth of the Churchill River. His book, *A Journey to the Northern Ocean*, reveals him to be a fresh-eyed travel writer. He was the first fur trader to examine with some objectivity the Chipewyans—Indian for "pointed skins," based on the cut of their caribou tunics. He was also an acute observer of wildlife. The naturalist surrounded himself with pets— weasels, beavers, wolves, bald eagles, whiskyjack jays and Lapland longspurs, squirrels, lemmings and frogs—and wrote of them with rare artistry.

Yet he was a scholastic failure as a London city boy. Orphaned at the age of three, he eventually became an eleven-year-old cabin boy in the Royal Navy. At twenty-one, he was hired to be mate of an H.B.C. whaling sloop. On the face of a granite rock in Sloop Cove, in the modern grain-shipping port of Churchill, Manitoba, one can see to this very day the inscription that the young adventurer carved out for posterity:

Sl Hearne, July ye 1, 1767.

One does not, however, glimpse his personality in the single portrait of him that survives. It shows him dandified in a gold-laced ruffled uniform, blond hair curled, feminine lips pursed, blue eyes staring out blankly from a rather pasty face. A fellow fur trader described him as "a handsome man six feet in height, of a ruddy complexion and remarkably well-made, enjoying good health." Good health was obviously vital to the athlete. Hearne tells how he used to toughen himself by camping out in winter with trading Indians, shooting ptarmigan and racing after moose, until he was "celebrated for being particularly fleet of foot in snowshoes."

He was also celebrated among his contemporaries for being a nonconformist who admired the satires of Voltaire. Perhaps this accounts for the satirical sketch he drew of Moses Norton, governor of the Churchill trading post. Norton was a half-blood, who apparently inherited the easygoing profligacy of his Indian mother along with the hypocrisy of his English father.

Hearne pictures Norton as a lecherous old man who wearied the souls of his officers with long-winded and saintly sermons on virtue. "But the selfish debauchee simply wished to engross every woman in the country to himself," said Hearne. "He kept, for his own use, five or six of the finest Indian girls he could select. But notwithstanding his own uncommon propensity for the fair sex, he took every means in his power to prevent the other Europeans from having intercourse with the women of the country.... He always kept a box of poison to administer to those who refused him their daughters or their wives.... He actually poisoned two of his women because he thought them partial to other men more suitable to their ages."

Just before his death in 1773, according to Hearne, the jealous old reprobate saw an officer putting a hand on one of his Indian concubines. Norton bellowed: "God damn you for a bitch! If I live, I'll knock your brains out!"

"A few minutes after this elegant apostrophe," said Hearne, "he expired in the greatest agonies that can possibly be conceived."

Norton did live long enough to send Hearne out on his three walking expeditions. The governor's instructions were explicit. Hearne was to drum up trade among Chipewyan Indians in the northern hinterland; to keep an eye out for the Northwest Passage; and, not least important, to track down an El Dorado of copper rumored to exist at the mouth of a fabled Far-off-Metal River that emptied into an unknown

Samuel Hearne, the marvellous hiker who from 1769 to 1772 explored by foot 5,000 miles on the cap of the continent, was the first white man to gaze upon the North American Arctic Ocean.   PUBLIC ARCHIVES OF CANADA

Fort Prince of Wales, the Hudson's Bay Company post at Port Churchill. Hearne, who thus sketched it, started his epic hike from this jumping-off point.

ocean. All that Hearne had to go by was a rude map of the north country drawn on a caribou skin with charcoal by an Indian who claimed to have found enormous lumps of copper ore.

Hearne made two false starts, partly because his guides were blundering rogues picked by Governor Norton from among his own Swampy Cree Indian relatives. Hearne was robbed by marauding Indians, his quadrant was smashed in a gust of wind, and his porters deserted with his supplies. Pulling his caribou skin sledge, Hearne trudged back to the fort, half-starved but resolved to try again. "I endeavoured, like a sailor after a storm," said Hearne with characteristic mildness, "to forget past misfortunes."

The Indian who guided his major hike of almost nineteen months epitomized, for Hearne, all the virtues and defects of the northern tribesmen. This was the great Matonabbee. Shortnecked, copper-colored, with a Roman nose and six-foot stature, the Chipewyan had an engaging personality. "I have met with few Christians who possessed more good moral qualities, or fewer bad ones," wrote Hearne, who developed a genuine affection for the chief. "To the vivacity of a Frenchman, and the sincerity of an Englishman, he added the gravity and nobleness of a Turk."

Matonabbee told Hearne that the reason for the failure of his two previous trips was elementary. The bachelor explorer had neglected to take along women to lug his packs.

"Women were made for labour," Matonabbee explained with a laugh. "One of them can carry or haul as much as two men. They also pitch our tents, make and mend our clothes of the hunt, keep us warm at night. More than this, women can be maintained at a trifling expense. For, as they always cook, the very licking of their fingers in scarce times is sufficient for their sustenance."

Matonabbee maintained seven strapping wives. They were built, Hearne dryly observed, like grenadiers. Yet Matonabbee was passionately jealous of his harem, even stabbing a young lover who tried to elope with one of them. Hearne could not understand why anybody would want to elope with these plodding drudges. "Their senses seem almost as dull and frigid as the zone they inhabit," he privately recorded. "Still, I suppose it only requires indulgence and precept to make some of them as lofty and insolent as any women in the world."

Hearne had occasion to note their coquettishness as his expedition tramped across the glassy ice of Partridge Lake in piercing February cold. The thighs and buttocks of one of Matonabbee's wives became encrusted with freezing snow.

"The pain the poor woman suffered was greatly aggravated by the laughter and jeering of her companions," he noted. "They said she was rightly served for belting her clothes so high. I must acknowledge that I was not in the number of those who pitied her, as I thought she took too much pains to shew a clean heel and good leg; her garters being always in sight."

Although acknowledging that he viewed them through prejudiced European eyes, Hearne was not very flattering about the comeliness of Indian women.

"Take them in a body, the women are as destitute of real beauty as any nation I ever saw," he generalized, "though there are some few of them, when young, who are tolerable. But the care of the family, added to their constant hard labour, soon make the most beautiful among them look old and wrinkled, even before they are thirty. . . .

"Ask a Northern Indian: What is beauty? He will answer: A broad flat face, small eyes, high cheekbones, three or four broad black lines across each cheek, a low forehead, a large broad chin, a clumsy hook nose, a tawny hide, and breasts hanging down to the belt."

And yet, with the perceptiveness of a balanced reporter, Hearne was able to recognize that perhaps *he* did not look so beautiful in the eyes of the Indians. He has an endearing journal entry in which he describes the point of view of a Copper Indian tribe who had never before seen a paleface:

"It was curious to see how they flocked about me, and expressed as much desire to examine me from top to toe as a European naturalist would a nondescript animal. They pronounced me to be a perfect human being, except in the colour of my hair and eyes. The former, they said, was like the stained hair of a buffalo's tail; and the latter, being light, were like those of a gull. The whiteness of my skin also was, in their opinion, no ornament. They said it resembled meat which had been sodden in water till all the blood was extracted."

Eventually, as he was forced to depend upon them for sustenance and good cheer, Hearne came to appreciate their amazing endurance in the face of starvation. His band of twenty Chipewyans sometimes tramped sixty miles in three days, wading through gluey muskeg swamps, yet joking about their stoical diet of melted snow water and a pipeful of tobacco. During one fast of seven days, Hearne, like Charlie

Chaplin in *The Gold Rush,* joined his comrades in devouring a boiled pair of boots. Indeed he came to relish uncooked Indian delicacies: unhatched snowbirds; a savory haggis of kidneys gobbled steaming out of a caribou just slain; a succulent unborn beaver ripped out of the belly of its mother.

He gave a sympathetic account of their rituals, and he found many of them enchanting. When two bands of Chipewyans met on the lone tundra, an orator from each would recite the calamities suffered since each party had last seen each other. This was followed by a crying match in which each party vied in howling their sympathy. The wailing concert invariably ended with a dance. Lines of Indians curtsied to each other formally, as though in a minuet, lifting their feet high like cranes to the pounding beat of a caribou-skin drum as they sang a sprightly chorus of *"Hee, hee, hee! Ho, ho, ho!"*

He regarded their religious rites with amused tolerance. Their conjuror was a wonderful magician, and it was truly remarkable the way he swallowed an entire dwarf willow the size of a barrel stave. Hearne found delightful their worship of the *nantena,* the mythic gods who were supposed to control the wind and the sea and the air. And the aurora borealis, with its lustrous curtains of yellows, crimsons and purples, was to them the *edthin* or "cloud caribou." On a still night Hearne swore that he could hear these "nocturnal lights" make "a rustling and crackling noise, like the waving of a large flag in a fresh gale of wind." Hearne, the natural scientist, was mystified. His good friend, Matonabbee, was not. Surely it must be the spirits of dead warriors dancing and making merry in the sky with the caribou. Hearne gravely accepted that superstition. He agreed with Matonabbee that one must have "liberality of sentiment," and not "ridicule any particular sect on account of their religious opinions."

When his nomadic band reached the banks of the Coppermine River on July 13, 1771, Hearne was far from amused. A village of Eskimos was camped near a waterfall and Matonabbee was determined to massacre the helpless natives in their sleep. Hearne vainly tried to dissuade Matonabbee from this "brutish slaughter," but his heretofore easygoing friend seemed to be fired with a fierce hatred for the hereditary enemies of his people.

With a discipline and murderous zeal that Hearne had not seen before, Matonabbee led a war party of about sixty braves in painting images of the sun and moon and the wolf on their caribou hide shields. They smeared red and black stripes on their faces and tied their hair back to keep the wind from blowing it into their eyes. "And though the mosquitos were so numerous as to surpass all credibility," said Hearne, "yet some of the Indians actually pulled off their jackets and entered the lists quite naked, except for their breech cloths and moccasins."

Creeping quietly to where the Eskimo families were sleeping in their tents, the Indians rushed down the bank, brandishing spears. Those men, women and children not immediately stabbed to death ran naked into the snow until the Coppermine River cut off their escape. The Indians hacked at one elderly Eskimo man "until his body was like a sieve." They poked the eyes out of an old Eskimo woman and slowly tortured her to death. A few Eskimos huddled in knee-deep water. Then the Indians formed a circle on the hill, raised their spears high and clashed their shields together, and to deride their victims, taunted, *Tima! Tima!*—Eskimo for "Good cheer! Good cheer!"

Hearne was aghast when a young Eskimo girl of about eighteen, skewered by an Indian spear, threw herself writhing and clutching at his feet. "She twisted round my legs, so that it was with difficulty I could disengage myself from her dying grasps. Two Indian men pursued this unfortunate victim. I solicited very hard for her life. But the murderers made no reply till they had stuck both their spears through her body and transfixed her to the ground. They then looked me sternly in the face, and began to ridicule me by asking, 'Do you want an Esquimaux wife?' They paid not the smallest regard to the shrieks and agony of the poor wretch, who was twining round their spears, like an eel."

Hearne pleaded with them to please dispatch the poor girl out of her misery. One of the Indians obligingly pulled his spear out and plunged it through her breast near the heart. Such was the love of life, said Hearne, that the Eskimo girl made feeble efforts with her arm to ward off this blow of mercy and then, at last, she died. "Even at this hour," Hearne wrote years later, "I cannot reflect on the transactions of that horrid day without shedding tears."

Dismayed and disenchanted, Hearne left this scene of carnage, known forever after as Bloody Fall. He was still downhearted as he and his band of "wanton" Indians proceeded down the Coppermine River to its mouth at the Arctic Ocean. There, peering through his pocket telescope, he saw a few forlorn curlews screaming over the marshland and several seals squatting on the edge of the ice. And there, at one o'clock in the morning of July 18, 1771, with the sun flickering through fog and drizzling rain, "I erected a mark, and took possession of the coast, on behalf of the Hudson's Bay Company."

His triumph was a bitter one. The fabled El Dorado of copper, supposed to be rich enough to fill an entire ship, proved "no more than an entire jumble of rock and gravel." A four-hour search yielded nothing but a single four-pound chunk of copper ore.

On his long and circuitous hike home, in which he also touched Great Slave Lake in the Northwest Territories, Hearne brooded despondently over his accomplishments. The first white man to reach the Arctic Ocean overland felt that his astounding feats were largely negative. "The continent of America is much wider than many people imagine," he mused. "As to a passage through the continent of America by way of Hudson Bay, it has been exploded."

The northern Indians he had encountered were more difficult to puzzle out. As a humanitarian, he had to confess that his role of inducing these brazen, independent, laughter-loving people to catch beaver skins in exchange for a skinful of brandy "is by no means for the real benefit of the poor Indians; it being well known that those who have the least intercourse with the Factories are by far the happiest."

And surely, despite their famines and their idolatry, they were "the happiest of mortals and the greatest philosophers. For nothing but personal or family calamities can disturb their tranquility; while misfortunes of the lesser kind sit light on them. Being destitute of all religious control, these people have, to use Matonabbee's own words, 'nothing to do but consult their own inclinations and passions; to pass through this world as contentedly as possible, with no painful fear of punishment in the next.'"

And Matonabbee himself, despite his participation in a bloody *grand guignol*, was surely no worse than any European warlord. Uncivilized he might be, but his guiding hiker and hunter, who had taught him to live off the land, remained to Hearne "the most sociable, kind, and sensible Indian I had ever met with."

Hearne was destined to die destitute in England at the age of forty-seven, just two months after a publisher agreed to pay him two hundred pounds for his sensitively written masterwork of a journal. He had retired from the fur trade censured for being a timid Caesar. He had surrendered Fort Prince of Wales to superior French forces; the seventy-four-gun battleship *Sceptre*, commanded by the Comte de la Pérouse, had blown up the H.B.C. fortress and taken Hearne prisoner. Matonabbee knew that his paleface friend who had survived with him the rigors of The Savage Country was no Caspar Milquetoast. In the winter of 1783, on learning that Hearne had been conquered, Matonabbee strung up a rope and hanged himself.

"This is the more to be wondered at," wrote Hearne, a naturalist humanly touched and yet philosophically puzzled by the self-sacrifice, "as he is the only Northern Indian who, that I ever heard, put an end to his own existence."

Six years later, in the summer of 1789, one of Matonabbee's Chipewyan Indian band served as guide in the next fur trade thrust to the Arctic Ocean. The twenty-five-year-old leader of this overland expedition was very different from Hearne.

Alexander Mackenzie was one of a new breed of explorers: the driving business executive. A haughty Stornoway Scot, he was as forceful as Hearne was unassertive. He was as tough as Scottish thistle, with blowtorch energy and machinelike precision—and was seemingly as aloof as an automaton.

One looks at the portrait of him painted by Sir Thomas Lawrence, now hanging in the National Gallery in Ottawa, and one wonders what sort of man he really was. The portrait is not very revealing. Undoubtedly it is as prettified as his ghost-written journal, *Voyages Through the Continent of North America to the Frozen and Pacific Oceans*, which won a knighthood for Sir Alexander Mackenzie.

The painting makes him appear as strikingly handsome as Adonis. Blond curls tumble over a godlike brow. The dark poetic eyes are Byronic. The lips are a cupid's bow. The stiff cravat and rich velvet waistcoat are impeccably correct. His chin—the only suggestive clue to his character—is thrusting and dimpled and stubborn.

We see nothing here of the roisterer who indulged in Bacchanalian all-night drinking bouts in the Beaver Club at Montreal; who could wolf down pounded moose *pemmican* as savagely as the Indians he contemptuously termed savages; who was described by his fellow Nor'Westers as vain, vindictive and arrogant; who was so lustful for power that he was indeed called a Caesar of *Le Pays Sauvage*.

The man who was first to conquer the second-longest river in North America—the colossal, imperious, cocoa-brown Mackenzie River, which coils some one thousand and one hundred tortuous miles into the modern Beaufort Sea—was born in the impoverished little isle of Lewis in the Hebrides. His mother died when he was an infant; his immigrant father, who fought on the side of the British Royalist forces in the American Revolution of 1776, died when Alexander was sixteen. The youth abandoned his schooling to become a Montreal counting house clerk. By the age of twenty-three he was one of the most aggressive partners in the North West Fur Trading Company. He prided himself on being a true Nor'Wester—an amalgam of Highland Scots and New

273

PUBLIC ARCHIVES OF CANADA

Sir Alexander Mackenzie, in this portrait painted in 1800 by Sir Thomas Lawrence, looks like an Adonis. But the Nor'Wester fur trader was a true Caesar in the Savage Country: tough as Scottish thistle and a born executive driven relentlessly by ambition. He conquered the colossal Mackenzie River, which flows 1,100 miles into the Beaufort Sea of the Arctic Ocean.

England freebooters who offered, literally, murderous cutthroat competition to the humble servants of the H.B.C.

One finds it hard to admire Mackenzie because he gives so little credit to his Nor'Wester partners who helped make him a front-ranking explorer. One was Simon McTavish, the Highlander who was the reigning grandee of the company. Known to his associates as "the Marquis" or "the Premier," he elbowed his way up until he became the richest merchant prince of Montreal. He acquired an elegant seigniory in the Quebec countryside, with liveried servants and four-horse carriages, and at the foot of Mount Royal built Montreal's tallest sandstone mansion. The autocrat evidently sensed that ambitious young Mackenzie had a commercial flair. So in 1787 the Marquis assigned him to the company's potentially most profitable sales territory to try his wings. This was the company's newly established trading outpost at Lake Athabasca in what is now the northeast corner of Alberta.

There Mackenzie took over the exploration dream of a visionary and violent Nor'Wester wintering partner named Peter Pond. "Odd in his manners," a colleague described Pond, "he thought himself a philosopher." He was odd indeed, this pugnacious, bombastic, semi-literate son of a shoemaker. Pond was a former Connecticut Yankee who believed in killing off his fur-trading competitors in bloody duels. "We met the next morning eairely," Pond wrote of one such killing, "and discharged pistels in which the pore fellowe was unfortenat."

Nevertheless Pond was a true pathfinder. He set out from Lachine, Quebec (so named because it was thought to be the embarking point for China), paddled across the interlacing lakes and rivers of western Canada, and discovered the Athabasca River (named by the Indians—"Where there are reeds"). He built a log cabin on its reedy shores just south of Lake Athabasca. Trading Indians told him of a great river that flowed out of Samuel Hearne's Great Slave Lake to the Pacific. So Pond sat in his cabin, and in weather so cold that the very inkwell froze, drew a landmark map of Canada's Northwest Territories. He dreamed of presenting this masterpiece of guesswork to the Empress of Russia and he dreamed of exploring the wonderful river himself. But he was forty-seven, an old man by the iron standards of the fur trade. Besides, he was charged with murdering two fellow fur traders, and the Nor'Westers were forcing him to retire.

Mackenzie, who was sent to serve as his second in command, had his imagination kindled by Pond's dream. In his published journal, however, Mackenzie is coldly disdainful of his mentor, who flung him the torch and taught him all the known geographical lore of the Athabasca country. The idea was, the egotist insisted, the "favourite project of *my own* ambition."

The only person who seemed to have a humanizing effect on the would-be explorer was his cousin, Roderick McKenzie. "Dear Rory," as Mackenzie calls him affectionately in his letters, was, unlike himself, a warm, generous, cultured Nor'Wester. He loved books, and had such a considerable library sent west by canoe across half a continent that eventually Fort Chipewyan won renown as the "Little Athens" of the Arctic regions.

In his letters, Mackenzie opens up his heart to Dear Rory. He thanks him for letting him borrow *The History of England.* He sends him by canoe express "a pair of mittens to keep your fingers warm" while Rory is in an outpost on the Saskatchewan River. He expresses regret at having drunk too many drams of H.B. Blackstrap rum, "so that my head is rather out of order at this late or early hour, as you choose to call it." He exchanges gossip about that boozing French Canadian *voyageur,* Pierre Jollie the Drunkard. He damns the "dastardly set of D- - - - -fools" who compete with them as rat-catchers. Mostly he groans about the sheer tedium and ennui of being imprisoned in a log cabin like a caged lion, while doling out firewater to those "troublesome Indians, asking for things for nothing."

One notable letter reflects an intense, highstrung temperament hidden behind that armor of dour reserve. He confesses to having had nightmares: "Although I am not superstitious, dreams amongst other things caused me much annoyance. I could not close my eyes without finding myself in company with the dead."

That letter was written after he had completed his epic canoe expedition, and one is grateful for it because his published journal seems so personally emotionless. His unedited diary, while reading like a series of terse business memos, was a little better; at least it conveys some impression of the man that he was. A magnificent commander of men he may have been, but Mackenzie was not a man who commanded their love. It was once summed up acutely by the late Canadian surveyor-explorer, J.B. Tyrrell. Unlike Samuel Hearne, he pointed out, Mackenzie was simply not interested in his men as individualized human beings. He was rather a masterful executive, and his canoe companions, "whether white men or natives, were merely so many instruments to be used in the accomplishment of any purposes which he had in mind."

Mackenzie's French Canadian voyageurs periodically rested while portaging alongside rapids. "Resting on a Portage" by H.Y. Hind.

Bartering with Indians for beaver peltries was part of the 1789 journey. "Indians Bartering" by J.R. Coke Smyth.

This was borne out by Mackenzie's chronicle. On June 3, 1789, he set out from Fort Chipewyan on his momentous exploration that was to occupy one hundred and two days. Since it was partly a business trip, his three yellow birchbark canoes were loaded with blue beads, mirrors, knives, and other trading gewgaws. His crew included four paddling French Canadian *voyageurs*, two of whom were attended by their "wives," and a man who was a German. Engaged for the expedition also was a party of Indian interpreters and hunters, headed by the chief Chipewyan guide, and two of his wives.

The *voyageurs*— those gay, volatile, chanson-singing muscles of the fur trade, who were to paddle at an amazing average speed of nearly one hundred miles a day downstream and better than thirty miles a day upstream—remain blank faces in Mackenzie's diary. The chief guide— nicknamed English Chief, since he had learned English on Hearne's safari to the Arctic—emerges as a less shadowy personality, but only because Mackenzie was so dependent upon him. Yet Mackenzie leaves no doubt about his lordly relationship with the lot of them.

"I had," he writes, "to watch the savage who was our guide, or to guard against those of his tribe who might meditate our destruction. I had, also, the passions and fears of others to control and subdue. Today I had to assuage the rising discontents, and on the morrow to cheer the fainting spirits of the people who accompanied me.... The voyaging Canadians are equally indolent, extravagant and improvident when left to themselves, and rival the savages in a neglect of the morrow."

In fairness, it must be said that Mackenzie was an inspiring leader and drove nobody more relentlessly than himself. He traveled in a kind of tightly controlled fury, for he was racing against time before winter's onset. Portaging and towing alongside the Slave River's foaming Pelican Rapids, his men were spurred on to run at a dogtrot while carrying ninety-pound backpacks slung by rawhide tumplines around their foreheads. Yet Mackenzie could barely contain his impatience.

"One of the Indian canoes went down the fall and was dashed to pieces," he brusquely recorded. "The woman who had the management of it, by quitting it in time, preserved her life, though she lost the little property it contained.... Our canoes being lightened, we passed on the outside of the opposite island, which rendered the carrying of the baggage very short indeed."

As it was, it took nineteen days before his little canoe brigade entered Mackenzie River proper. He was stalled by solid ice that crusted Great Slave Lake; swarms of mosquitoes and gnats bit implacably; he was blitzed by a tempest of wind and rain; and evidently his *voyageurs* were having their own internecine spats.

"My Steersman had a misunderstanding with his Lady last night and arranged for her to remain at the campment," Mackenzie scribbled in his unedited notebook on June 26. "But his Cousin (her seducer) got her on board and the Husband said nothing to the contrary."

His descent down the river highway was not altogether a dash to the Arctic. He had to pause periodically to call upon Indian customers. They were largely edge-of-the-wood neighbors of the Chipewyans. There were Yellowknives (so called because they used copper implements); Dogribs (who believed they were descended from a supernatural dogman); Slaves (reputedly as docile as slaves); Hares (as meek as their food staple of arctic hare); and the Loucheux (erroneously believed by the French to be squint-eyed).

Mackenzie's visits to their riverbank villages were conducted with shrewd showmanship, as though he were leading a troupe of gypsies in a travelling carnival. In Nor'Wester salesmanship tradition, he first shaved himself and wore his finest beaver top hat; his canoemen spruced up in their gaudiest scarlet leggings, purple capots and sashes, with yellow feathers tucked in their red wool caps. Then Mackenzie would have himself carried regally from his *canot du maître* on his *voyageurs'* shoulders.

After overcoming their initial fear at seeing the palefaces clad in godlike habiliment, the natives crowded around like curious children. Mackenzie sometimes gained their awe by firing his "thunderstick." At other times the white medicine man solemnly promised them that a dose of his Turlington's Balsam mixed with water would drive away the evil spirits.

Invariably English Chief delivered a long harangue. The tribesmen were urged to bring their beaver skins to the new trading post being established at Great Slave Lake. They were beseeched, and sometimes bribed, to supply a pilot to help guide the party downstream to the next village.

The palaver was followed by an exchange of gifts, not always satisfactory to either party. The Indians were particularly appreciative of blue-colored beads, but balked at the alien tobacco and grog that Mackenzie dispensed. "I believe," the paleface salesman recorded in his notepad, "they accepted those civilities more through fear than inclination." On his part, Mackenzie found delicious those forty-pound water hogs of the north, the whitefish; but he could not conceal his distaste for Indian presents of weevily reindeer meat which was "so rotten and stunk so abominably that we did not accept of it."

Neither did he accept of their entertainment very gracefully. The hospitable Indians threw parties for their guests and danced and serenaded Mackenzie with festive songs. The condescending Scot endured it all with attempts at pawky humor. He felt their singing sounded as unharmonious as the howling of wolves. (Evidently he did not consider that their yodelling may have been produced by his H.B. Blackstrap rum, a cordial known to have worked similar results on himself.)

Their dancing he dismissed as orgies of promiscuity. "The women have no covering on their private parts, except a tassel of leather which dangles from a small cord, as it appears, to keep off the flies," he observed primly. "Indeed their want of modesty would make a person think they were descended from Adam. Probably had he been created at the Arctic Circle, he would not have had occasion for Eve, the Serpent, or the Tree of Knowledge to have given him a sense of his nakedness."

Considering that he himself is known to have had an Indian mistress and begat an illegitimate half-blood son named Andrew, Mackenzie's published remarks about the licentious savages smacks of hypocritical prudery. In his unpublished diary, he speaks more uninhibitedly of the promiscuity of his own so-called civilized crew.

"They are not very tempting objects," he writes of the Slave women, "for they are as ugly and disagreeable beings as can be. Notwithstanding which one of our married men and one of the hunters got the better of their feelings, and prevailed upon two of the above objects to accept a share of their bed for the night. The reward was a small knife. But in place of a seducing each they had three, the young men having invited their companions to partake of their favours. However, the recompense was augmented in proportion."

In point of fact, too, Mackenzie admits that he sometimes used force to make a Slave tribesman serve as his conductor downriver. The Indians were fearful of the Eskimos who inhabited those northerly regions. They were winged giants, the legend was whispered, and they could kill you with one glare of their eyes, and they could devour a large beaver with a single gulp.

"We would be several winters getting to the Sea," one soothsayer warned Mackenzie, "and we should all be old men by the time we would return, and we would encounter many Monsters."

Mackenzie says he personally scoffed at these fabulous tales, but they had a powerful effect on both English Chief and the superstitious Indian pilots pressed into service. A gift of Mackenzie's own best traveling jacket helped soothe English Chief's fears, but no bribe was tempting enough to prevent their pilot from deserting.

"We therefore compelled another of these people, very much against his will, to supply the place of his fugitive countryman," wrote Mackenzie. "We also took away the paddles of one of them who remained behind, that he might not follow us on any scheme of promoting the escape of his companion, who was not easily pacified."

The "serpenting river," as Mackenzie described it, proved more full of magic and mystery and surprises than any Indian swami could have imagined. From Mackenzie's terse bulletins one can piece together a little of the sense of wonder he must have felt as he first gazed upon the harsh yet eerie beauty of The Savage Country.

At the river's source in Great Slave Lake, he observed "one continued view of mountains and islands and solid rock, covered here and there with moss, shrubs and trees, the latter quite stunted in their growth for want of soil to nourish them; notwithstanding this barren appearance you can hardly land upon those rocks but you will meet with gooseberries, cranberries, whortleberries, juniper berries, raspberries." As he went north the riverbanks became jungled with black jackpine and silver birch, and even within sight of the Arctic Ocean he was startled to see stands of white spruce towering one hundred feet tall.

He never knew what tricks the river would play beyond its next treacherous twist. Sometimes the rapids "hissed and boiled" like a tea kettle and the currents creamed up "the colour of asses' milk." Sometimes the water changed from "being limpid to muddy" and it curled sluggishly through tangles of reeds and tongued through coulees winy with the smell of wild strawberries and rancid with scummy silt.

Sometimes the sky was a metallic bowl "steel-blue" and the sultry "heat was insupportable"; the sun blazed so constantly overhead that his men couldn't tell night from day. Sometimes he waded through a porridge of swamp muskeg up to his armpits and sometimes the skin of permafrost ground was so tough his dagger couldn't penetrate beyond a depth of six inches. Sometimes he was assailed by hailstones, "boisterous hurricanes whose gusts blew our tents away," and sometimes the frost was "so severe our axes became almost as brittle as glass."

Sometimes his canoemen paddled by golden plovers, "very beautiful," and sometimes they glided by a frieze of white herons and swans, standing in a silver filigree of marsh sedges and silhouetted in a design as lovely as anything to be found on a Japanese fan. Sometimes talc-like cliffs gleamed out of the mists and their shiny peaks "were called by the Indians *manetou aseniah* or 'spirit stones'," and sometimes they were aproned with exquisite rock gardens of yellow arnica, milky avens, blue lupins and purple-pink fireweed. "Yet, in odd contrast," marveled Mackenzie, "though the hills are covered with blossoming flowers and verdure of beautiful appearance, the valleys are full of ice and snow, the earth not thawed above four inches from the surface."

Mackenzie was such a methodical geographer that a traveler today can still detect some of his famous landmarks. At one point English Chief spotted an entire riverbank afire and the apparent coal mine gave off a "very sulphurous smell." That seam of lignite burned like a torch in the wilderness until the next century. And, not far off, English Chief pointed out another riverbank, dripping with "*petrolium*, which bears a resemblance to yellow wax, but is more friable." Both points were in the vicinity of modern Norman Wells, now owned by Imperial Oil, a subsidiary of Standard Oil of New Jersey. With all his business acumen, Mackenzie never suspected that his Indian guide had sniffed out the wellsprings of a potential treasury more fabulous in value than all the beaver skins ever trapped in the some three quarter million square miles of basin drained off by the Mackenzie Valley.

On July 10, Mackenzie reached Point Separation, and he admits bewilderedly in his diary, "I am much at a loss here how to act." It was little wonder. Here the great river fans out into its delta: a gigantic jigsaw puzzle about eighty miles wide and one hundred miles long. It is an intricate maze of meandering channels, soupbowl lakes, pothole ponds, and puddlelike sloughs. Hundreds of islands are matted with the coniferous forests called "taiga." Tens of hundreds of silted quagmires swirl and loop around offshoots of the river, the biggest of which is called Butter's Doughnut. And erupting from the wrinkled tundra are more than one thousand and four hundred "pingos," volcanolike oddities which are equivalent to ice plugs that form in the top of a bottle of milk as it freezes. Even today there is something hostile and primeval about the tortured landscape, something out of the unfinished beginnings of the world, and yet Mackenzie did not flinch.

"All this discouraged my hunters and I am confident that were it in their power they would leave me, as they are quite disgusted with the Voyage," he wrote. "I satisfied them a little by telling them I would go on seven days more, and that if I did not come to the Sea in that time I should return."

He must have cheered on his *voyageurs* considerably. They paddled down one of the sinuous channels, singing their *chansons*, and they put up their tents on a marshy riverbank. Though probably not so, one would like to think it was near the site of modern Aklavik (Eskimo for "Place where there are bears") or possibly near the mellifluous-sounding Eskimo outpost of Tuktoyaktuk ("It looks like a caribou").

Wherever it was, Mackenzie took time out to scribble a rare commendation of his *voyageurs*. "My men express much sorrow that they are obliged to return without seeing the Sea, in which I believe them sincere," he recorded. "For we marched *exceeding* hard coming down the River, and I never heard them grumble; but on the contrary in good spirits, and in hopes every day that the next would bring them to the Sea of the West, and declare themselves now and at any time ready to go with me wherever I choose to lead them."

The next two days were a series of highs and lows for Mackenzie. On Monday, July 13, he records: "We had no sooner retired to rest last night, if I may use that expression in a country where the sun never sinks beneath the horizon, than some of the people were obliged to rise and remove the baggage, on account of the rising of the water." Along with English Chief he tramped up to the top of a high hill, and all that he could see was a limitless expanse of pale blue, jagged, irritated and shifting ice.

So it was *not* the Pacific Ocean, and Mackenzie must have been heartbroken. If so, he kept his feelings under control. All we hear in his journal is that he sat up writing and presumably brooding until three o'clock in the morning. About nine o'clock he was awakened by one of his men, who "saw a great many animals in the water, which he at first supposed to be pieces of ice."

But Mackenzie perceived immediately that they were white beluga whales sporting among the ice floes; and "being curious to take a view of the ice," in a wild spirit of exhilaration the extraordinary man ordered his men to prepare the canoes and give chase to the arctic creatures. It was as though he knew he had lost his great gamble, and he had to release his frustrations somehow. But it was a short-lasting fling; soon the cool executive had his emotions under control.

In the stilted language of a business memo, he expresses regret for his temporary spirit of abandon: "It was, indeed, a very wild and unreflecting enterprise, and it was a very fortunate circumstance that we failed in our attempt to overtake them, as a stroke from the tail of one of these enormous fishes would have dashed the canoe to pieces. We may, perhaps, have been indebted to the foggy weather for our safety, as it prevented us from continuing our pursuit. . . . We were in a state of actual danger, and felt every corresponding emotion of pleasure when we reached the land."

On July 14, 1789, on an Arctic islet he named "Whale Island," which no geographer has been able to identify precisely (though it may have been modern Garry Island), Mackenzie took possession of the end of the road of what he disappointedly called his River of Disappointment. "I ordered a post to be erected close to our tents," he wrote in muted prose, "on which I engraved the latitude of the place, my own name, the number of persons which I had with me, and the time we remained there."

On the arduous trip home, however, tempers became as taut as the towlines used by the *voyageurs* to haul their canoes upstream. English Chief grew increasingly edgy. His youngest wife was threatening to elope with one of his handsome young hunters. Mackenzie, of course, was already simmering with frustration. It was aggravated by English Chief who seemed reluctant to help him glean information from Indian tribesmen about another possible river route across the Shining Mountains to the west.

A blowup was bound to arise, and on August 13 the seemingly imperturbable Mackenzie finally let off steam. His excuse came when English Chief led his Indian hunters in pillaging the belongings of a band of frightened Slaves.

"I severely rebuked the English Chief for his conduct," he says. "The English Chief was very much displeased that I had reproached him, and told me so. This was the very opportunity which I wanted to make him acquainted with my dissatisfaction for some time past."

Mackenzie then gave him a thorough tongue-lashing. "I stated to him that I had come a great way, and at a very considerable expense, without having completed the object of my wishes; and that I suspected he had concealed from me a principal part of what the natives had told him respecting the country, lest he should be obliged to follow me; that his reason for not killing game was his jealousy. . . . "

English Chief burst into a violent passion. He threatened not to accompany Mackenzie any farther. "As soon as he was done his harangue he began to cry bitterly; and his relations assisted the vociferations of his grief; though they said that their tears flowed for their dead friends."

Mackenzie let them wail uninterrupted for two hours. "But as I

Simon McTavish, "The Premier" of the clannish Nor'Westers, squeezed out Mackenzie when the explorer tried to gain dynastic control of the entire Canadian fur trade. Mackenzie died in 1820, and having made the Northwest Passage "by land," predicted nobody would persist in attempting it by sea. He was wrong.

could not do well without them," the realist acknowledged, "I was obliged to use every method to make the English Chief change his mind, and at last he consented with a great reluctance."

That evening, while his *voyageurs* were unloading the canoes, Mackenzie went for a walk along the riverbank. He gazed at the far-off, cloud-plumed Shining Mountains bulking against the sky, which may have been the Camsell Range, and he pondered reflectively. Then he made a decision, which showed that he was not completely the automaton, for it prompted the most human entry in his journal:

"I invited the English Chief to sup with me," he wrote. "I gave him a dram or two, which dispelled all his heart-burning and discontent, and we were as good friends as ever.

"He informed me that it was a custom of the Chipewyan chiefs to go to war after they had shed tears, in order to wipe away the disgrace attached to such a feminine weakness, and that in the ensuing spring he should not fail to execute his design; at the same time he declared his intention to continue with us as long as I should want him. I took care that he should carry some liquid consolation to his lodge, to prevent the return of his chagrin. The weather was fine, and the Indians killed three geese."

By September 12, 1789, Mackenzie was back at Fort Chipewyan again, and he could contemplate his achievement. He had traced to its mouth North America's only truly navigable waterway coursing into the Arctic Ocean. The tugboat skippers who each summer shepherd millions of dollars worth of cargo down that "skinny, shallow-bottomed, snake-backed river" in their skeins of barges attest to his commercial and geographical feat. But in Mackenzie's day his fur-hungry Nor'Wester partners considered it a River of Disappointment, a splendid highway to nowhere. After consultation back east with the company Premier, Simon McTavish, Mackenzie wrote emotionlessly to his Dear Cousin Rory, "My expedition was hardly spoken of, but that is what I expected."

Four years later, lured by what Indians had told him of mysterious rivers flowing across the Shining Mountains, the indefatigable Mackenzie made his second great expedition. With nine canoemen and a dog, he pushed up the Peace and Parsnip Rivers, skirted the headwaters of the Fraser River, and plunged down the Bella Coola to the Pacific Ocean. Then with a mixture of vermilion and bear grease he methodically painted on the southeast face of a rock jutting into Dean Channel his celebrated inscription: "Alexander Mackenzie, from Canada, by land, the twenty-second of July, one thousand and seven hundred and ninety-three."

He had made the first truly transcontinental crossing, the Northwest Passage, "by land."

Again Mackenzie seemed doomed to disappointment. The roaring rivers of the Rocky Mountains were deemed by his Nor'Wester partners to be commercially valueless. Mackenzie could not accept that verdict. He was an ambitious executive, with imperial visions in his head, and he wanted to dominate the entire fur trade: to seize control of both the North West Company and the Hudson's Bay Company. The would-be Caesar spent the rest of his life trying to attain that dynastic power.

He almost made it, but not quite. He went to England, hired a gifted forger and ghostwriter named William Combe (author of *Dr. Syntax*) to add literary touches to his unpolished journals, and was lionized in the salons of London society. He was knighted; he was painted by the King's Painter-in-Ordinary; he won the patronage of a royal duke. He bought for twenty thousand pounds a handsome estate and mansion at Avoch on the Black Isle in Ross-shire; he married a thirteen-year-old Scottish belle named Geddes Mackenzie, said to be "one of the most beautiful women I ever saw," and had three children by her; and by canny investment became a wealthy magnate, who used pressure to try to amalgamate the rival fur-trade companies.

In the end he was thwarted. The "Indian Business," as he termed it, was ruled by clannish Scots as autocratic as himself. He had a business confrontation with The Marquis, Simon McTavish, and if the testimony of a Nor'Wester shareholder is to be believed, the clash of those two egocentric fur barons must have been as fierce as any modern proxy fight on Wall Street:

"Mackenzie is out. The latter went off in a pet. The cause, as far as I can learn, was who should be first—McTavish or Mackenzie. And as there could not be two Caesars in Rome, one must remove."

The ousted Mackenzie found it hard to forgive and forget. "I was so out of temper," he brooded in a letter sent to his comrades back in the Indian country, "that I could not write upon any subject without mixing something of my own Private Concern and that in an acrimonious style, which I knew can never please those who are the friends of Both Parties. . . . But McTavish and his relatives' treatment of me is such that I may for a time forget I had friends. . . . as an Indian Trader."

In the last letter he ever wrote to his Dear Cousin Rory, Mackenzie gains our sympathy. He wrote it from his hearthside at Avoch in the year 1819. He was then fifty-five, an old man by fur-trade standards, and he was an old man withering away with Bright's disease.

He strives to paint a cozy domestic picture. While scratching away with his quill pen, he writes, "Lady Mackenzie is sitting by me and the children are playing on the floor."

But the picture is not really that bright. The roisterer, who once gloried in his capacity to drink every Nor'Wester under the table, now admits he is an enforced temperance man. His gullet may swallow pills every evening, but he is under doctor's orders not to touch a dram of H.B. Blackstrap. "I have," he writes disgustedly, "become a water drinker and milk sop. I have not tasted wine, spirituous or malt liquor for several months."

And most pathetic is his confession that old age and sickness have rusted away his steel mettle. No longer is he the man of iron who could boast of a "constitution and frame of body equal to the most arduous undertakings." No longer is he the demonic force who used to awaken his *voyageurs* before dawn with the revitalizing command, "*Alerte! Lève, lève, nos gens!*" No longer is he the prodigious traveler, who could squeeze the last ounce of nerve and daring and loyalty from his canoe brigade and lead them at the end of a back-breaking expedition on a wild chase after arctic whale.

"The exercise of walking," he confides to Dear Rory, "particularly if uphill, brings on a headache, stupor or dead pain, which at once pervades the whole frame, attended with a listlessness and apathy which I cannot well describe. Exercise in a carriage, if not violent, has a beneficial effect.... I have been overtaken with the consequences of my sufferings in the North West."

One year later, on March 20, 1820, they buried Mackenzie at Avoch. Before his death the business executive had predicted that the fur-trade companies would go bankrupt unless they consolidated their forces. He was right. Within a year of his death, in 1821, the Nor'Wester swashbucklers and the humble servants of the Honourable Company were compelled by the economics of the fur trade to unite under the banner of the H.B.C.

Before his death, too, the explorer had declared that it was foolhardy to persist in seeking a thoroughfare in the arctic latitudes, "the Sea being eternally covered with ice." His first overland expedition, he predicted, "has settled the dubious point of a practicable Northwest Passage; and, I trust, it has set that long agitated question at rest, and extinguished the disputes respecting it for ever."

There he was wrong. The Savage Country continued to tantalize other iron men, and the would-be Caesars continued in their aspirations to conquer it.

Christmas in the Hudson's Bay Territory. In the century ahead Arctic wintering became commonplace for explorers of the Savage Country.

Notes and Acknowledgements

This is the first of two self-contained volumes on the lives of Arctic explorers. It takes us from the earliest Viking sea darers to the fur-trade pathfinders at the close of the eighteenth century. The second volume will continue with the life stories of the American, British, Scandinavian and Canadian North Pole adventurers who transformed the nineteenth century into the golden age of Arctic discovery.

Any reader who glances at the following bibliography I have compiled for my two volumes might well ask: "Why another book on Arctic exploration?"

The answer is simple. None of the hundreds of books I have consulted has attempted to portray the entire pantheon of major Arctic explorers as *people.* When I embarked on my own voyage of exploration through the seas of polar literature for five years, I was amazed by this literary vacuum. I was amazed and yet delighted, for the biographical omission presented a journalistic sleuth like myself with a most exhilarating challenge for personal discovery.

The questions that crowded my mind kept begging for answers: What were these personalities really like? Where did they come from? What influences shaped their lives and their characters? Who sponsored their voyages of discovery? How did their wives fare while the menfolk were occupied on their one-to-five-year odysseys of adventure? When the explorers entered the alien world of ice and Eskimos, how were they prepared, and how did they cope with the encounter? How did they relate to their fellow explorers? And how did they feel when they either failed or succeeded in their missions? Above all, what motivated them? Why were so many impelled to hurl themselves time and again into the terrible, beautiful void of the Arctic solitudes?

I do not pretend to have come up with all the answers. It has been difficult, and sometimes impossible, to ferret out these intimate things. Documents dealing with the early voyages are particularly scanty. And because I have followed the rule of relying primarily on first-hand contemporary evidence, some of the explorers must remain shadowy figures. Having lived out their destinies, they are dead now. Their footsteps in the snow have long vanished, perpetuated only by a few cairns, old bones, and the moldering records.

Ancient artifacts and yellowing documents are such poor substitutes for meeting human beings in the flesh. This thought recurred time and again during the course of my seemingly vain pursuit after elusive clues. I was a journalist on the trail of historical phantoms, and they escaped my touch no matter how hard I tried to conjure them up in their former settings. I thought repeatedly of the apparent futility of my quest.

I thought about it as I paced the seven miles of red granite gorges on the banks of the Avon River overlooking the port of Bristol, and I tried to imagine John Cabot smelling the identical fragrance of blooming bluebells and yellow primroses that May day in 1497 when his little *navicula, Mathew*, slipped out of the cobblestoned quay below and set sail for the spiceries of Cathay.

I thought about it as I peered at the inscription scratched out on a lichen-filigreed rock at Churchill on the lonely shores of Hudson Bay, "*Sl Hearne, July ye 1, 1767*," and I imagined I could see the wraith of the Hudson's Bay Company hiker stepping out of the stone gateway of the ruins of the fur-trade fortress nearby, seven cannon ringing a salute in his ears, when he jauntily began his epic walk to the fabled Far-Off-Metal River.

I thought about ghosts again as I fingered the original manuscript of Samuel Hearne's modestly written *Journey from Prince of Wales's Fort ... to the Northern Ocean* and compared it with the strident prose of Thomas Simpson reporting from Fort Confidence to the Old Lady of Fenchurch Street ("Our subsequent progress along the Coast was one incessant—we may say desperate—struggle with the same cold, obdurate foe.... "), and I marveled to find two such dissimilar narratives reposing after so many years in the same vaults of Beaver House in London.

And I thought of the futility of stalking spectres as I stood on the gneiss crags fringing Holsteinsborg Harbor on the west coast of Greenland, and I tried to imagine how William Baffin felt the morning of July 22, when he saw forty Eskimos swarm from the very spot where I was standing and take revenge for a former white man's kidnap outrage by killing his captain.

I thought about failed missions again as I flew over the marshy, chocolate-brown delta oozing at the edge of the Beaufort Sea, and I made a hopeless attempt to reconstruct the emotions of that seemingly emotionless automaton, Alexander Mackenzie, the July day in 1789 when he had reached the end of his tether and the end of his River of Disappointment, and had urged his *voyageurs* to paddle in mad pursuit after arctic beluga.

I felt as though I had embarked on my own wild whale chase as I pored through the Arnamagraeiske Collection at the University of Copenhagen Royal Library, and touched the yellowish brown parchment folio of the mediaeval Norse *Flateyjarbók*, and tried to evoke from this first written-down version of the sagas an image of Leif the Lucky coursing down the ice-strewn coast of Baffin Island to Vinland.

And once again I thought I heard the taunt of mocking phantoms when the trail finally led me to the bubbling mudholes of Iceland's Thingvellir, the origin of the world's first parliament and of the first voyage of discovery to Greenland. There, as a white blizzard raged over the desolate black lava fields, I tried to imagine Eric the Red being outlawed by the *Althing* parliament for his bloody murders away back in 982 A.D. But the old red-bearded *knarr* voyager eluded me, and all I could summon up was Eric's ghostly laughter roaring in the wail of the wind.

How much one would have enjoyed sitting down with Eric and interviewing him in the flesh, I thought. Stripped of his Wagnerian helmet and Viking battle axe, and without his Odin war cries, perhaps he would have relaxed and revealed a human side of his nature only hinted at in the sagas. Surely there was more to him than the legendary hell-raiser. Perhaps the old pagan was just another henpecked husband and he was so restless because he wanted to escape from the domination of his Christianized wife, Thjodhild. The sagas merely tell us with frustrating lack of detail that Thjodhild "vexed him very much" because she "would not live with Eric as man and wife once she had taken the faith."

Perhaps Sebastian Cabot, too, if he submitted to a journalist's interview, might not be altogether as slippery a rascal as depicted in the sketchy historical accounts. Perhaps Sebastian was also an escapist, seeking surcease from his bossy Spanish wife, Catalina. Perhaps it was ambitious Catalina who drove him to filch credit for the discoveries made by his father, and "to seke strange regions" on his own. It is not implausible, for she was reputedly a sort of Lady Macbeth who urged her husband to poison mutineers on one of his voyages. Or so the meagre historical records claim. How wonderful it would be if Sebastian, a teller of wonderful tales, could now speak out from the grave and tell his side of the story.

And how one longs to have talked to Martin Frobisher and find out if the pirate did actually chop off the right hands of quarrelsome mariners during his Arctic gold rush; to have questioned John Davis about his feelings when his faithless wife, Faith, absconded with a lover while he was off searching for the Northwest Passage using the crystal-ball spirit, Madimi, as his guide; and to have asked poor Henry Hudson what really happened that tragic day in 1611 when his mutinous crew cast the old man adrift with his son and seven sailors in a little shallop among the blue icebergs of "Hudson, his Bay."

Though I have tried to breathe life into the bare bones of these complex personalities, you will not find imagined scenes in these pages. Everything is based on documented fact. Except where it suggests the flavor and atmosphere of the period, I have tended to modernize the Old English spellings and antiquated syntax. But I have scrupulously refrained from inventing dialogue. Nor have I attempted to put fictional thoughts into their heads. I have felt that the unvarnished life stories of these men are so extraordinary, often so brimming with pathos and comedy and drama, that they require no embellishment.

Wherever possible, too, I have attempted to use illustrations that were sketched or painted on the scene by members of the discovery expeditions. In all candor it must be said that these were often done from memory, years after a voyage, and their larger-than-life distortions must be accepted with a stalactite of salt. No explorer's journal published was felt to be complete without its pictures of ravening polar bears, savagely attacking walruses and outlandish-looking "Esquimaux." I have included some of these grotesques, just as I have reproduced some of the drawings of melodramatic scenes that appeared in contemporary magazines and boys' adventure books, because they reflect the quaint attitudes and stereotypes held about the arctic regions.

Most of the Arctic explorers were remarkably literate and some were gifted artists as well. Unfortunately, the early editions of their original journals are long out of print and are hard to come by except in specialized libraries. For those readers who would like to pursue the subject, I would suggest they begin with the volumes of George Francis Lyon and Knud Rasmussen for their warm charm; perhaps dip into the Norse sagas to savor their Grimm fairytale-like quality; take Barents and Amundsen for lively adventure; McClintock and John Ross for naval thrills; Hearne to gain understanding of the northern Indians; Kane and Hall for the sheer fun of their Yankee yarn-spinning; Simpson, Bellot and Cook for their poetic fireworks; and work up to Nansen and Stefansson for their intellectual brilliance.

Unfortunately, with the single exception of the translated memoirs of the Christianized native Greenlander, Hans Christian Hendrik, the Eskimos had no written language and therefore have left us no journals. This is especially regrettable, for one would dearly love to know what the aborigines thought of the intruding white men.

Wherever possible, I have taken pains to suggest events from the Eskimo viewpoint. In some chapters, when presenting the clash of the two cultures, the narrative may appear "racist" by today's enlightened standards. I sincerely hope that Eskimo readers understand that my intention is not to denigrate the *Inuit*, surely the most courteous and unfailingly hospitable people on this earth. I am merely citing with historical accuracy the bigoted attitudes of the early *Kabloona* explorers. Almost invariably the white men were more "barbaric" and "cannibalistic" than the so-called uncivilized "savages" they brutalized. Yet the maltreated natives had the kindness to teach the invaders how to survive in their land.

At the same time I have tried to do justice to the Kabloona explorers who often failed to learn from their Eskimo mentors. Some of them, to be sure, were fools (like Belcher), or swaggerers (like Gilbert), or a trifle pompous (like Franklin and Parry), or outright arrogant (like Simpson and Peary). I have not whitewashed their blemishes, as some of their early idolatrous biographers have done. Yet, despite their frailties, I have always tried to keep in mind that all of them were arctic worthies of a very high order. It took tremendous guts to sail a little bark or even a naval vessel of stout oak into the uncharted Seas of Darkness, to fight for your life against crested waves and easterly gales and blinding mists, and then to stumble about in an unmapped world of bergs and sleet and snow.

If one were to generalize about these exceptional, strong

individualists, one might say that they were driven men. Some were driven by a hunger for glory or for wealth. Some were driven by an almost masochistic need to test their strength and cunning against a hostile environment, as though stricken with a death wish. Some were driven by the scientist's, the collector's, the sportsman's instinct. And some were driven by the simple trailblazer's desire to be the first to break into new country.

A strange love-hate compulsion drove almost all of them to return to the High Arctic. Its harsh, luminous, compelling beauty exerted a curious fascination. They might rail against the cold indifference of its lunar landscapes, and yet they were impelled to come back again and again, even if it killed them. If some failed to unlock its mysteries and neglected to come to terms with its pitiless demands, they gave their lives at least knowing they had fulfilled man's Faustian yearning and absorbing curiosity to seek out the unknown. Theirs was a shining triumph of courage, of imagination, of human tenacity. They were the gleaming land's white first-comers, and theirs was a splendid sunburst of the explorer's achievement.

For their unstinting aid and kind encouragement in helping an amateur historian enter their professional domain, I am first of all indebted to the two eminent Arctic scholars who read through the preliminary drafts of every chapter in this volume and generously shared their expert knowledge: Alex Stevenson, Chairman, Northwest Territories Historical Advisory Board, Department of Indian and Northern Affairs, Ottawa; and Graham Rowley, retired Scientific Adviser, Department of Indian and Northern Affairs, Ottawa.

I am also grateful to those two Arctic worthies, both retired officers from the Royal Canadian Navy and both distinguished navigators of the polar seas, who took time out to help my manuscript steer a clear course through the unfamiliar "ice jargon": Commodore O.C.S. Robertson, who as captain of the Canadian ice-breaker *Labrador* in 1954, became the first to skipper a heavy, sea-draft ship through the Northwest Passage and the first to circumnavigate North America on a single voyage; and his messmate, Captain Thomas C. Pullen, whose icemanship and piloting skill were largely responsible for the successful voyage in 1969 of the mighty one-thousand-and-five-foot icebreaking tanker, *U.S.S. Manhattan,* the first commercial vessel to conquer the Northwest Passage.

I am equally indebted to Frank Stevenson, retired Toponymic Research Officer of the Canadian Permanent Committee on Geographical Names, Ottawa, who cheerfully clarified and unscrambled for me the bewildering jigsaw puzzle of Arctic geography, patiently scrutinized each chapter to make sure the pieces and place names fitted properly, and who tolerantly forgave me when I insisted on using the more modern spellings of McClure and McClintock instead of the outmoded, though more toponymically accurate, M'Clure and M'Clintock.

I am likewise beholden to two specialists on Eskimo culture: Dr. William E. Taylor, Director of the National Museum of Man, Ottawa, for checking my opening chapter to make sure I had not made any mistakes about the Inuit anthropologically; and my friend, Len Peterson, the Canadian playwright, whose dramas champion Eskimo rights, for checking all chapters to make sure I had not violated the Inuit sensibilities spiritually.

I owe thanks to many northern travellers who made research for this book a pure delight, for they enabled me to travel to far-flung spots right across the Far North. Thanks, then, to Murray Watts, the Canadian mining explorer, who flew me on his private Lear Lodestar on a vast sweep from the roof of Baffin Island to the roof of Alaska, who stood with me on mountain peaks overlooking Lancaster Sound and the Bering Strait, and helped me understand the feeling of exultation that must have moved the early discoverers to unravel the geological mysteries beyond the next glimmering mountain peak.

Thanks to Captain Don Tetrault, skipper of the Arctic Cruise Lines *Norweta*, for the supreme thrill of allowing me to take over the pilot's wheel of his riverboat as she began her maiden voyage from Great Slave Lake *down*—not *up*—the Mackenzie River to the Beaufort Sea.

Thanks to Tommy Gordon, the Eskimo pilot from Reindeer Airways in Inuvik, Northwest Territories, for gliding me over the Beaufort Sea with such dexterity in his tiny Cessna, while I was holding on for dear life to the legs of photographer Richard Pierre, who was half way out the window shooting pictures of the seals and polar bears on the ice floes below.

Thanks also to Bob Bruce of Winnipeg, who gave me a lift to Churchill on the Canadian National Railway's annual "Explorers of Hudson Bay" excursion train; to Richard Rohmer, founder of the Mid-Canada Development project, for letting me hitch train and plane rides to the subarctic regions of Labrador and Ungava; to George E. McGrath, New York representative of Icelandic-Loftleider Airlines, for enabling me to explore Iceland by plane, bus and pony; and to Stanley Tapson, Toronto representative of Scandinavian Airlines, for the jet flights to the museums of Norway and Denmark and the helicopter trips over the glaciers of Greenland.

I am indebted to a host of scholars and institutions who graciously opened up their doors to me. I would particularly like to acknowledge the hospitality of Dr. Gordon G. de Q. Robin, director, Alan Cooke, manuscript curator, Clive Holland, assistant curator, and H.G.R. King, librarian, of the Scott Polar Research Institute in Cambridge, England. They permitted me to study the original letters of Lady Franklin and the other Franklin-expedition searchers for one week, and then had the kindness to forgive me for mussing up their rare collection.

Other guides who helped ease my tortuous trail include: Colonel Jorgen V. Helk, director of the Arktisk Institut of Denmark, who took the trouble to collate and translate into English for me all the known biographical data pertaining to Knud Rasmussen; Dr. Helge Ingstad, who spent many hours with me at his charming home overlooking a fjord in Norway chatting about his own search to discover the archaeological ruins of Vinland in Newfoundland; Kaare Z. Lundquist, deputy director of the Norsk Polar Institutt in Oslo; Dr. Gutorm Gjessing, director of the Norwegian Ethnological Museum in Oslo; Dr. Jorgen Meldgaard, curator of the Arctic Division of the Danish National Museum in Copenhagen; and Dr. Thor Magnusson, curator of the Icelandic Museum in Reykjavik.

In England, for the warm courtesies they extended, I owe special thanks to: Sir Lawrence P. Kirwan, director of the Royal Geographical Society in London; Christine Kelly, the Society's archivist; Lieutenant Commander George P.B. Naish, keeper emeritus, Ann Shirley, assistant keeper, and Edward Archibald, curator, at the National Maritime Museum in Greenwich; Dorothy Lindsay, registrar, who allowed me to examine original paintings of all the Franklin-search figures in the catacombs of the National Portrait Gallery in London; Joan Craig, Hudson's Bay Company archivist at Beaver House in London; Judith Phillips, associate archivist of the City Archives in the port of Bristol; and Lord Tweedsmuir, John Norman Stuart Buchan, who mixes his Scotch and his Arctic knowledge at the House of Lords at Westminster with equal finesse.

In Canada I received considerable aid from Edith Firth, who guards the rare Arctic collection in the Baldwin Room of the Toronto Public Library; Jean Gibson, who does likewise at the John Robarts Library of the University of Toronto; Michael Bell, print curator, Public Archives of Canada; Hugh A. Dempsey, archivist for the Glenbow

Foundation, Calgary; Barry Hyman, assistant archivist at the Manitoba Archives in Winnipeg; Dr. Walter Oscar Kupsch, director of the Institute for Northern Studies, Saskatoon; Oblate Brother J. Volant, curator of the Eskimo Museum in Churchill; and Dr. Edward C. Shaw, the dedicated curator of Red River House Museum in St. Andrews, Manitoba, undoubtedly the only museum devoted to enshrining an Arctic explorer —Captain William Kennedy.

The Film Department of the Toronto Public Library was kind enough to screen for me four little-known documentary movies dealing with the lives of Knud Rasmussen and Vilhjalmur Stefansson—which was as near as I got to actually seeing the apparitions of the great dead explorers in live action.

Finally I must thank my wife, Brenda. Not only did she help edit each chapter, but the forbearing woman withstood my extended five-year *Wanderjahr* of polar research with a patience and fortitude perhaps equalled only by Jane, Lady Franklin, herself.

A Select Arctic
Bibliography

Amundsen, Roald. *The Northwest Passage.* 2 vols. London: Archibald
    Constable, 1908.
    The South Pole. 2 vols. London: John Murray, 1912.
    Our Polar Flight. In collaboration with Lincoln Ellsworth. New
    York: Dodd, Mead, 1925.
    My Life as an Explorer. Garden City, N.Y.: Doubleday, Doran,
    1928.

Andrews, Roy Chapman. *Beyond Adventure: The Lives of Three Explorers.*
    New York: Duell, Sloan & Pearce, 1958.

Andrist, Ralph K. *Heroes of Polar Exploration.* New York: American
    Heritage, 1962.

Angell, Pauling K. *To the Top of the World: The Story of Peary and Henson.*
    Chicago: Rand, McNally, 1965.

Armstrong, Alexander. *A Personal Narrative of the Discovery of the North-
    West Passage.* London: Hurst & Blackett, 1857.

Asher, G.M. (Editor). *Henry Hudson, the Navigator.* London: Hakluyt
    Society, 1889.

Back, George. *Narrative of the Arctic Land Expedition to the mouth of the
    Great Fish River.* London: John Murray, 1836.

Bacon, Edgar Mayhew. *Henry Hudson, His Times and Voyages.* New York:
    Putnam's, 1907.

Baffin, William. *The Voyages of William Baffin.* Annotated by Clements
    R. Markham. London: Hakluyt Society, 1831.

Bain, J. Arthur. *Life and Explorations of Fridtjof Nansen.* London: Walter Scott, 1897.

Baliksi, Asen. *The Netsilik Eskimo.* Garden City, N.Y.: Natural History Press, 1970.

Barrow, John. *A Chronological History of Voyages into the Arctic Regions.* London: John Murray, 1818.
    Voyages of Discovery and Research within the Arctic Regions from 1818 to the Present Time. London: John Murray, 1846.

Bartlett, Robert A. *The Log of "Bob" Bartlett.* New York: Putnam's, 1928.

Beazley, C. Raymond. *John and Sebastian Cabot.* London: T. Fisher Unwin, 1898.

Belcher, Sir Edward. *The Last of the Arctic Voyages.* 2 vols. London: Lovell Reeve, 1855.

Bellot, Joseph René. *Memoirs of Lieutenant Joseph René Bellot.* 2 vols London: Hurst & Blackett, 1855.
    Journal d'un Voyage aux Mers polaires exécuté à la Recherché de Sir John Franklin en 1851 et 1852. Paris: Perrotin, 1854.

Berry, Erick. *Mr. Arctic: An Account of Vilhjalmur Stefansson.* New York: David McKay, 1966.

Biggar, H.P. *The voyages of the Cabots and of the Corte Reals to North America and Greenland.* Paris: Macon, Protàt Frères, 1903.
    The Precursors of Jacques Cartier, 1497-1534. Ottawa: Public Archives of Canada Publications, 1911.

Birket-Smith, Kaj. *The Eskimos.* London: Methuen, 1955.

Borup, George. *A Tenderfoot with Peary.* New York: Frederick A. Stokes, 1911.

Brebner, J.B. *The Explorers of North America, 1492-1806.* Garden City, N.Y.: Doubleday, 1955.
    Canada. Ann Arbor, Mich.: University of Michigan Press, 1960.

Brendon, J.A. *Great Navigators and Discoverers.* Toronto: George C. Harrap, 1929.

Brogger, A.W. *The Viking Ships.* Oslo: Dreyer, 1951.

Brown, John. *The North-West Passage and the Plans for the Search for Sir John Franklin: A Review.* London: Stanford, 1858.
    A Sequel . . . to the North-West Passage. London: Stanford, 1858.

Browne, W.H.J. *Ten Coloured Views taken during the Arctic Expedition of H.M.S.* Enterprise *and* Investigator. London: Ackermann, 1850.

Bruemmer, Fred. *Encounters with Arctic Animals.* Toronto: McGraw-Hill Ryerson, 1972.

Seasons of the Eskimo: A Vanishing Way of Life. Toronto: McClelland & Stewart, 1971.

Burpee, Lawrence J. *The Search for the Western Sea.* Toronto: Musson, 1908.

Campbell, Marjorie Freeman. *A Century of Crime.* Toronto: McClelland & Stewart, 1970.

Caswell, John E. *Arctic Frontiers.* Norman, Oklahoma: University of Oklahoma Press, 1956.

Chappell, Lieut. Edward. *Narrative of a voyage to Hudson's Bay on H.M.S. Rosamond.* London: J. Mawman, 1817.

Christie, Miller. (Editor). *The Voyages of Captain Luke Foxe of Hull and Captain Thomas James of Bristol.* 2 vols. London: Hakluyt Society, 1894.

Collinson, Captain Richard. *Journal of H.M.S. Enterprise ... in search of Sir John Franklin's ships by Behring Strait 1850-55.* Annotated by Major General T.B. Collinson. London: Sampson, Low, Marston, Searle & Rivington, 1889.

(Editor). The Three Voyages by Martin Frobisher. London: Hakluyt Society, 1887.

Cook, Dr. Frederick Albert. *My Attainment of the Pole.* New York: The Polar Publishing Co., 1911.

Return from the Pole. Annotated by Frederick J. Pohl. New York: Pellegrini & Cudahy, 1951.

Cooper, Paul Fenimore. *Island of the Lost.* New York: Putnam, 1961.

Corner, George W. *Dr. Kane of the Arctic Seas.* Philadelphia: Temple University Press, 1972.

Courtauld, Augustine. *From the Ends of the Earth: An Anthology of Polar Writings.* London: Oxford University Press, 1958.

Creighton, D.G. *Dominion of the North.* Toronto: Macmillan, 1944.

Cresswell, Samuel Gurney. *A Series of Eight Sketches in colour ... of the voyage of H.M.S. Investigator (Capt. M'Clure) during the discovery of the Northwest Passage.* London: Day & Son, 1854.

Croft, Andrew. *Polar Exploration.* London: A. & C. Black, 1939.

Crouse, Nellis M. *The Search for the Northwest Passage.* New York: Columbia University Press, 1934.

In Quest of the Western Ocean. London: Dent, 1928.

The Search for the North Pole. New York: Richard R. Smith, 1947.

Cumming, W.T. *The Discovery of North America.* In collaboration with R.A. Skelton and D.B. Quinn. Toronto: McClelland & Stewart, 1971.

Cyriax, Richard Julius. *Sir John Franklin's Last Arctic Expedition.* London: Methuen, 1939.

Davis, John. *The Voyages and Works of John Davis, the Navigator.* Annotated by Albert Hastings Markham. London: Hakluyt Society, 1830.

Deacon, Richard. *John Dee: Scientist, Geographer, Astrologer, and Secret Agent to Elizabeth I.* London: Muller, 1968.

De Poncins, Gontram. *Kabloona.* New York: Reynal & Hitchcock, 1941.

De Veer, Gerrit. *The Three Voyages of William Barents in the Arctic Regions.* Annotated by Lieut. Koolemans Beynen. London: Hakluyt Society, 1876.

D'Israeli, Isaac. *The Occult Philosopher, Dr. Dee.* Paris: Amenities of Literature, 1843.

Dodge, Ernest S. *Northwest By Sea.* London: Oxford University Press, 1961.

    The Polar Rosses: John and James Clark Ross and their Explorations. London: Faber & Faber, 1973.

Dunbar, Moira. *Arctic Canada from the Air.* In collaboration with Keith R. Greenaway. Ottawa: Queen's Printer, 1956.

Eames, Hugh. *Winner Lose All: Dr. Cook and the Theft of the North Pole.* Boston: Little, Brown, 1973.

Elder, William. *Biography of Elisha Kent Kane.* Philadelphia: Childs & Peterson, 1958.

Elias, E.L. *The Book of Polar Exploration.* London: George C. Harrap, 1928.

Ellsworth, Lincoln. *Beyond Horizons.* New York: Book League of America, 1938.

    Search. New York: Brewer, Warren & Putnam, 1932.

Euller, John. *Arctic World.* New York: Abelard-Schuman, 1958.

Evans, Admiral Sir Edward. *British Polar Explorers.* London: Collins, 1943.

Fell-Smith, Charlotte. *John Dee: 1527-1608.* London: Constable, 1909.

Fiske, John. *The Discovery of America.* 2 vols. Boston and New York: Houghton Miflin, 1892-1902.

Fox, Margaret. *The Love-Life of Dr. Kane, Containing the Correspondence, and a History of the Acquaintance, Engagement, and Secret Marriage between Elisha Kent Kane and Margaret Fox.* New York: Carleton, 1866.

Franklin, Jane. *A Letter to Lord Palmerston, K.G. from Lady Franklin.* London: James Ridgway, 1857.

Franklin, Sir John. *Narrative of a Journey to the shores of the Polar Sea in the years 1819-20-21-22.* London: Dent, 1819. Reprint (annotated by Louis Melzack). Edmonton: Hurtig, 1969.
    Narrative of a Second Expedition to the Shores of the Polar Sea in the years 1825, 1826, and 1827. London: John Murray, 1828. Reprint (annotated by Leslie H. Neatby). Edmonton: Hurtig, 1971.

Freeman, Andrew A. *The Case for Dr. Cook.* New York: Coward-McCann, 1961.

French, Peter J. *John Dee: The World of Elizabethan Magus.* London: Rutledge & K. Paul, 1972.

Freuchen, Peter. *I Sailed with Rasmussen.* New York: Viking Press, 1961.
    Arctic Adventure: My Life in the Frozen North. New York: Farrar & Rinehart, 1935.
    Book of the Eskimos. New York: Fawcett World Library, 1961.
    Book of Arctic Exploration. New York: Coward-McCann, 1962.

Gell, E.M. *Sir John Franklin's Bride.* London: Murray, 1930.

Gerson, Noel Bertram. *Passage to the West, the Great Voyages of Henry Hudson.* New York: Messner, 1963.

Gilbert, Sir Humphrey. *The Voyages and Colonising Enterprises of Sir Humphrey Gilbert.* 2 vols. Annotated by David Beers Quinn. London: Hakluyt Society, 1940.

Godfrey, William C. *Godfrey's Narrative of the last Grinnell Arctic Exploring Expedition.* Philadelphia: J.T. Lloyd, 1851.

Gordon, W.J. *Round About the North Pole.* London: John Murray, 1907.

Gosling, William G. *Life of Sir Humphrey Gilbert.* London: Constable, 1911.

Greeley, A.W. *Handbook of Polar Discoveries.* Boston: Brown, 1907.
    True Tales of Arctic Heroism in the New World. New York: Charles Scribner Sons, 1912.

Green, Fitzhugh. *Peary: The Man Who Refused to Fail.* New York: Putnam's, 1926.

Hagen, Anders. *The Viking Ship Finds.* Oslo: Universitetets Oldsaksamling, 1968.

Hakluyt, Richard. *Divers Voyages Touching the Discovery of America.* Annotated by J.W. Jones. London: Hakluyt Society, 1850.

Hall, Anna Gertrude. *Nansen.* New York: Viking Press, 1940.

Hall, Charles Francis. *Life with the Esquimaux.* Reprint (annotated by George Swinton). Edmonton: Hurtig, 1970.
    Narrative of the North Polar Expedition U.S.S., Polaris , Captain Charles Francis Hall Commanding. Annotated by C.H. Davis. Washington: U.S. Government Printing Office, 1876.

Narrative of the Second Arctic Expedition made by Charles F. Hall. Annotated by J.E. Nourse. Washington: U.S. Government Printing Office, 1879.

Hannon, Leslie F. *The Discoverers.* Toronto: McClelland & Stewart, 1971.

Hanssen, Helmer. *Voyages of a Modern Viking.* London: Routledge, 1936.

Hanson, Earl Parker. *Stefansson, Prophet of the North.* New York: Harper & Brothers, 1941.

Harrisse, Henry. *Jean et Sebastien Cabot.* Paris: E. Leroux, 1882.

    Découverte et Évolution Cartographique de Terre-Neuve. Paris: C. Delagrave, 1900.

    John Cabot, the Discoverer of North America, and Sebastian his Son. London: B.F. Stevens, 1895.

Hartwig, Dr. G. *The Polar and Tropical Worlds.* Guelph, Ont.: J.W. Lyon, 1874.

Hayes, Isaac Israel. *An Arctic Boat Journey in the Autumn of 1854.* London: Richard Bentley, 1860.

    The Open Polar Sea. New York: Hurd & Houghton, 1867.

Hayes, James Gordon. *Robert Edwin Peary: A Record of his Explorations.* London: Richards & Toulmin-Cayme, 1929.

    The Conquest of the North Pole. London: Butterworth, 1934.

Hearne, Samuel. *A Journey to the Northern Ocean.* Annotated by Richard Glover. Toronto: Macmillan, 1958.

Hendrik, Hans Christian. *Memoirs of Hans Hendrik, the Arctic Traveller.* Translated from the Eskimo language by Dr. Henry Rink. Edited by Dr. George Stevens. London: Trubner, 1878.

Henson, Matthew A. *A Black Explorer at the North Pole.* Toronto: Ryerson Press, 1969.

Hoare, J. Douglas. *Arctic Explorations.* London: Methuen, 1906.

Hobbs, William Herbert. *Peary.* New York: Macmillan, 1936.

Hoyer, Liv Nansen. *Eva Og Fridtjof Nansen.* Oslo: J.W. Cappelens Forlag, 1954.

Huish, Robert. *The Last Voyage of Captain Sir John Ross.* In collaboration with William Light, steward. London: Saunders, 1835.

Ingstad, Helge. *Westward to Vinland.* London: Jonathan Cape, 1969.

Jenness, Diamond. *The People of the Twilight.* University of Chicago Press, 1928.

    The Indians of Canada. Ottawa: National Museum of Canada, 1955.

Johansen, Frederik Hjalmar. *With Nansen in the North.* London: Morange, 1898.

Jones, Lawrence F. *Pathfinders of the North.* In collaboration with George Lonn. Toronto: Pitt, 1969.

Jones, Gwyn. *The Norse Atlantic Saga.* London: Oxford University Press, 1964.

Kane, Elisha Kent. *The U.S. Grinnell Expedition in search of Sir John Franklin.* New York: Harper & Bros., 1854.
   Arctic Explorations in the years 1853, '54, '55. 2 vols. Philadelphia: Childs & Paterson, 1856.

Keating, Bern. *The Northwest Passage.* Chicago: Rand McNally, 1970.

Kennedy, William. *A Short Narrative of the Second Voyage of the Prince Albert, in search of Sir John Franklin.* London: W.H. Dalton, 1853.

King, Richard. *The Franklin Expedition from First to Last.* London: John Churchill, 1855.

Kirwan, L.P. *The White Road.* London: Hollis & Carter, 1959.

Krogh, Knud J. *Viking Greenland.* Copenhagen: National Museum, 1967.

Lamb, G.F. *Franklin, Happy Voyager.* London: Benn, 1956.

Lamb, Harold. *New Found World.* New York: Doubleday, 1955.

Lamb, W. Kaye. *Canada's Five Centuries.* Toronto: McGraw-Hill of Canada, 1971.

Lanctot, Gustave. *A History of Canada.* Toronto: Clarke, Irwin, 1963.

Lantis, Margaret. *Alaskan Eskimo Ceremonialism.* New York: J.J. Augustin, 1947.

Laut, Agnes. *The Adventurers of England on Hudson Bay.* Toronto: University of Toronto Press, 1964.

Leacock, Stephen. *Adventurers of the Far North.* Toronto: University of Toronto Press, 1964.

Le Bourdais, D.M. *Stefansson, Ambassador of the North.* Toronto: Harvest House, 1962

Lewis, Lorna. *Nansen.* London: Thomas Nelson, 1937.

Ley, Willy. *The Poles.* New York: Time, Inc., 1962.

Loomis, Chauncey. *Weird and Tragic Shores.* New York: Knopf, 1971.

Low, A.P. *Report on the Dominion Government Expedition ... on D.G.S. Neptune.* Ottawa: Government Printing Bureau, 1906.

Lyon, George Francis. *A Brief Narrative of an Unsuccessful Attempt to reach Repulse Bay.* London: Murray, 1825.
   The Private Journal of Captain G.F. Lyon. Annotated by James A. Houston. Barre, Mass.: Imprint Society, 1970.

Macdonald, R. St. J. *The Arctic Frontier.* With colleagues. Toronto: University of Toronto Press, 1966.

MacGahan, J.A. *Under the Northern Lights.* London: Sampson, Low, Marston, Searle & Rivington, 1876.

MacInnes, C.M. *Bristol: A Gateway of Empire.* London: Arrowsmith, 1939.

MacKay, Douglas. *The Honourable Company.* Toronto: McClelland & Stewart, 1949.

Mackenzie, Alexander. *The Journals and Letters of Sir Alexander Mackenzie.* Annotated by W. Kaye Lamb. Toronto: Macmillan, 1970.

Voyages from Montreal . . . to the Frozen and Pacific Oceans. London: R. Nobe, 1801. Reprint (edited by John W. Garvin). Toronto: Christino Edition, 1927

Maclean, J. Kennedy. *Heroes of the Farthest North and Farthest South.* In collaboration with Chelsea Fraser. New York: Crowell, 1923.

MacMillan, Donald B. *How Peary Reached the Pole.* Boston: Houghton Miflin, 1934.

Four Years in the White North. Boston: Hale, Cushman, & Flint, 1933.

McClintock, F. Leopold. *The Voyage of the* Fox *in Arctic Seas.* London: Murray, 1908.

Reminiscences of Arctic Ice-Travel in Search of Sir John Franklin. Dublin: Journal of Royal Dublin Society, 1857.

M'Dougall, George F. *The Eventful Voyage of the H.M.S. Discovery Ship Resolute to the Arctic Regions.* London: Longman, Brown, Green, Longmans & Roberts, 1857.

McFee, William. *The Life of Sir Martin Frobisher.* London: John Lane. The Bodley Head Ltd., 1928.

McIlraith, Rev. John. *Life of Sir John Richardson.* Longmans, Green, 1868.

Mangles, Commander James. *Papers and Dispatches relating to the Arctic Searching Expeditions of 1850-51-52.* London: Francis and John Rivington, 1852.

Markham, Captain Albert. *Life of Sir John Franklin.* London: George Philip & Son, 1891.

Markham, Clements R. *A Life of John Davis, the Navigator, Discoverer of Davis Straits.* London: George Philip, 1889.

Life of Admiral Sir Leopold McClintock. London: Murray, 1909.

The Lands of Silence: A History of Arctic and Antarctic Exploration. Cambridge: Cambridge University Press, 1921.

May, Walter William. *A Series of Fourteen Sketches made during the Voyage up Wellington Canal.* London: Day & Son, 1855.

Miller, Francis Trevelyan. *The World's Great Adventure: One Thousand Years of Polar Exploration.* New York: Miller Illustrated Press, 1930.

Mirsky, Jeannette. *To the Arctic!* New York: Knopf, 1948.
 Elisha Kent Kane and the Seafaring Frontier. Boston: Little, Brown, 1954.

Morison, Samuel Eliot. *The European Discovery of America: the Northern Voyages A.D. 500-1600.* New York: Oxford University Press, 1971.
 Admiral of the Ocean Sea. Boston: Little, Brown, 1942.

Morris, Charles. *Finding the North Pole.* New York: Scull, 1909.

Morton, W.L. *The Kingdom of Canada.* Toronto: McClelland & Stewart, 1963.

Mowat, Farley. *Canada North.* Toronto: McClelland & Stewart, 1967.
 Westviking. Toronto: McClelland & Stewart, 1965.
 Ordeal by Ice. Toronto: McClelland & Stewart, 1960.
 The Polar Passion. Toronto: McClelland & Stewart, 1967.
 Tundra. Toronto: McClelland & Stewart, 1973.

Nansen, Fridtjof: *Farthest North.* 2 vols. London: Constable, 1897.
 In Northern Mists. 2 vols. London: Heinemann, 1891.
 First Crossing of Greenland. London: Longmans, Green, 1890.
 Eskimo Life. London: Longmans, Green, 1893.
 To Siberia, the Land of the Future. New York: Stokes, 1914.
 Letters (Brev). 4 vols. Oslo: Universitet Sforlaget, 1961-1966.

Nanton, Paul. *Arctic Breakthrough.* Toronto: Clarke, Irwin, 1970.

Neatby, Leslie H. *In Quest of the Northwest Passage.* Toronto: Longmans, Green, 1958.
 Search for Franklin. Edmonton: Hurtig, 1969.
 Frozen Ships, the Arctic Diary of Johan Miertsching, 1850-1854. Toronto: Macmillan, 1967.
 Conquest of the Last Frontier. Athens, Ohio: Ohio University Press, 1966.

Nobile, Umberto. *My Polar Flight.* London: Muller, 1961.

Noice, Harold. *With Stefansson in the Arctic.* Toronto: Ryerson, 1943.

Nourse, J.E. *American Explorations in the Ice Zones.* Boston: Lothrop, 1884.

Oleson, Tryggvi J. *Early Voyages and Northern Approaches 1000-1632.* Toronto: McClelland & Stewart, 1963.

Ortzen, Len. *Famous Arctic Adventures.* London: Barker, 1972.

Osborn, Sherard. *Arctic Miscellanies: Souvenir of the late Polar Search.* With colleagues. London: Colburn, 1852.

　　The Discovery of the Northwest Passage by Captain Robert Le Mesurier M'Clure. Reprint (edited by William C. Wonders) Edmonton: Hurtig, 1969.

　　Stray Leaves from an Arctic Journal. London: Longman, Brown, Green & Longmans, 1852.

　　The Career, Lost Voyage and Fate of Sir John Franklin. Edinburgh: William Blackwood, 1865.

Parry, Ann. *Parry of the Arctic: The Life Story of Admiral Sir Edward Parry.* London: Chatto & Windus, 1963.

Parry, Captain William Edward. *Journals of the First, Second, and Third Voyages for the Discovery of a Northwest Passage.* 5 vols. London: Murray, 1828.

Partridge, Bellamy. *Amundsen.* London: R. Hale, 1953.

Peary, Josephine Diebitsch. *My Arctic Journal.* New York: Contemporary Publishing Co., 1893.

Peary, Robert E. *Nearest the Pole.* New York: Doubleday, 1907.

　　The North Pole. New York:Stokes, 1910.

　　Northward over the "Great Ice." 2 vols. New York: Stokes, 1898.

　　Secrets of Polar Travel. New York: Century, 1917.

Phillips, R.A.J. *Canada, the Yukon and Northwest Territories.* Toronto: McGraw-Hill of Canada, 1966.

Pohl, Frederick J. *Atlantic Crossings before Columbus.* New York: W.W. Norton, 1961.

Pond, Seymour Gates. *The History and Romance of Exploration.* New York: Cooper Square Publishers, 1966.

Powys, Llewelyn. *Henry Hudson.* London: J. Lane, 1927.

Purchas, Samuel. *Hakluytus Posthumus; or Purchas, his Pilgrimes.* 20 vols. Glasgow: J. MacLehose & Sons, 1905-1907.

Rae, Dr. John. *Narrative of an Expedition to the shores of the Arctic Sea in 1846-47.* London: Boone, 1850.

　　Rae's Arctic Correspondence, 1844-1855. Annotated by E.E. Rich and A.M. Johnson. London: Hudson's Bay Record Society, 1953.

Rasky, Frank. *The Taming of the Canadian West.* Toronto: McClelland & Stewart, 1967.

Rasmussen, Knud. *Greenland by the Polar Sea.* New York: Stokes, 1920.

　　The People of the Polar North. London: Kegan Paul, Trench, Trubner, 1908.

Across Arctic America: Narrative of the Fifth Thule Expedition. New York; Putnam's, 1927.

Report of the Fifth Thule Expedition. With colleagues. 10 vols. Rasmussen reports in vols. 7 to 10. Copenhagen: Danish Government, 1931-1942.

Rawlins, Dennis. *Peary at the North Pole: Fact or Fiction?* Toronto: Musson, 1973.

Rawnsley, Willingham Franklin. *The Life, Diaries and Correspondence of Jane, Lady Franklin.* London: Erskine Macdonald, 1923.

Read, John Meredith. *A Historical Inquiry Concerning Henry Hudson.* Albany, N.Y.: Joel Munsell, 1866.

Robinson, Bradley. *Dark Companion.* New York: McBride, 1947.

Rich, E.E. *Hudson's Bay Company 1670-1870.* 3 vols. Toronto: McClelland & Stewart, 1960.

Richardson, Sir John. *Arctic Searching Expedition.* New York: Harper & Bros., 1854.

The Polar Regions Edinburgh: Adam & Charles Black, 1861.

Ross, Captain John. *A Voyage of Discovery in his Majesty's ships Isabella and Alexander.* London: Murray, 1819.

Narrative of a Second Voyage ... 1829-1833. London: Orlando Hodgson, 1835.

Observations on a work ... by Sir John Barrow, Being a Refutation of the numerous Misrepresentations contained in that Volume. Edinburgh and London: Pamphlet, 1846.

Rowse, Alfred Leslie. *The England of Elizabeth, the Structure of Society.* London: Macmillan, 1950.

The Elizabethans and America. London: Macmillan, 1959.

The English Spirit. London: Macmillan, 1966.

Sabine, Captain Edward. *Remarks on the account of the late voyage of Discovery to Baffin's Bay.* London: Pamphlet, 1819.

Shackleton, Edward. *Nansen the Explorer.* London: Witherby, 1959.

Simpson, Alexander. *The Life and Travels of Thomas Simpson.* Reprint (annotated by John Gellner). Toronto: Baxter, 1963.

Simpson, Thomas. *Narrative of the Discoveries of the North Coast of America.* London: Richard Bentley, 1843.

Skewes, J. Henry. *Sir John Franklin, the True Secret of the Discovery of his Fate, a "Revelation."* London: Bemrose, 1890.

Smith, I. Norman. *The Unbelievable Land.* With colleagues. Ottawa: Queen's Printer, 1965.

Smith, James K. *Alexander Mackenzie, Explorer, the Hero Who Failed.* Toronto: McGraw-Hill Ryerson, 1973.

Smith, Murray D. *Arctic Expeditions British and Foreign.* London: Thomas C. Jack, 1880.

Smith, William D. *Northwest Passage.* New York: American Heritage Press, 1970.

Smucker, Samuel M. *Arctic Explorations and Discoveries during the 19th Century.* New York: William L. Allison, 1886.

Sorensen, Jon. *The Saga of Fridtjof Nansen.* New York: American-Scandinavian Society, 1932.

Steensel, Maja Van. *People of Light and Dark.* With colleagues. Ottawa: Queen's Printer, 1966.

Stefansson, Vilhjalmur. *My Life with the Eskimo.* New York: Macmillan, 1913.

    The Northward Course of Empire. New York: Macmillan, 1924.

    The Standardization of Error. New York: Norton, 1927.

    Unsolved Mysteries of the Arctic. New York: Macmillan, 1938.

    The Three Voyages of Martin Frobisher. 2 vols. Annotated in collaboration with Eloise McCaskill. London: Argonaut Press, 1938.

    Ultima Thule. New York: Macmillan, 1940.

    The Friendly Arctic. New York: Macmillan, 1943.

    The Fat of the Land. New York: Macmillan, 1956.

    Discovery. Toronto: McGraw-Hill Book Co., 1964.

Sverdrup, Otto. *Sverdrup's Arctic Adventures.* Annotated by T.C. Fairley. Toronto: Longmans, 1959.

Taylor, E.G.R. *Late Tudor and Early Stuart Geography 1583-1650.* New York: Octagon Books, 1968.

Thomson, D.W. *Men and Meridians: History of Surveying and Mapping in Canada.* Ottawa: Queen's Printer, 1966.

Traill, Henry Duff. *The Life of Sir John Franklin.* London: John Murray, 1896.

Turley, Charles. *Nansen of Norway.* London: Methuen, 1933.

    Roald Amundsen, Explorer. London: Methuen, 1935.

Tyrrell, J.W. *Across the Sub-arctics of Canada.* Toronto: William Briggs, 1908.

Tyson, George E. *Arctic Experiences: Containing Capt. George E. Tyson's Wonderful Drift on the Ice-Floe.* Annotated by E. Vale Blake. New York: Harper & Bros., 1874.

Valentine, Victor F. *Eskimo of the Canadian Arctic.* In collaboration with Frank G. Vallee. Toronto: McClelland & Stewart, 1968.

Victor, Paul-Emile. *Man and the Conquest of the Poles.* New York: Simon & Schuster, 1963.

Villarejo, Oscar M. *Dr. Kane's Voyages to the Polar Lands.* Philadelphia: University of Pennsylvania Press, 1965.

Villiers, Captain Alan. *Men, Ships and the Sea.* Washington: National Geographic Society, 1962.

Vogt, Per. *Fridtjof Nansen: Explorer, Scientist, Humanitarian.* With colleagues. Oslo: Dreyer, 1961.

Wallace, W. Stewart. *By Star & Compass.* Toronto: Ryerson, 1953.

Waters, D.W. *The Art of Navigation in England in Elizabethan and Early Stuart Times.* New Haven, Conn.: Yale University Press, 1958.

Weems, John Edward. *Race for the Pole.* New York: Holt, 1960.
  Peary: The Explorer and the Man. London: Eyre & Spottiswoode, 1967.

Weyer, Edward Moffat. *The Eskimos: Their Environment and Folkways.* New Haven, Conn.: Yale University Press, 1932.

Whitehouse, John Howard. *Nansen, a Book of Homage.* With colleagues. London: Hodder & Stoughton, 1930.

Whitney, Harry. *Hunting with the Eskimos.* New York: Century, 1911.

Whittaker, C.E. *Arctic Eskimo.* London: Seeley, Service, 1938.

Wilkinson, Doug. *Arctic Fever.* Toronto: Clarke, Irwin, 1971.

Williamson, James A. *The Cabot Voyages and Bristol Discovery under Henry VII.* Cambridge: Hakluyt Society, 1962.
  The Voyages of John and Sebastian Cabot. London: G. Bell & Sons, 1937.
  The Ocean in English History. Oxford: Clarendon Press, 1941.

Woodward, Frances J. *Portrait of Jane: A Life of Lady Franklin.* London: Hodder & Stoughton, 1951.

Woollacott, Arthur P. *Mackenzie and his Voyageurs.* London: Dent, 1927.

Wright, Helen S. *The Great White North.* New York: Macmillan, 1910.

Wright, Noel. *Quest for Franklin.* London: Heinemann, 1959.

Wright, Theon. *The Big Nail: The Story of the Cook-Peary Feud.* New York: John Day, 1970.

Young, Delbert A. *According to Hakluyt.* Toronto: Clarke, Irwin, 1973.

PERIODICALS, NEWSPAPERS, OTHER SOURCES

North-Nord (Journal of Department of Indian and Northern Affairs, Ottawa)

Arctic (Journal of Arctic Institute of North America, Montreal and Washington)

Polar Record (Journal of Scott Polar Research Institute, Cambridge)

The Beaver (Journal of Hudson's Bay Company, Winnipeg)

The Musk-Ox (Journal of Institute for Northern Studies, Saskatoon)

The Bulletin (Journal of National Museum of Canada, Ottawa)

The Geographical Journal (Journal of Royal Geographical Society, London)

National Geographic (Washington)

Maclean's (Toronto)

Penny Illustrated Times (London)

The Graphic (London)

Illustrated London News

London Times

John Bull

New York Times

New York Herald

New York Evening Post

Toronto Star

The Arctic "Blue Books" (British Parliamentary Papers, numbers 45210-45250 from 1848 to 1858)

Dictionary of National Biography (21 vols., Oxford University Press, London)

Dictionary of American Biography (11 vols., Scribner, New York)

Dictionary of Canadian Biography (3 vols., University of Toronto Press, Toronto)

The Oxford Companion to Canadian History and Literature (by Norah Story, Oxford University Press, Toronto)

Index

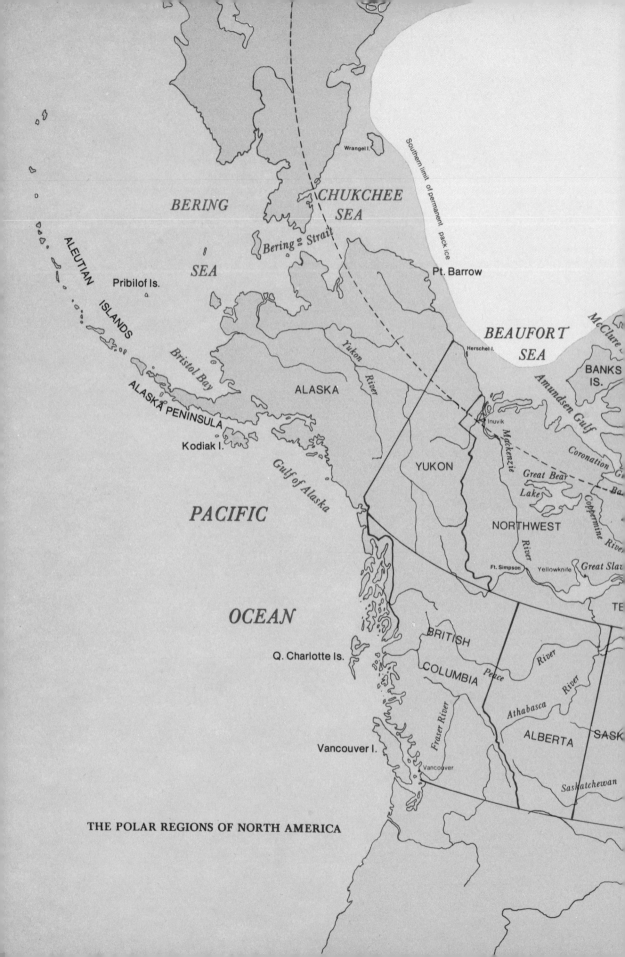

THE POLAR REGIONS OF NORTH AMERICA